Journey To Light

PEACE PORTAL ALLIANCE
CHURCH LIBRARY

Copyright © 2005 Larry Breitkreutz
All rights reserved.
ISBN: 1-4196-0272-1

To order additional copies, please contact us.
BookSurge, LLC
www.booksurge.com
1-866-308-6235
orders@booksurge.com

LARRY BREITKREUTZ

JOURNEY TO LIGHT

A NOVEL

2005

Journey To Light

*For my wife Hazel,
without your support this book would not have been
possible.*

*With special thanks to those who read the manuscript and
offered encouragement and suggestions. I am grateful to:
Carolyn, Janet, Marilee, Maria, Noni, Rebecca, Robert
and Trish.*

ONE

Omar felt an unusual apprehension when he awoke. The soft, early morning light playing on the cedar-panelled walls contrasted sharply with the trouble stirring his soul. He jumped out of bed, grabbed a red linen tunic from a peg on the wall and slipped it over his large, muscular body. Reaching for a clay jar on the floor, he poured water into a colourful clay basin on a small mahogany table beside the bed. He splashed the cool liquid over his face and beard, then rubbed it vigorously with a plush cotton towel. He studied his reflection in a brass mirror carefully as he ran his fingers through thick, soot-black, curly hair. Then he walked through the spacious, airy living area of the house and out the front door where his ears were struck by the shrill, trilling chorus of a garden full of songbirds.

"Good morning, Sigmund," Omar greeted a majestic full-maned lion lapping at a large, splashing fountain in the centre of the garden. Sigmund raised his head. Then, as he shook his great mane, sunbeams bounced and danced on the spray that filled the air.

"Easy boy," exclaimed Omar as the giant cat bounded toward him. Omar planted his feet firmly on the ground to avoid being knocked over as the wet head thrust into his stomach. He scratched the lion's head vigorously as it reached up to lick his face. They tussled playfully for several minutes in the fragrant garden, pushing and shoving in a friendly match of strength.

Hooves thundering on the hard packed dirt road leading to the house interrupted their play. The earlier apprehension tightened around Omar's heart as a horse and rider galloped toward them. The horse stopped abruptly when it reached the path leading through the garden to the house. A young man jumped from the horse. As he rushed up the path toward Omar the cloud of dust following the horse's hooves drifted through the air and settled over the lush garden.

"Good morning, friend." Omar walked toward the horseman. He recognized the blue stripes on the tunic. A king's courier. The earlier apprehension closed around his heart with a clammy coldness.

"Good morning, Governor," said the rider as he bowed.

"What's the news? What brings you here so early in the morning?" The courier held a papyrus scroll before him. Omar took the scroll and unrolled it. As he read, colour drained from his face. His hands shook, sudden nausea swept through him. His knees sagged as his head spun in the crisp morning air. Afraid he was going to faint, Omar looked around for a rock and sat down, staring at the scroll in disbelief.

The message was from Sorna, the viceroy.

***

Noble Omar, Governor of Cormath, the message began.

It is with great sadness that I must inform you of a terrible tragedy that has taken place in our land. Your father, the noble and good King Ulis, King of Fabia, was attacked and killed by two vicious men from the Province of Pasidia. The king's golden breastplate of authority was torn from his body and taken by the killers.

Your mother is safe, but deeply grieved.

Please come to Aklavia as quickly as possible.

Report to me when you arrive as we have some urgent details to discuss.

Awaiting your presence.

Sorna—Viceroy of Fabia

***

Omar dropped the scroll and sat with his head between his hands, staring at the ground. He was stunned, and silent, as incredulity and sorrow collided in his soul. His body shook as the reality of the tragedy seeped through his being. Tears poured from his eyes. Sigmund, sensing his friend's agony, nuzzled his face against the governor's legs. Omar pushed the lion's head absently until the majestic animal settled down at his feet.

The courier waited as waves of pain washed over Omar so powerfully that his heart hammered in his breast, his breathing became laboured gasps. Grief leached through his body and slowly settled into the innermost depths of his spirit like a giant ball of throbbing, molten lava.

"How could this happen?" he muttered quietly. "How could this happen?" he repeated over and over and over...

Where was Elconan? His mind questioned. *Where was the God his people trusted?* Ulis had taught his family the customs and traditions of the elders well. Elconan was the great creator, the sustainer. The people of Fabia believed in a high and holy one, who was good, who loved his people, who provided sun and rain for food. One whom they could trust for protection. And love.

As a child Omar experienced doubt about the teachings. *Where was Elconan?* He often wondered. *Why can't I see him? Touch him? Hear him? Why is he so elusive and hidden? Does he really care about us? Is he really real?*

Knowing no alternative, Omar followed the customs and traditions of the elders along with the rest of Fabia. But the doubts of his childhood always lay in the back of his mind, and he longed for visible evidence to erase them.

The people of Fabia lived in peace and harmony with one another. The custom of the elders that was passed on from generation to generation was simple, Aoght—each person lived for the highest good of all, the whole. As society followed this custom each person felt the love and support of the rest of the community.

The killers had violated Aoght, the spirit of the culture. *Where was Elconan, and why didn't he stop them?*

As he sat on the rock, dazed with despair, the birth pangs of a new world thrust through his soul and pushed him into a terrible, new dawn. The intense grief and pain he felt sparked powerful new emotions in his breast. He was disappointed and angry that Elconan didn't protect his father. Fueled by grief so deep that it numbed the heart and dulled the senses, anger rose up within him like a volcanic eruption. His veins pulsed with hot rage at the Pasidians who had cruelly murdered his father.

He was shocked by the intensity of emotion that swept through his soul. He had never felt such anger before. He wanted to strike back. To punish, get even. To kill. Thoughts of Aoght faded from his mind as he recognized the strength of this terrible stranger, for it seemed to calm the molten lava in his heart and focus it into sharp purpose.

The horrific act could not go unpunished. He would avenge his father's death. A steely resolve settled into his soul. He knew what he had to do.

Omar wiped his tears and looked at the courier, his face a mask of grief, etched with resolve.

"I'm sorry about your father," said the courier. Omar nodded absently.

"Thanks."

A strained silence hung between them.

Finally, after several minutes, Omar spoke. "When did you leave Aklavia?"

"Two days ago."

"You didn't stop to rest?"

"No. I got fresh horses along the way and kept riding. Sorna asked me to get here as quickly as possible."

"You must be tired." Omar stood to his feet. "Come to the house."

"Your father was a good man," said the courier as they walked through the garden.

"Too good to die like this," Omar's voice was brittle. "Do the people know what happened?"

"The news spread through the capital quickly. Aklavia's mourning. Everyone loved your father."

"Not all, I guess. How do we know the killers were from Pasidia?"

"Two council members saw them."

Omar shook his head sadly. "This is like a horrible dream. Why would they do it?" When they reached the entrance Omar turned to Sigmund. "Outside, I have company." Reluctantly the giant cat turned and walked into the garden.

The men entered Omar's spacious home. Like many homes in Cormath, it was built with light grey cut rock. Inside, the walls were panelled with smooth cedar. The marble floor was covered with reed mats of intricate design and colour. Finely crafted teak and mahogany furniture was scattered throughout the house. Omar had selected each piece carefully to compliment the style and design of the home.

Beside the main living area was a small room containing a bronze basin on a small mahogany table. On the floor, beside the table, stood a large clay jug, full of water. Omar pointed to the room and said, "You can wash there. I'll get something for you to eat."

***

With sluggish, deliberate movements Omar placed some bread and a bowl full of oranges, pears, figs and dates on a low table. Then the men sat down on the soft cushions around the table. "Please, give thanks," said Omar. "I don't feel very thankful right now."

The courier raised his face and prayed. "Blessed are you, Elconan. You provide us with food daily. For this we are thankful."

Omar moved the bowl toward the courier. "Go ahead. Eat. Riding all night, you must be hungry."

"Thanks." The courier picked up a pear, then handed the bowl to Omar.

"No thanks. I don't feel like eating."

The courier bit into the juicy fruit. "Hmmm, wonderful," he exclaimed. "From your garden?"

"Yes."

"Obviously well taken care of."

"My governor's duties don't allow much time for gardening. The people do most of it."

"You live alone?"

"Yes, I'm still single."

"A large house for a single man."

"I'm engaged. We're planning to be married in two months."

"Who's the lucky girl?"

"Ester. Daughter of Egan, Governor of Vinx."

"Lucky guy! I've heard she's very beautiful."

"Thanks. I think so."

The courier reached for a piece of flatbread and tore off a chunk. "I'd like to go back with you," he said, munching.

"You need rest. You can stay here, in my house. Rest today and tonight. There's fresh bread and lots of fruit and vegetables in the garden. Then tomorrow you can head back."

"But I'd like to be there for the king's burial."

"Don't worry." Omar paused as grief swept through him. When he regained his composure he continued. "The spices will preserve the body. People will want to come from all over Fabia for the funeral, so we'll have to wait a few weeks anyway."

"Thanks. I guess I am tired."

"How's Sorna handling this?"

"She's a woman of great strength. She's handling it well. But deeply grieved."

"Please keep eating," Omar said as he rose to his feet. "I'm going to pack."

"Will anyone be riding with you?"

"No. I want to leave immediately. I'll ride alone." Omar went to his bedroom. His mind was dazed, his spirit torn by grief. With slow mechanical movements he packed a fresh linen tunic, his ceremonial robe and a few personal items into a shoulder bag. Then he took a fresh papyrus scroll and quickly wrote instructions to Abu, his deputy on the provincial council. He picked up his shoulder bag and walked back into the living area.

"Before you retire you must go to the town centre and proclaim the sad news. Tell the people I've left for Aklavia. Then, please give this scroll to Abu." The courier rose and accepted the scroll. Omar put his hands on the courier's shoulders and looked directly into his eyes. "Thank you, for coming so quickly. I appreciate what you've done for me."

"My pleasure, Governor. I wish I could have brought better news." Omar's eyes filled with tears. He turned and walked toward the door. "Safe journey, Governor," said the courier. "May Elconan be with you."

"And with you," Omar replied blankly. He walked into the garden and whistled. A few minutes later a large, golden stallion trotted toward the house. His hair glistened in the soft morning light; his white mane flowed freely in the breeze.

"Good morning, Kaspar," said the governor, as his favourite horse approached. "We've got some hard riding to do." He laid a cotton blanket on the stallion's back, jumped onto the horse and with a simple hand signal to the animal's neck they were off toward Aklavia. What Omar didn't realize was that, with the brutal death of his father, Fabia had changed. It was no longer safe for anyone to ride alone at night.

TWO

Omar usually rode through the streets of Asker, his home city, slowly. He'd wave at the residents, often stopping to talk to them and interact with the people openly and warmly. Today was different. The stallion moved over the cobbled streets quickly as Omar rode with his jaw set, his face resolute and his eyes focused forward. His grief was a silent, but strong, barrier between him and the people.

Asker, the capital of Cormath, lay on the south bank of the East Yasa River. The east side of the city ran to the edge of the Great Sea. As he rode, Omar passed beautiful homes built of cut rock and cedar surrounded by large, lush gardens that were intricately landscaped and tended with great care. The people thrived on the abundant nuts, fruits and vegetables from their gardens.

When they reached the edge of the city, cobbled streets became a road of packed clay. Omar leaned forward and gave Kaspar the order to run at top speed. The horse responded, lurched forward, hooves thundering as they sped across the plain. Omar crouched over the horse's neck, his face buried in the flowing mane, horse and rider moved across the land as one. Simple hand signals to the neck directed the horse with the wishes of his human cargo.

The first part of the journey led across an open plain that stretched through Cormath from the edge of the Great Sea to the forest near the Yaseb River. Here the road joined another highway that led from the Province of Pasidia to Aklavia, the capital of Fabia. The stallion was soaked with sweat when they reached Cornea, the first of several villages scattered along the road. As they entered the village Omar signalled Kaspar to slow down. Reluctantly, the great horse slowed to a walk. Omar noticed that the streets were unusually empty. The village was desolate, as if deserted. An oppressive heaviness hung in the air. The sun was shrouded by dark clouds, the leaves on the trees drooped and the flowers turned their faces down to the earth. Even the birds were quiet and the animals were still as nature joined the people in mourning. The king's couriers had travelled throughout the provinces of Fabia informing the people of the assassination of Ulis.

The meeting place was a large, grassy area in the centre of the village. It was normally a happy place where the people met to celebrate joyful occasions; to sing and dance, and to worship Elconan. Today the villagers had come here to mourn. Their faces were long and drawn, eyes weeping. They cried, they wailed and they prayed. Omar stopped the stallion at the watering trough near the village centre. He slid off the horse and said, "Have a drink, my friend, and get some rest. I'll be back shortly. We have a long road ahead of us." He gave the stallion an affectionate slap, then walked toward the mourning villagers. A quiet whisper rippled through the crowd as he approached. Every eye was on the slain king's son.

The village overseer bowed as Omar approached, then greeted him with a warm embrace. "It's good to see you, Omar," he said. "I'm terribly sorry about your father."

"Thank you, friend. May I speak to the people?"

"Of course."

Omar walked to the front of the crowd and spoke. "Friends, I greet you in the name of Elconan. For many years we have enjoyed his goodness and blessing in our great land of Fabia. A land of freedom and goodness. A land where justice and love prevail." The crowd listened intently as Omar spoke. "In Fabia we have lived together as brothers and sisters, each of us caring about our neighbour. It has been a good life in a wonderful land." He paused, studied the crowd, then continued. "But evil has crept in among us. An evil such as we have never known, where brother rises against brother to kill and destroy." Quiet sobbing moved through the audience.

"As you already know," Omar continued. "Two days ago my father, the King, was murdered by evil men." The people moaned.

"We've never seen anything like this before, we need to pray that we'll never see it again. I'm on my way to Aklavia to be with my mother and to meet with the viceroy. You will be notified of the date of burial as soon as plans are finalized." The people grew quiet.

"It's been my privilege to be your governor. Your love and support is deeply appreciated. I must be on my way. May the blessing of Elconan be with you." As Omar turned to leave, the people pushed forward to crowd around him.

"May Elconan be with you," they cried. Some shook his hand warmly, others hugged and cried with him. Omar moved through the crowd slowly, touching as many as possible as he pushed his way out from the throng. Finally, he reached the edge of the meeting place where he escaped the crush of people and slipped away to his horse. As the sad-faced villagers watched, he mounted Kaspar, waved and sped away.

The scene was repeated in village after village as Omar followed the road across the fertile plain. In each village the beautiful homes of dressed rock and cedar were surrounded by lush green gardens bursting with the vibrant colours of roses, lilies, bougainvillaea and many other flowers and shrubs. Expertly pruned trees laden with figs, pears, apples, oranges and other fruits and nuts filled large orchards at the back of each house. Ample vegetable gardens, swollen with beans, peas, carrots, cucumbers, yams and other staples, were carefully tended by each household. Beyond the villages lay a large open plain where lions, tigers, deer, elk, giraffes, elephants, camels and many other animals roamed freely. In Fabia, humans, as well as all animals, ate only plants. No animal preyed upon another. The lion and the lamb frolicked together, without fear of each other, or of humans.

The last rays of the sun in the western sky struggled against the encroaching darkness as Omar and the stallion entered the village of Gathe. As usual, they stopped at the water trough by the town centre. The meeting place was empty, the village hushed and quiet. The villagers had spent the day in communal mourning, but they were now in their homes for the evening meal. Omar left the horse at the trough and walked up the cobbled street to the home of Morla, the village overseer. Morla lived in a large house with her husband Oleb and five children. Omar followed a path of flat stones that led from the street through a brilliant flower garden. It contained three small pools filled with colourful fish swimming among the lotus plants. A cascading fountain beside the entrance to the house supplied the pools with fresh water full of oxygen.

Several children played in the garden. When they saw Omar they ran into the house. A few moments later a tall, slender woman wearing a colourful linen robe appeared in the doorway. "Good evening, Governor, this is a pleasant surprise," said Morla in a strained voice as she greeted him with a bow. Grief etched Morla's face, her eyes were red.

"Good evening, Morla."

"I'm very sorry to hear about your father, Omar. You must be crushed. That's so awful."

Oleb joined her at the entrance. "Governor, Omar," he exclaimed. "It's good to see you." He bowed. "We've been thinking about you all day. I'm terribly sorry about what happened to your father."

"Good evening, dear friend. I'm on my way to Aklavia. I need a fresh horse."

"Come in," said Morla. "Please join us. We're ready to eat our evening meal."

"Thank you. I've been riding all day. I'd love something to eat."

"Refresh yourself." Morla pointed toward a small room off the main living area, the family washroom. On a small teak table was a basin, some water and towels.

Later, as Omar and the family were sitting on cushions around a low table, enjoying a meal of coconut bread, a cucumber pepper salad, oven roasted vegetables, sweet potato balls and roasted nuts, finished by a tantalizing apple cake served with freshly brewed coffee, Morla said, "You should stay here tonight, we have plenty of room."

"Thank you, but I want to get to Aklavia as quickly as possible. I'm going to ride through the night."

"But where will you sleep?"

"Sleep? I'm far too upset to sleep. I just want to get there and get after the killers. Can you loan me a fresh horse?"

"Of course. We have many. But I still think you should spend the night here. It's dark out already."

"The moon will guide me. The stars will keep me company. If I get tired I'll stop and take a nap." He paused, looked directly at the overseer. "How's your village doing, Morla?"

"The news of your father was a big shock. We spent the day in the meeting place mourning and praying. The people want to know when the burial will take place. A lot of them want to be there."

"We'll send couriers throughout Fabia once the date's been set. They're waiting for me to get to Aklavia."

"Is it true that the killers were from Pasidia?" asked Oleb.

"Apparently. That's what I've been told."

"Isn't Governor Kuman a friend of yours?"

"Yes. We've been best friends since childhood. We grew up together in Gara, when my father was the governor. We attended school together."

"Kuman must be distraught."

"Yes. My father was like a second father to him. They were very close. The fact that the killers were from his province would trouble him deeply."

"I'm sure the council will have a plan to capture the killers," said Oleb. "What do you think should happen to them?"

A soft silence hung between them as Omar reached deep within himself to respond. "I've thought about that." His words were slow and deliberate. He knew they would upset his hosts, but he continued. "I'm very angry. I want to see them punished. I'd like to beat them with my bare hands. I want to see them suffer."

"Omar," exclaimed Morla softly. "I don't think anyone can fully understand how painful this is for you. But revenge? It's not Elconan's way."

"Where was Elconan when my father needed him?" Omar retorted sharply. "Father trusted him. What did that get him? A knife in the back?"

The air became brittle and strained.

Oleb placed a hand on the governor's shoulder. "Our hearts go out to you and your family, Omar. This is a great loss. But we can't forget Aoght. The way of our people is to love and forgive."

"But first I'll get even. Then we can talk about forgiveness."

"Is that what your father would want you to do, Omar?" asked Morla gently.

"Unfortunately, I can't ask him. So we'll never know, will we?"

"Your father always spoke about the power of forgiveness, and overlooking an offence."

"So, does that mean the killers should be allowed just to go free?"

"No," said the overseer. "They must face justice. But you must not be bitter toward them, or your heart will become like theirs."

"I don't intend to kill anyone. At least not anyone innocent."

"But the guilty?"

"They've earned their fate." Omar rose from the table. "I really need to get back on the road. It's getting late."

The family members rose to their feet.

"Are you sure you won't spend the night here?" Morla's soft eyes showed deep concern.

"No, I really have to go. Thanks for the great meal. You're a wonderful cook." He hugged the overseer warmly.

"We'll pray for you and your family," said Morla softly. "And for the council. We'll pray that Elconan's wisdom and love will prevail. And that you'll have the courage to do what's right."

"Thank you. I couldn't ask for anything more." He turned to Oleb. "Can you take care of my stallion until I return?"

"Of course. Come, I'll get a good horse for you."

***

JOURNEY TO LIGHT

The horse Omar chose was a tall, spirited, energetic, brown mare with a black tail, mane and stockings.

"Good choice," said Oleb. "That one runs like the wind."

Omar spoke to the horse and stroked her gently for several minutes until she felt comfortable with him. Then he took his blanket from the stallion and placed it on the brown mare.

"Thank you, my friend. I'll take good care of her and see that she gets back to you."

"Any time."

The friends embraced heartily. Then Omar mounted the mare and they took off. The usual brilliance of the stars and light of the moon was obscured by the dark clouds that had hung in the sky throughout the day. After they had travelled for several hours in the darkness Omar began to feel sleepy. In the darkest hour of the night even the rocking of the horse failed to keep him awake. He laid his face into the mane on the horse's neck and slept as the road left the plain and led into the forest near the Yaseb River. The horse was unable to see clearly in the dark forest, so she slowed to a walk. The change in pace roused Omar. Suddenly, as if sensing danger, the horse stopped. Omar awoke, and sat up straight. Alert.

"What is it girl? Why did you stop? Are you tired?" The horse stood rigidly, its ears cocked forward. Omar shivered as cold apprehension settled around his heart. It throbbed loud, rapid beats. The hair on his neck stiffened. His body tensed. He waited. Slowly, out of the darkness ahead of them, two riders emerged.

"Hello," Omar was surprised at the quiver in his voice. The riders came closer, soon one was on each side of him. Suddenly he felt a rope slip around his body, his arms slammed against his side.

"Go!" one of the riders yelled. His horse lurched ahead. Omar was jerked from the mare. Pain shot through his body as he hit the ground. The second rider jumped from his horse and quickly tied Omar's hands behind his back with a rope.

"Who are you? What's going on?" Omar shouted. In the darkness he could barely make out the forms of his captors. They were two large men with long, bushy hair and full beards. He was jerked to his feet.

He smelled the foul breath of the bearded face that looked at him intently in the darkness and asked, "Who are you?"

"I am Omar, Governor of Cormath. What's going on here?"

"Good," said the assailant, ignoring the question. "Just who we're looking for." Omar recognized the accent. The man was from Pasidia.

One of the assailants placed a rope around the neck of the mare and brought her to Omar. "Get on!" he ordered.

"How can I, with my hands tied?" The captors grabbed Omar and shoved him onto the mare. "Who are you? What are you doing?" he asked.

"Keep your mouth shut!" said the Pasidian. He took a piece of cloth, rolled it and tied it around Omar's head, covering his mouth. "That'll keep you quiet." The assailants mounted their horses and rode into the forest leading Omar's mare. They followed a narrow trail for several hours, riding slowly in the darkness, relying on the horses to find their footing as they walked single file. Omar studied the sky whenever it was visible through the tree tops. They were heading west, toward the Yaseb River. The deep darkness of night began to weaken with soft light when the riders reached a clearing in the forest. A faint sound of rushing water purred in the distance.

Omar noticed the remains of a fire at the edge of the clearing. When they reached it the riders stopped, dismounted and tied the horses to a sapling. They pulled Omar off the mare and moved him to a tree close to the fire. "Sit here!" the Pasidian ordered. Omar leaned a shoulder against the rough bark, with his hands still tied he slid slowly and awkwardly to the ground. His captor tied a rope around Omar's body and the trunk, securing him so he couldn't move. In the early light Omar noticed a thick scar across the Pasidian's cheek underneath his right eye. He also noticed a long, broad knife in a sheath hanging from the man's belt. Omar had never seen such a knife. It was made of a strange kind of bluish-black metal. Not like the simple knives used in the garden. Each side was a cutting edge, the tip was pointed and sharp. The handle was a hard, white material that looked like dry bone. Omar shuddered.

The men wore cotton tunics that stopped at mid-thigh. Their shoes were hand-carved wood secured with rope. The men had been quiet on the trail, but now they spoke to each other freely, both with Pasidian accents. Omar noticed that the second man had a red rope tied around his forehead, keeping the long hair out of his face. The man with the scar said, "Get the fire going. I'll get us something to eat." He walked toward the river.

What will he find to eat by the river? Omar wondered. The red-roped man busied himself with the fire and soon it sparked and crackled. He stood by the flames warming himself. He ignored Omar who was sitting on the ground, unable to move, and getting cold.

The light was growing stronger when Omar saw his scarred captor returning from the river dragging a large humped object behind him. When he got closer to the fire a deep chill shuddered through Omar. The man was dragging a dead beaver. Omar watched in dismay as the men skinned the animal. He sensed a pained cry from the blood soaked ground as it swallowed the animal's life force. They carved the carcass into pieces, placed chunks of meat on sticks and hung them over the fire. The smell of roasting meat burned Omar's nostrils and made his heart sick. While the meat roasted the men sat around the fire engaged in small talk, drinking greedily from a small clay jug. Eventually, as the sun broke above the trees, the scarred man poked the meat with his knife and said, "Looks like it's done."

"Let's eat. I'm hungry," slurred the other.

"Should we give him some?" asked the scarred one pointing to Omar.

"Meat?"

"I guess not." They both laughed derisively. "He won't be hungry much longer."

Who are these men? Omar wondered. *What were they going to do with him? What did they mean by, 'He won't be hungry much longer'?* He shivered with cold in the early morning mist. His stomach gnawed. He fought the icy fear that crept through his veins and threatened despair. He was helpless, he realized, and the prisoner of some great evil. But he determined to stay focused and look for an opportunity to outwit his captors and escape. Habitually, Omar whispered quietly to Elconan, praying for wisdom, courage. But then, sadly, he thought, *Didn't help my father. Will he help me?*

The men sliced small pieces of meat from the chunks over the fire and ate using their knives and hands. Bones were chewed clean and tossed into the fire. The men ate with grunts of satisfaction and drank frequently from the clay jug, which they passed back and forth to each other. The morning light grew stronger as the men ate and drank. Finally, Scarface belched. "Guess I'm getting full," he said. "Just need another drink of tekara." He raised the jug to his mouth and gulped repeatedly. Then, smacking his lips, he handed the jug to his partner. Scarface sighed. Rubbed his stomach. "Can't eat any more." He burped. "Gotta get some shuteye." He spread a blanket on the ground beside the fire and lay down. His friend did the same on the opposite side of the fire. Soon they were both fast asleep.

They were snoring loudly when Omar noticed an object moving toward him from the river. He watched carefully as it moved closer until, to his surprise, he realized it was a beaver. *Probably looking for its slain mate*, Omar thought. The beaver hesitated, then moved closer. Omar looked at the animal intently attempting to make eye contact, but the beaver kept moving toward the fire. It stopped, hesitated. Then it noticed Omar. With his eyes he signalled warmth and friendship to the beaver. It began moving toward him. He held its gaze and kept signalling to it. With eye and head movements he kept the beaver coming toward him. The animal sensed his distress and drew closer. He tried to move his shoulder while signalling to the animal. The beaver came next to him, placed its front paws on the tree, and began chewing the ropes. A few chomps of the beaver's strong front teeth and the ropes fell off. Omar was free. He held his hands out toward the beaver. It chewed through the ropes and freed his hands. Omar patted the beaver's head and said quietly. "Thank you for your help. I'm really sorry about your mate but you better get out of here or these evil men will eat you too."

Very quietly, he walked over to the mare, untied the rope, and led her toward the river. He decided not to go back through the forest to the highway as that's where his captors would probably go looking for him once they discovered his escape. Rather, he would take the more difficult, but direct, route along the river to Aklavia. He led the mare carefully until they were out of hearing's reach from the fire, then he mounted the horse and rode to the river's edge. Here they turned left and sped along the banks of the surging water.

THREE

Two days later, the western sky danced with the fiery hues of the sinking sun when Omar and the mare broke out of the highland forest and saw Aklavia spread out before them across the valley along the Yoleb River. Excitement surged through Omar at the sight of the familiar buildings. His journey had taken him along the Yaseb River to its headwaters in the Fabian mountains. Here he connected with a road leading down through the forested highlands to the capital.

A pained quietness hung in the air as Omar rode into the subdued metropolis. The murder of the king had shaken the city, and its grief was tangible, like a festering sore.

The homes in Aklavia were built with cedar and set in clusters, like small villages. Each cluster had its own communal garden and an overseer to organize its care. Many of the residents were involved in government, others in trade, manufacturing and commerce. Aklavia was the seat of government, of learning and culture, with several large public buildings built of hewn rock dominating the river's edge.

Both Omar and his horse were tired and hungry, but the sight of the city renewed their energy. They travelled through the streets quickly. The residents were in their homes for the evening meal, so Omar's arrival was largely unnoticed.

When they reached a large cedar home faced with rock near the city centre they turned onto a path paved with clay bricks that led them through a vibrant flower garden, around to the back of the house where a cedar stable stood beside a small orchard. Omar dropped a metal bucket into the well by the orchard, then drew it up with the flax rope attached to it. He took the water to the mare, then released her in the stable to a manger of freshly cut hay. The yard was quiet, lonely. His father's absence flashed pain through his heart with such force that his body shook, his shoulders slumped. He dragged himself up the short flight of steps that led to the main entrance of the house where an elegant cedar door was faced with hand-carved scenes of the countryside and forest. Omar knocked, waited. After a few seconds the door swung open. The slender form of his sister, Anna, filled the doorway.

"Omar," she cried as she reached for him. "It's so good to see you." They clung to each other.

"And I'm glad to see you, Anna. How is mother?" Anna broke the embrace and looked at him.

"You're a mess. Looks like you've been living in the bush."

"I have."

"Come in. Mother will be happy to see you." She held his hand as they walked into the house. "Mother, Omar's here," Anna announced as they entered a small garden courtyard in the main living area. A tall woman, grief visibly etched on her face, rose from a chair gracefully, but painfully.

"Omar, I'm so glad to see you." They embraced. She clung to him and wept.

"I came as quickly as I could, Mother," he said with a soft voice. Omar decided not to mention being captured on the way. She had enough grief on her heart and he didn't want to add worry to it. He loosened his embrace. "How are you doing, Mother?"

"I'm okay," she said as she wiped her tears with a soft hand cloth. "I'm very glad you're here. But look at you. The Governor of Cormath looks like he's been living in the forest."

"Yes. I need to clean up."

"You must be hungry," Anna said.

"Yes, I am. Very hungry."

"The meal is ready," said Miriam. "We were about to eat. Clean up and join us. We can talk while we eat."

***

JOURNEY TO LIGHT

The morning air was fresh and brisk. A heavy dew covered the garden as Omar left his mother's house for the short walk to the office of the viceroy in the administrative centre. The council-of-elders would meet later in the morning. Sorna asked Omar to meet with her before the council meeting. The administrative centre was a large complex of stone buildings in the heart of the city. It was located at the intersection of two major roads that ran through Fabia. One road connected the northern provinces with the south, the other road ran west, across the Plain of Shinar to the West Coast. This intersection served as the hub of Fabian trade, commerce and travel. The western perimeter of the administrative centre was the Yoleb River. It connected the major marine movements of people and goods throughout the nation. The hall-of-justice, a large building constructed of cut rock, faced west toward the river. It contained the judgement seat, a large chair of hand carved oak, overlaid with pure gold, on which each new king was installed with elaborate ceremony and celebration. The king sat on this chair when listening to disputes and settling differences, and when ratifying the authority of the provincial governors after they were elected by the people.

The council-of-elders was a national body of twenty-four members, two from each province, elected by the people to oversee the nation's affairs. The elders elected the king and viceroy from among themselves. The golden breastplate of authority was vested to the king by the council and was worn whenever the monarch sat in the golden chair.

The breastplate was surrounded with much mystery and tradition. Its gold was bright and vibrant, shining like the sun. So bright that people had to shield their eyes when they looked at it. Excellent goldsmiths had tried in vain to produce a similar metal. None could produce the lustrous shine. Tradition said that the breastplate was illumined by the power of Elconan at the beginning of time, with instructions to rule with justice, love and equity. Subsequently, it had been passed down through the generations. It was Elconan's presence among the people, and the king ruled as a representative of the supreme deity.

Each province elected a governor, but the governors were responsible to the king and the council-of-elders. This arrangement of shared responsibility gave maximum voice to the people, but also ensured a stable and responsible federal administration.

The offices of the king and the viceroy were located in the hall-of-justice along with the meeting chambers for the council-of-elders. A deep sadness settled through Omar's soul as he walked up the marble steps. His father would not be there to meet him. Instead, he would meet with his substitute, to discuss the king's death and burial. He stopped at the top of the stairs and looked out over the garden of trees, shrubs and splashing fountains. The pain that tore his heart dulled his senses to the beauty before him.

He turned and walked to a polished cedar door, elegantly carved with images of the land and accented with gold. He knocked. The door opened and the large shape of the viceroy's assistant filled the frame. "Good morning, Governor," he greeted Omar with a bow. "It's good to see you. Come in. The viceroy is waiting." They walked through the entry lobby to a door standing ajar. The assistant stepped through the door. "Governor Omar," he announced, then stepped back.

"Good morning, Governor." A woman of medium height, with a full, firm body stepped around the desk. Her long, black hair was streaked with grey, braided and curled into a bun which sparkled with gem-tipped pins as she walked toward Omar. "I'm terribly sorry about what happened to your father," she said as she embraced him warmly. "Our hearts ache with you." She released the embrace slowly, stood back and looked at her young visitor, her warm blue eyes filled with sympathy. "How are you doing, Omar?"

"I can't believe what's happened to our country, Viceroy. Where did this evil come from?"

"Hearts that have lost their love for Elconan and their neighbour. They've replaced it with love for themselves. They've placed their desires and their interests above the common good."

Omar shook his head sadly. "But we've always lived for Aoght."

"Until five days ago. It looks like things have changed. Sit down, Governor." She pointed to large cushions near the window that looked out across the gardens and to the river beyond. Once they were seated she continued. "The council meets later this morning. I want you to attend."

"I can't believe that the golden breastplate was taken."

"Yes," Sorna sighed. "That's a big problem. We can't replace the king without the breastplate."

"But you have authority to rule."

"Only in the interim. Until your father is buried. Then, according to our custom, we must select a new king."

"But you can't without the breastplate."

"That's correct. The authority to rule is given to the king through possession of the breastplate."

"So, what do we do?" asked Omar

"We must find the breastplate and bring it back here."

"Fabia is a large country. There are many places to hide."

"Yes. But tell me, king's son, why would anyone want the breastplate? Gold is plentiful in Fabia."

"Authority, I guess."

"Can you exercise authority in secret?"

Omar reflected on the question for a few moments. He felt Sorna's intense gaze. Waiting. "I guess not," he said. "Authority relates to people. It must be public."

"So, if someone is going to use the breastplate as a sign of authority, it would be done publicly. As a declarative statement. Expecting the loyalty of the people to follow."

"But, they wouldn't"

"Why not? Our tradition is that people respect and honour the authority of the breastplate."

"Even if it's taken illegally? And a murder's been committed?"

"We shouldn't underestimate the power of tradition. Our nation would be torn. Some would feel obligated to honour the breastplate. Others would feel as you do."

"That would be tragic."

"A tragedy we can't allow to happen."

"How do we prevent it?"

"You're aware that the killers were from Pasidia, aren't you?"

"Yes. So I've been told. Who saw them?"

"Abdu and Bithar. Two of our most trusted council members."

"What did they look like?"

"Large burly men. Long bushy hair with full beards. One had a thick scar under his right eye." A cold chill crept through Omar. "The other had a red rope tied around his forehead."

Omar jerked upright. "I met those men."

"You did?" Sorna's eyes widened.

"Yes." The viceroy listened intently as he described the details of his capture and escape.

When he reached the end of his story she said, "They knew you'd be travelling on that road and were waiting for you."

"What would they want with me?"

"They might be concerned that the loyalty of the people could easily transfer from the king to his son. You are a threat to them. They probably feel that if you're dead they can gain the loyalty of the people more easily."

"But that's not the way it's done. The king is selected by the council-of-elders, from among its members."

"The killers, obviously, don't respect our customs."

"Who is behind all this?"

"We're not sure. But we've heard some disturbing rumours about Pasidia. People not getting along. Not caring for one another. All not treated as equals. New words must be created to explain it."

"Like?"

"Selfishness, caring about oneself without regard to how others are affected. Greed, grasping for more possessions than are necessary, even if others are hurt by it. And hatred. This one is difficult to describe, but its kind of like the opposite of loving and caring for one another. It's a very strong negative emotion that results in disrespectful acts. We could go on."

"How is the council dealing with this?"

"I'm glad you asked, because it involves you."

"Me?"

"Yes. You're a close friend of Governor Kuman, aren't you?"

"Yes. We've been friends since childhood."

"We're concerned about Governor Kuman and Pasidia. The last time he attended our governors' meeting he seemed distant and removed. That was several years ago. Since then he hasn't been back. He's always sent someone else to represent himself."

"I noticed that. But I thought maybe he was just burdened by the responsibility of governing."

"That may be. But we're not sure. The council members feel that, since you're the one closest to him, you should be the one to speak to the governor. Find out what's going on in Pasidia."

"What about the killers?"

"Kuman must help us find them. Before someone declares himself as king."

"What will we do with them?"

"We must heal their wounded souls."

"But what about my father?" Omar exclaimed. "They killed my father."

"Your father would want us to deal with them with love and forgiveness, so they might be restored."

"I know that's the custom in Fabia, Viceroy. But my heart is torn with feelings of anger and hatred. I want to see them punished, without mercy."

"Tell me, Omar do those feelings arise from your relationship with Elconan?"

"Why would Elconan allow this to happen? Why would someone be allowed to kill my father? Doesn't Elconan care about us? Or has he become impotent?"

The viceroy leaned forward and placed a hand gently on Omar's shoulder. With a voice full of love and tenderness she said, "Omar, I can't even begin to imagine how terrible you must feel. You have lost a wonderful, loving father. I know that your grief, and the grief of your mother and family, is beyond anything we can understand. We all grieve with you, for Ulis was dear to all of us. But you must not turn against Elconan. He gave us a free-will so that we can make our own choices. We can choose whether or not we will love and trust him. Just because some have used that free-will to turn against him and the wonderful world he placed us in, does not mean he doesn't care. It's because he cares so much that he does not interfere and take away our free-will."

"Sometimes I wish he did."

"The free-will of others, yes. But not our own, right?"

"Something like that." Omar dropped his head.

"But who are we to decide? Our knowledge is limited to our experiences on earth. But there is greater knowledge. And it's committed to our highest good."

"But, my father's murder was not for the highest good."

"No, Omar. Your father's murder was an act of free-will by evil men. And I can't even imagine how much pain you're feeling right now. But I know that in your grief you can find solace and healing in Elconan. Trust him."

"I'm having difficulty with that. I feel like Elconan let us down. He should have protected my father." He paused. Anger and grief struggled in his heart. He stared out the window, seeing nothing. Then, sighing deeply, he continued. "But if I turn against Elconan, I become like those who killed my father."

"A powerful insight, Governor. Come, it's time for the council meeting."

FOUR

The next morning, as the first light of dawn tinted the eastern sky, Omar and four companions rode out of the sleepy city. They travelled north, across the highlands to the headwaters of the Yaseb River. From here they would travel by boats to Gara, the capital of Pasidia. This was the fastest route between the two cities, several days shorter than travelling by land.

After a heated debate the council decided that, for his safety, Omar should not travel alone.

"I don't want an escort," Omar told the elders. "Should we react in fear just because of one bad incident? No. Then we would become their slaves."

But the council persisted, and four strong men now surrounded Omar. They felt awkward and uncomfortable with the long gardening knives the council insisted they tuck into their waist sashes.

The strongest of the quartet was swarthy Maki. Short, but stocky, with a firm athletic build, he was a fierce competitor in throwing the disc. Broad shouldered Asher was the tallest of the four. His strong arms and competitive spirit helped him win many sporting events. Raphu, although thin and small, was wiry and strong, and could defeat men much bigger and heavier than himself. The fourth was Shaphat, a nephew of Sorna. With a quick wit and easy laugh, he was well liked and had many friends. Sorna entrusted him with the responsibility to ensure that Omar got to Gara and back safely.

The highlands cut a diagonal across Fabia from the Northwest to the Eastern Coast. From the treeless summit the landscape dropped on both sides and stretched out through the forests and across the plain to the great sea. The riders followed a road of packed clay through dense forests of cedar, pine and hemlock. Birds twittered and chirped, deer, bear and other forest creatures grazing along the side of the road lifted their heads and watched the riders curiously as they passed. At midday they stopped beside a stream briefly to rest the horses and to enjoy a quick lunch of flatbread, cheese, raisin cakes, tree ripened figs and nuts.

The shadows cast by the riders were long when they reached the secluded village of Otta, nestled on the river's edge. Omar and his companions stopped at the inn, a large stone building, with a stable for horses in the back. They were greeted by a short, fat, balding man with a clipped beard shot through with streaks of grey.

"Welcome, friends," he greeted them warmly.

"Good evening," Omar replied. "Do you have room for five?"

The innkeeper shook his head. "I'm sorry, we're full."

"Full? What's the occasion?"

"A delegation from Gara took all the rooms."

"Gara?" Omar's face brightened. "Is the governor here?"

"No. Only underlings."

"That's a large delegation."

"Yes." The innkeeper looked around cautiously. "Gara is changing. Their government representatives travel in large groups."

"Where are they headed?"

"Refta."

"In Vinx?" The innkeeper nodded. "I'm familiar with the city," said Omar brightly. "I'm pledged to marry a woman there."

The innkeeper studied Omar carefully. Recognition flashed behind his eyes. "Forgive me, Governor. I didn't recognize you," he said, as he bowed. "I'm terribly sorry about what happened to your father."

"Thank you for your thoughtfulness. His death has been a blow to all of us."

"Yes. And what brings you here, so far from Asker?"

"I'm on my way to Gara to meet with Governor Kuman on behalf of the council. When you said you had a delegation from

Gara I thought the governor might be with them and perhaps I could meet him here."

"Have you seen Governor Kuman recently?" asked the innkeeper.

"He's a good friend, but I haven't seen him for several years."

The innkeeper shifted, looked out the window, his eyes far away. After several long seconds he turned to Omar. "It's good you're going to Gara. I wish you success on your journey." He paused. Sighed. Reflected for a moment, then continued. "I don't have any room, but I'll put up your horses till you return. Go up that street." He pointed away from the river. "At the top of the hill you'll see a large cedar house with a big tree in the front garden. That's the home of Lady Elga. She'll put you up for the night. She helps me when I'm full and have special guests."

"Thank you, friend," said Omar. "You're very kind. We'll be back for the horses in a few days."

"They'll be well taken care of." Omar and his companions turned and walked up the street.

***

Omar awoke as the enticing aroma of fresh bread baking on hot clay drifted through the house. Lady Elga had risen at the first light of morning and was preparing breakfast for her guests. She was a large woman, with a warm, cheery disposition. Since her husband died three years ago she lived alone, and so she enjoyed the company of travellers when they came to her home.

Later, as Omar and his friends were seated around a low table eating freshly baked bread, fresh peaches, pears, raisin cakes, cheese and a bowl of walnuts, Elga turned to Omar and said, "I knew your father well."

"How did you meet him?"

"We were neighbours when we were children. He used to tease me a lot. But he always had that special something. Like, you just knew he'd be great some day. It's so sad." She dabbed at her eyes with her apron.

"Can you come to the funeral?"

"When is it?"

"In four weeks."

"On The Plain of Shinar?"

"Yes. In the Kings' Tombs."

"I'll be there. I'm fortunate that I'm only a day's journey from Otta. But people will be coming from all over Fabia. They'll be travelling many days."

"Yes. We expect a lot of pilgrims. Aklavia is preparing for the visitors. Many will open their homes to strangers, like you have."

"I wish I had relatives in Aklavia."

"Don't worry. You can stay with us."

"Oh, but I couldn't. Your mother...she's still grieving."

"You put us up last night. The least I can do is return the favour. Mother will be glad to have your company."

"But only if you insist."

"I insist. You'll be like a member of the family."

"Thank you, Governor Omar. And for that you must stay here on your return from Gara. And I won't accept any payment from you." Omar winked at his friends. He had anticipated this and left enough zorn under his pillow to pay for them all.

"Thank you for your kindness, Lady Elga," Omar said as he rose from the table. "But we must be on our way." The men each thanked their hostess as they left the table. As they walked out the door Omar turned to Lady Elga and said, "May this house be blessed by Elconan."

"May Elconan go with you," Elga replied. The men walked to the river in the early light. Five long boats, each with four oarsmen, waited for them at the dock. The oarsmen were short, muscular men accustomed to long periods of travel on the waterways. They wore short tunics, from the waist to mid-thigh. Their deeply bronzed backs glistened as the sun's rays reflected in the clear river.

"Good morning, Governor," said the bright young captain with a bow. Energy and intelligence shone from his eyes. "Welcome to our boats."

"Good morning, Captain," Omar replied. "How long will it take to get to Gara?"

"We'll be there by late afternoon. Well before the evening meal."

"Good. Let's be off."

Shaphat turned to Omar and said, "Asher and I will ride in the two front boats. You can follow us. Maki and Raphu will stay behind you."

"Whatever you say, my friend," Omar replied nonchalantly. He got into the boat assigned to him by Shaphat. "Let's be off men," he shouted. Five boats slid into the current. The men picked up their oars and began the rhythmic singing that co-ordinated their movements and raised their spirits as the boats glided through the water.

The soft sun of early morning grew warm and bright as the convoy moved down the river. Both banks were lined with trees, broken only occasionally to reveal a village nestled near the river. Fish jumped in the water. Deer, antelope and other creatures of the forest came to the edge of the banks to drink and stare at the boats as they passed.

"It's a great world," Omar said to the men in his boat. But they didn't reply, just kept up the rhythmic singing. "Praise be Elconan," Omar shouted. "Praise be Elconan, creator of heaven and earth." It was good to be on the water. After the long ride across the plain from Asker, his experience with the captors, meeting the council, comforting his mother, and the ride over the highlands, he was tired. The singing of the oarsmen, the water hitting the sides of the boat, the warm sun overhead, the lightness in his spirit, all contributed to heavy eyelids. The Governor of Cormath stretched out in the boat and slept, unaware of the challenge that awaited him at Gara.

FIVE

"Governor." Omar awoke at the sound of the captain's voice. He sat up, rubbed his eyes and looked around. The captain pointed ahead. "Gara." Omar saw that buildings broke the horizon ahead. Large cut rock structures stood like giant sentries on the river's edge. As the boats drew closer Omar studied the buildings with increasing curiosity and amazement. Omar had never seen anything this massive.

Large marble pillars lined the front of each building. The walls were graced with detailed stone carvings of animals and plants set in Fabian landscapes. Wide marble steps led up to each entrance. The steps were lined on each side with huge stone statues of lions, elephants and other large beasts. Lush, green lawns, accented with abundant, bright flowers and proud marble statues, surrounded the buildings. Stone walkways ran through the gardens, across the well-manicured grass and led past noisy fountains that splashed and played in shimmering pools sunk into the ground.

"What are those massive structures?" Omar asked.

"Governor Kuman has built many new buildings," replied the captain. "A new residence for the governor, and new buildings for the government."

"So large? They're even bigger than the capital buildings in Aklavia."

"Governor Kuman loves to build."

In the distance, on the highest hill in Gara, Omar noticed an elevated scaffold swarming with thousands of workmen. The scaffold was lined with immense sheets of cloth material so that the workmanship was not visible. A large cloud of dust rose out of the shroud, drifting into the sky and out over the city. "What's he building there, on top of the hill?"

"It's Governor Kuman's secret. He hasn't told the people what it is."

"But how does he get the people to work on a project that they know nothing about?"

"Things have changed in Pasidia. Here people are forced to work."

Shock and disbelief rocked through Omar's soul. "Forced? What do you mean, forced?"

"Governor Kuman groomed a large group of men to carry out his wishes. Soldiers, he calls them. And together they form an army. The soldiers took men from their homes and forced them to work."

Confusion and incredulity collided in Omar's brain. It felt like the door to a terrible nightmare had opened before him and he was being sucked into a vortex of evil such as he had never even imagined. Men groomed and empowered to force others against their will. To enslave them to the wishes of another. His mind numbed with the impact of what he had just heard.

The boat touched the dock. "Here we are, Governor. Welcome to Gara." Omar sat motionless, staring at the hilltop.

"But don't...," he stammered. "Don't the men tell others what they're building?"

"The workmen are kept isolated from the rest of the city. They live in special barracks and are not allowed to contact anyone."

"But their families...they're separated from them?"

"Apparently. They haven't been allowed to speak to anyone." The captain jumped onto the dock and extended a hand toward his passenger. Omar ignored the gesture and got up unassisted. "Since you're visiting Governor Kuman, perhaps you'll get some answers to your questions."

"Perhaps. Thank you for a safe journey, Captain. Will you wait here for me?"

"Not in Gara. This place is too unfriendly. We'll move down river to the next village. When do you want us back here to pick you up?"

"How long is the trip back?"

"Against the current, a day and a half."

"Then we'll leave at noon tomorrow, so we can get back to Otta by the next evening."

"As you say, Governor. We'll be here." The captain bowed and stepped back into the boat.

"These men will go with you," Omar said pointing to his four travelling companions. "There's no danger, here in Gara."

"We'll look after them," replied the captain. Omar turned to walk up the dock. He was surprised to see two burly men walking toward him, long knives with elegant bone handles hanging from their belts. They wore strange tunics. Omar studied them inquisitively, then, to his dismay, realized the tunics were made of animal skins.

"Good day, friends," said Omar.

"What's your business in Gara," asked one of the men without acknowledging Omar's greeting.

"I am Omar, Governor of Cormath. I've come to visit Governor Kuman."

"Do you have an appointment?"

"Appointment? No. Governor Kuman is my friend. I come to visit him as a friend, and with business from the council-of-elders."

"You need an appointment to see the governor. Doesn't matter who you are."

Omar was surprised at the man's rudeness. "Please tell him I'm here. I know he'll see me," Omar persisted.

"He's busy. We can't interrupt him. All appointments are made through the secretary."

"Well then, please tell the secretary that I'm here, and I need to see Governor Kuman. I'm a friend."

"Everybody wants to be a friend of the governor, it seems."

"We've been friends for a long time. We grew up together, here in Gara, when my father was the governor. We even went to school together, under Kara. Please tell him I'm here. I'm sure he'll see me."

The two burly men looked at each other. One of them shrugged, "Guess we could tell the secretary. After all, he is a governor."

"I guess," shrugged the other. He turned to Omar. "Come with us." They escorted him off the dock toward the massive stone steps of the new government building. Omar admired the solid columns that rose for several stories in front of the entrance. They supported a portico faced with intricate carvings of lions, tigers, elephants as well as pomegranates, wheat and grapes. The top was so high he couldn't distinguish the details in the carvings. *A marvel of engineering and construction*, Omar thought.

Across the top of the steps stood several muscular men in animal skin tunics with long knives strapped to their waists. They stood straight and tall, like statues, with their arms rigid at their sides. On their feet they wore tall, heavy boots made of animal skin attached to hand-carved wooden soles.

Omar was led to a narrow door beside the steps to the main entrance. The door opened into a small, bare room. High on the wall a weak shaft of light poked through a narrow window. Omar was surprised to see iron bars over the window.

"Wait here," ordered one of his escorts. "I'll speak to the secretary." With that he left. The second man stayed with Omar. He stood by the door, his back straight and rigid. He was unfriendly and not willing to talk. Omar folded his legs under him and sat down on a small carpet in a corner of the room and waited. He sensed an oppressive heaviness in the room. It created anxiety in his soul, uneasiness and apprehension. As he waited he prayed quietly to Elconan, thanking the good and high one for a safe journey and asking for wisdom in his meeting with Kuman. After about an hour the burly one returned. He was accompanied by a delicate, young lady wearing a flowing purple robe that was embroidered with colourful geometric designs around the cuffs of the sleeve and around the hem that brushed the marble floor. Her light blond hair fell in soft curls over her shoulders. Large, round, hazel eyes danced and sparkled in the soft oval face which was accented by full, red lips enhanced by deep red pigment.

"You're fortunate," said the burly one as he entered the room. "Obviously, a good friend of the governor."

The young lady stepped forward. "Welcome, Governor Omar," she said with a bow. "I am Leeah. Governor Kuman has invited you to dine with him tonight. Please follow me and I'll help you prepare for the evening." Omar followed Leeah out of the room. They walked along a path of flat stones around the side of the building and across a large carefully manicured courtyard toward a massive cedar structure faced with rock accents. Omar noticed that a rock wall, the height of a man, ran around the building. The path led to a heavy wooden gate on each side of which men in animal skin tunics stood rigidly with long, shiny knives strapped to their waists. One of the guards nodded to Leeah and opened the gate for her and Omar.

"What's this building?" he asked.

"The governor's palace," Leeah replied.

"Why the wall? And the guards?"

"To protect the governor and his family."

"From what?"

"Evil."

"Evil? In Fabia?"

"Wasn't our king murdered?" Pain shot through Omar's heart. He didn't respond. *Yes,* he thought. *His father would be alive if he had been protected like this.* Leeah led Omar around the side of the palace to a long, low building at the back that was separated from the palace by a lush, green courtyard lined with flowering bushes and trees along the perimeter, bursting with brilliant flowers throughout. A fountain bubbled and splashed in a large ceramic pool in the centre of the courtyard. Cedar lounging chairs covered with soft cushions were spread around the pool.

"What's this building?" asked Omar.

"It's the palace guest-house." They stopped in front of the second door along the side of the guest-house. "This is your room. You'll stay here tonight. A set of clothes that is proper for the banquet is in the room. The boys will bathe you." She pointed to a small cedar building beside the pool. Several young boys dressed in short purple skirts that reached from the waist to the top of the thigh milled around the building. Steam rolled out the top. "After you've cleaned up, put on the clothes in the room. Stay here until I call for you. Refreshments are in the room."

"Who are these other people?" Omar noticed a man and a woman enter one of the rooms.

"Guests of the governor. There is a delegation here from Calda. You will meet them at the banquet."

A young boy, about twelve years old, walked up to them. His blond, curly hair was neatly trimmed around the ears. Leeah smiled at the boy. "Georgie, this is Governor Omar from Cormath."

"Welcome to the palace," said Georgie as he bowed. "I am at your service."

"I'll be back in about an hour," Leeah said. "Georgie will look after your bath." She bowed and slipped away.

"Your bath is ready," said Georgie. "Follow me." When they reached the bathhouse Georgie turned to Omar and said, "You can hang your clothes there." He pointed to a row of wooden pegs along the wall. "Then step into that stall," he pointed. "We'll wash you." Omar was uncomfortable. Undress in front of these boys? *This is immodest,* he thought. He looked at his clothes. He certainly needed to be cleaned up if he was going to a banquet. He looked around self-consciously. No one was watching. He slipped off his tunic and sandals and stepped into the stall. Four naked boys entered the shower with basins of hot scented water. Two of them climbed up to a platform near the top of the stall. As they poured the water over Omar's head the other two washed his hair, then lathered his body with soap. As the boys on top continued to pour water, the other two took soft cloths and scrubbed Omar's body. Finally, they towelled him dry with plush cotton towels.

"You boys are good," Omar said to Georgie as he wrapped himself with a towel. "How long have you been doing this?"

"Six months."

"What about your schooling?"

"We go to school in the morning. It's a special governor's school, so we learn fast," he said proudly.

"Are there no baths in the morning?"

"Oh yes. That's another shift. They go to school in the afternoon."

"Why do you do this?"

"Governor's orders."

"What about your parents? Don't they mind you working here?"

"They said I'd get better schooling this way. And since I'm gone from home they can both work."

"You don't live at home?"

"No. We live here, in palace quarters."

"How often do you see your parents?"

"I get to go home for two days every month."

Omar cringed. "Do you enjoy working here?"

"It's not bad," Georgie replied. "It's lots of fun when we wash the women. That's the best part." He laughed. Disbelief registered on Omar's face. "You look shocked," Georgie exclaimed.

"I am. Is there no modesty in Pasidia?"

"It's not a big deal. It's natural, isn't it?"

"Just because it's natural doesn't mean it's public," Omar replied.

Two strangers entered the bathhouse. Omar greeted them. "Good afternoon, I'm Omar, Governor of Cormath."

"Good afternoon," the men chorused tersely. They began undressing. Omar left the bathhouse quickly and went to his room.

The inside walls were lined with fresh sawn cedar and its pungent aroma filled Omar's nostrils as he entered. The room contained a small oak table, a chair and a low bed. On the table stood a clay jug of water, a flask of purple liquid, and several delicate tumblers. The bed was covered with a sheet of purple linen, very carefully crafted and embroidered with colourful images of pomegranates, grapes, pears and apples. Across the sheet, near the top of the bed, the words, *Welcome to Pasidia*, were stitched in yellow. A purple tunic and a long purple robe of fine linen lay on the bed. Omar slipped on the tunic, the soft, delicate linen felt good against his freshly laundered skin. He wrapped the robe around himself and secured it with a bright yellow sash. The hem of the robe, the sleeves and the shoulders were embroidered with colourful geometric designs. The outfit was completed with a pair of yellow soft reed sandals.

The windows were draped with purple linens embroidered with large bright flowers. A simple charcoal-on-papyrus drawing of the palace hung near the door. On another wall, across the room from the bed, hung an exquisite painting of a Fabian landscape done with pigment on papyrus.

Omar studied his image in a polished brass mirror on the wall. His dark complexion, black hair and beard contrasted sharply with the purple robe, but he didn't like the way the boys combed his hair at the bathhouse, parted in the middle. He looked around for a comb. There was none. He ran his fingers through his hair eliminating the part. "That's better," he muttered.

Omar filled a tumbler with the purple liquid. *Grape juice*, he thought. He sat on a cushion beside the bed and relaxed, enjoying the drink. *Very unusual grape juice*, he concluded. He refilled his tumbler and drank deeply. His head began to swirl. *Whew. What's happening with my head?* he wondered. *I better lie down.* He fell on the bed and lay still as his head swam.

SIX

A persistent knock on the door awakened him. "Governor Omar." It was Leeah's voice. "Are you ready?"

Omar rose from the bed, shook his groggy head and opened the door.

Leeah smiled at him, "I'm sorry to wake you," she said apologetically. "But it's time for the banquet."

Omar looked at Leeah attentively as his mind cleared. He held up the empty flask. "What kind of grape juice is this?"

Leeah laughed. "Oh, I'm sorry, I forgot that Governor Kuman's new discoveries haven't spread throughout the rest of Fabia."

Omar was puzzled. "New discovery? What is it? It made my head spin."

"That's wine. It's made by fermentation. One should drink it slowly. You must have enjoyed it," she giggled. "I see you drank the whole flask."

Omar set the empty flask on the table. He splashed cold water over his face, dried it with a plush towel and then, looking in the brass mirror, brushed his hair. "Okay, I'm ready," he said.

"Follow me," said Leeah. She led him through the courtyard along a meandering path lined with flowers and shrubs. They walked past the pool to a set of stone steps that led to the palace entrance. Two muscular, young men in purple tunics stood beside the entrance with solemn faces. Their backs straight, their feet firmly fixed. As Leeah and Omar approached, one of the rigid men opened the door. "Thank you," said Omar. The doorman bowed.

They entered a large lobby with a high cedar beamed ceiling. The walls were panelled with various colours of wood intricately carved with scenes of the Pasidian countryside. The floor was slabs of colourful, shiny marble. Plush linen hangings of white, purple and yellow linen, covered with intricate embroidery of fruits and flowers, draped the windows. The walls were decorated with paintings on a surface that Omar was not familiar with. He looked closely at the material and was dismayed to discover that it was animal skin.

The sound of frivolous conversation filled the air. Men and women were scattered throughout the lobby, all dressed in the purple robes and yellow sashes provided by Kuman. Attendants brought more people into the room. Young men and women in purple tunics moved among the people offering drinks and delicacies. A bright young lady with a clear complexion, sparkling blue eyes and soft brown curls that fell over her shoulders held a tray in front of Omar, looked into his eyes and smiled. The pleasant aroma of cooked food caused Omar's stomach to growl. He studied the items on the tray carefully. "What is it?" he asked.

"Pan-seared shrimp, medallions of cow heart, and stuffed mushrooms," she announced as she pointed to each in turn. A heaviness wrapped around his heart. He took a mushroom.

"Drink?" asked a handsome young man as he held a tray of small tumblers before Omar.

"This place is full of surprises. I better ask, what's in there?"

"Tekara. It's a new drink, made by distillation. Very strong, but good."

"I see Governor Kuman is full of new ideas."

"Yes," replied the young man. "We're very fortunate to have him as our governor. The rest of Fabia is coming here to learn." Omar thought of the cow heart medallions and wanted to say, eating animals is not great learning. But he held his tongue. This young man was not the one responsible. His curiosity prodded him.

"I'll try some of your new drink." Omar slowly took a sip. His face scrunched up. "Wow. That's powerful."

"Governor Omar," a familiar voice struck his ears. Moving across the room toward him was his good friend, Kuman. Tall, with flowing, yellow hair, a face cleanly shaven and a smile that revealed a row of flashing white teeth. His bright blue eyes sparkled and danced as he walked across the room. His muscular body rippled under a long white robe of shimmering silk which was secured with a wide purple sash around the waist. "It's so good to see you, my friend," he exclaimed as he welcomed Omar with a warm embrace. "This is a pleasant surprise. I didn't know you were coming. Shocking business about your father. I'm terribly sorry."

"Thank's for your sympathy. I know he was dear to you as well."

"Yes, of course. Like a father. I was crushed by the news." Kuman's face brightened. "And to what do we owe this great privilege of your presence in Gara?"

"I'm here at the request of the council. We have some urgent business to discuss."

"The council. Yes, of course. But we'll leave that for tomorrow. Tonight we celebrate. I'm honoured to entertain a special delegation from Calda. They've come to see the progress and changes we're making."

"I'm concerned about the changes I've seen."

"What's wrong? Didn't my servants treat you well?"

"Very well. But young boys serving in the bathhouse? Shouldn't they be at home, being schooled by their parents?"

Kuman laughed.

"Old restrictive ways, my friend. Welcome to the new Pasidia."

As the friends spoke they were approached by a tall slender woman who walked with an easy grace, her hips moved gently under the yellow sash, the robe filled by large, firm breasts. Lips, painted a deep red, revealed a perfectly formed set of white teeth when she smiled. Kohled eyes contrasted sharply with her smooth, clear, light complexion. Her freshly shampooed hair bore a sheen like red satin and fell over her shoulders in cascades of soft curls.

"Marshia," Kuman exclaimed. "It's good to see you. I was hoping you'd be here."

"They couldn't keep me away, Kuman," she replied with raised chin. "Your hospitality is irresistible."

"Thank you, Marshia, I'm honoured by your compliments, and delighted by your presence. Have you met my friend, Governor Omar?" he asked.

"I don't believe I've had the privilege," she replied in a soft voice.

"Marshia, this is Omar, Governor of Cormath...Omar, this is Marshia, daughter of Deputy Governor Kamasar of Calda."

"Pleased to meet you, Governor," she said with a bow.

"I'm pleased to meet you, Marshia," replied Omar. "I know your father. I didn't realize he had such a beautiful daughter."

"Beautiful and charming," Kuman interjected.

Gong...gong...gong...echoed through the room. The deep, full sound silenced the chattering guests. "Excuse me," said Kuman. He hastened from the lobby toward the banquet hall. "Friends," he said with raised voice. "Welcome to Pasidia. I'm delighted that you were able to come to my palace tonight to join us on this festive occasion. The meal is ready. Please allow my servants to seat you." He moved into the banquet room and took his place at the centre of a table on a raised platform at the end of the room. Male and female servants spread through the crowd quickly seating the guests at rectangular tables.

"Governor Omar," said a familiar voice. "Please follow me." It was Leeah. He followed her into the room, brightly lit with candles and oil lamps. The walls were decorated with elaborate brocade coverings of colourful linen. Omar followed Leeah across thick plush carpets that lay scattered over the marble floor. As they approached a table on the platform a petite woman with soft, sad eyes stood to greet him.

"Omar, it's so good to see you," she said brightly.

"Tamara, this is a pleasant surprise." He embraced her warmly. "How is the wife of my friend, the Governor of Pasidia?"

"I am well, Omar." Her face darkened. "I'm deeply sorry about your father. He was such a good king, and friend."

A deep sadness swept through Omar. "Yes, I miss him," he said sadly.

"How's your mother doing? She must be devastated," said Tamara, her voice filled with sympathy.

"Anna is with her. I'm going back tomorrow. She's mourning deeply, but mother is strong. She'll be fine."

"Have you decided when your father will be buried? I want to attend."

"It's going to be in about four weeks. We haven't decided on an exact date yet. But couriers will announce the news as soon as the date is set."

"Governor Omar, please be seated," Leeah said quietly. She pulled out the chair and motioned for him to sit down.

"How delightful. I get to sit beside you," Omar said as he sat down on Tamara's left. Kuman was on her right. Beyond that, at Kuman's right, sat Kamasar.

"Who are these people?" Omar asked when they were seated.

"A large delegation from Calda," Tamara replied. "And Kuman's top administrators. They've been in meetings all day."

"There are a lot of changes in Pasidia."

"Yes. My husband has a very creative mind."

"This house. It's very elaborate. Even greater than the king's residence in Aklavia. How is he paying for all this?"

"Taxes."

"Taxes? What's that?"

"Kuman requires the people to pay him a portion of everything they earn. This gives him a large treasury to work with."

"Incredible. The people don't mind paying these taxes?"

"My husband tells the people that taxes are good. He'll use them to improve their lives and provide for those who have less."

Omar spoke in a skeptical tone. "You mean he takes money from the people to do for them what they've always done for themselves, and there's enough left over to build a magnificent palace and host large delegations from the other provinces?"

"He also builds roads and schools and pays healers to help those that are sick."

"But this has always been done by voluntary contributions. The people don't mind this requirement?"

"Some do."

"What happens to them?"

"They are forced. Those who resist the governor are taken from their homes and made to work wherever he decides." A cold chill shuddered through Omar as he heard Tamara's words. This was foreign to Fabia, forcing others to one man's will. Where was respect, brotherhood and the common good? Tamara continued, "He has many construction sites. Some work here at the palace, the rest elsewhere. Many work on the structure."

"The structure?"

"Yes. Didn't you see it? The large scaffolding on the hill."

"Oh yes, I noticed that. What is it?"

"My husband's secret. He won't even tell me what he's doing there."

Their discussion was interrupted by a procession of servants entering the banquet hall. They were led by musicians playing drums, the lyre and trumpets. Four muscular men followed carrying a large object on a pallet set on top of two long poles that stretched between them. Behind this came male and female servants dancing and singing. The procession stopped in front of Kuman. He rose, an imposing figure in white and gold amidst the sea of purple robes that he had provided. *Unique amidst forced conformity*, flashed through Omar's mind.

Kuman waited until the crowd became quiet. "Ladies and gentlemen," he began. "We humble Pasidians are honoured by your presence here tonight." Kuman spoke with warmth and sincerity. "We welcome Deputy Kamasar and the delegation from Calda." He began clapping and all of the Pasidian dignitaries followed his cue. When the applause died Kuman continued. "Our discussions and negotiations over the past several days have been very fruitful. Tomorrow morning, in the hall-of-justice, we will formalize the agreement we made today. The future of our two provinces is bright. As we work together we will all enjoy more prosperity and wealth." The audience broke out in applause. Omar thought of the forced labour on the scaffold, he didn't move his hands.

JOURNEY TO LIGHT

"We are also delighted by a surprise visit by my good friend, Governor Omar of Cormath." Kuman gestured toward Omar. The audience applauded. "Governor Omar and I have been friends since childhood. We are all deeply grieved by the unfortunate and untimely death of his father, King Ulis." The audience became quiet. "Ulis was a great king, and a dear friend..." He paused. "On behalf of all of us gathered here I extend our deepest sympathy to the governor, his mother and their family. Welcome to Pasidia, Governor." The audience joined Kuman in applause.

"Our kitchen staff has prepared a great meal and I know you are anxious to enjoy it." The audience murmured agreement. "But first, I propose we drink to the future success and prosperity of our two provinces." Omar rose with the audience. They clinked their tumblers and drank of the fine Pasidian wine. When the audience was seated Kuman continued. "Now, ladies and gentlemen, let me introduce our feature of the evening." Servants raised the heavy lid on the pallet. Omar gasped.

"Roast suckling pig," Kuman exclaimed. The audience broke into applause. Kuman signalled to the servants and they began serving the meal. Some carved the pig. Others carried it to the tables along with trays of baked stuffed potatoes, sweet potato balls, sautéed vegetables served with delicious sauces, stuffed eggplant, spicy chick peas, a fine cabbage salad, along with a variety of breads.

Omar turned to Tamara. "What's happened to Pasidia?" he asked. "Isn't there any respect for animals?" He refused the pork offered to him.

"Kuman says that eating only vegetables is an archaic and outdated custom. It denies the people their right to eat what the earth has provided."

"What about our relationship with the animals?"

"My husband says he has no relationship with the animals. They're supposed to serve us. And since he dominants them, he feels he can kill and eat them."

"What about the poor and weak in Pasidia, are they also vulnerable?"

"He has no empathy for them. If they can't pay the taxes he puts them to work on the hill."

"Kuman has changed," said Omar sadly. "His ideas are foreign to Fabia."

"Not much longer. He's spreading his ideas to the other provinces. Those who agree with him are bound in covenant agreements. That's why Calda is here."

"In Otta we passed a large Pasidian delegation heading for Vinx."

"He sends delegations to the provinces to communicate his ideas. Those who want to learn more are invited here. He hopes eventually the whole country will agree with him."

"Where does that leave our king? And our traditions? What about Elconan and the teaching of the elders?"

"He ignores me when I ask about that. By the way, speaking of Vinx, how is Ester?"

Omar's heart brightened. "I haven't seen her for a couple of months. But we write to each other. She's busy preparing for the wedding. I can hardly wait."

"It must be difficult to govern Cormath as a single man."

"Yes, it is. The people are anxious for me to have a wife. Three more months."

"I've only met her once, but liked her instantly. She's a very beautiful woman, and very talented. How did you meet her?"

"I accompanied my father on an official visit to Vinx nine months ago. The governor's daughter was part of the welcoming committee."

"I've heard that your courtship blossomed very quickly."

"Yes. It was love at first sight. The moment I saw Ester it was like I was struck by a trance. And I haven't recovered." Omar paused, he remembered the tall slender girl whose blue eyes danced with an inner joy as she walked toward him with the confidence of an inborn grace and charm. The light auburn hair that fell over her shoulders glistened in the soft morning sun and framed the sharp features of a face that shone with inner light and sensual beauty as she greeted him with warmth and sincerity. His heart was captivated. No woman had ever affected him like this. Reluctantly he broke his reverie and continued. "I never knew love could be so wonderful, and so powerful."

"And she responded?"

"By the end of the day we both realized we had found our soul-mate."

"How romantic."

"I was supposed to be in Vinx for three days, but I stayed for two weeks. We saw each other everyday, and by the time I left we were beginning to make wedding plans."

"Wow! Even for someone as decisive as you are, that's moving pretty fast."

Omar laughed. "You'll come to the wedding, won't you?"

"Definitely! Wouldn't miss it."

The guests ate the sumptuous meal with relish. "This pork is wonderful. These vegetables melt on the tongue. This wine is superb," they said, as they smacked their lips and tipped the goblets. Their veins became inflamed and their talk grew boisterous and loud. Servants with large pitchers moved around the tables constantly keeping the goblets full.

When the guests had eaten all they could and began pushing back from their plates, servants cleared the tables quickly. An orchestra of drums, trumpets, lyres and tambourines entered the banquet hall. Kuman rose. "Ladies and gentlemen," he began. "I trust that you enjoyed the meal." Applause erupted from the audience. He continued, "Tonight we are honoured to have a very special guest from Calda in our midst. Marshia, daughter of Kamasar is well known in our provinces as a gifted and talented dancer. I'm delighted that she has agreed to perform for us, for your enjoyment. Ladies and gentlemen, please welcome Marshia of Calda."

As the audience cheered and clapped the orchestra began a rhythmic beat, the entrance burst open and Marshia swung into the room; swirling, twisting, twirling. She wore a short loose-fitting silk robe and leg coverings that waved and flowed as she moved around the tables. The audience was enchanted by her provocative movements and the expertise of her dance. They clapped and cheered as she flitted among them; teasing, charming, engaging.

She danced toward the head table where she focused on Omar. Swaying and bending, pleading, she used her eyes and her body to convey a message of desire and availability. Omar's pulse quickened, his heart thumped heavily as the sensuous woman enticed him. His face flushed as the audience roared their approval.

Her final act was a frenzied display to the crowd as the orchestra pushed their instruments frantically; pounding, striking, blowing, to an ecstatic crescendo as Marshia swayed, twisted and spun. The show ended as the drumbeats faded slowly and Marshia bowed to the audience. They jumped to their feet, clapping, cheering and whistling. Marshia blew kisses to the crowd, then she turned, blew a kiss to Omar, smiled mischievously and hurried out of the room.

***

Later, Omar sat in his room reflecting upon the evening. The change he saw in Kuman troubled him. He was leading Pasidia to forsake customs that held together the fabric of life in Fabia, the teaching of the elders that was passed down from generation to generation, and which was the foundation of Fabian society: worship of the Creator Elconan, love for one another, equality of all people, respect for animals, order and structure in society based on a commitment to Aoght.

What would he say to Kuman when he met with him in the morning? They would meet in the hall-of-justice, after Kuman finalized his agreement with Calda. *Why was Kuman making agreements with the provinces?* That was the king's role. Never before had a province tried to gather power unto itself. Omar's heart was heavy, concerned. He longed for his father. Ulis was a man of great wisdom and would have given Omar advice and direction. But his father was dead. A deep loneliness settled on his soul.

His custom was to meditate and pray, both in the morning and at the end of the day. As he reflected on the events of the past few days he wondered if it did any good at all. *Where was Elconan when his father needed him? Where was he now? Did he really exist?* Doubts struck his mind as he sat quietly in the night silence.

Omar was deep in meditation when the sweet fragrance of freshly crushed roses wafted in through the window. A few moments later he heard a knock on the door. He rose from his contemplation; as he opened the door the soft candlelight from the room fell across Marshia, standing in the darkness. A soft tunic covered her body. It was tight, accentuating her round hips and full breasts. "Good evening, Governor," she said coyly. "Got time for a lonely girl?" Desire surged through his loins. He hesitated. She brushed past him into the room, closed the door and put her arms around Omar's neck. The softness of her body against his caused a ripple of excitement through his flesh.

He felt her full lips close on his as she pulled him tightly to her.

"*Elconan help,*" flashed through his mind. He took her arms gently and pushed her back. "It's not right, Marshia," he said, catching his breath. "You shouldn't be here."

"Why not? We're both adults."

"But, I'm pledged to Ester."

"She doesn't need to know. I won't tell her if you don't."

Omar reached deep within his soul for courage. "Please leave, Marshia. You are a very beautiful woman. But it's not right that you are here." She was about to reply when they heard a knock on the door.

"Governor Omar." The voice was Leeah's. "I'm just checking to see if there's anything you need before you go to sleep."

"Yes, Leeah. Please come in." He opened the door. "Can you show Marshia to her room?"

SEVEN

The next morning when Leeah brought breakfast to Omar's room she handed him a large papyrus scroll, edged with gold and tied with a purple ribbon. "This scroll contains the governor's seal," she said. "You'll need it for admission to the hall-of-justice."

"Admission? To a provincial hall-of-justice?" he asked with surprise.

"Yes," Leeah responded. "No one is allowed to come before the governor unless he has pre-approved their admission."

"But what about access by the people? How do the citizens of Pasidia reach the governor?"

"They don't. The governor is too busy with his building projects and his negotiations with the provinces to speak to the common people. They only get to speak to his aides. There is no recourse to the governor."

"That explains something the council asked me to speak to the governor about. Why no disputes had come before the king from Pasidia for several years."

He decided to give Leeah a short history lesson. "The custom in Fabia has always been that disputes not settled to everyone's satisfaction by any governor can be brought before the king in the federal hall-of-justice in Aklavia. In the past five years Pasidia is the only province from which no dispute has been brought before the king." He paused. "Are the people content with this arrangement?"

"It's not what the people want that's important in Pasidia. The governor is leading us in a new direction. He has great wisdom, and the people follow."

"All of them? Even those in forced labour?"

"Not all of them." She became quiet, paused, grew distant. "I shouldn't be talking about this," she said. "Please let me know if you need anything else." She slipped out of the room.

Omar was troubled, confused. This was not the Kuman he knew, that he had played with as a child and studied together with in school. He had often felt like he was in Kuman's shadow because his friend was gifted in speaking and was persuasive with people. But Kara, their tutor, had always favoured Omar, because he worked harder at his studies. A heaviness sat on his heart as he left the room and walked to the justice hall.

He felt very small and insignificant beside the massive columns that stood before the entrance. He walked up the giant stairway. When he reached the top a guard stopped him. Omar showed the scroll Leeah had given him to the guard, who then bowed and opened the large oak door that was covered with elegant hand carved images of lions, tigers and elephants. Omar stepped through the doorway into a large lobby with dressed marble walls and floor. Soft light entered through windows cut high in the walls. Across the lobby was the entrance to the hall-of-justice.

Two guards dressed in purple linen tunics stood at the doorway. Their hair and beards were neatly trimmed and short knives with bone handles were tucked into sheaths attached to a belt. They stood with rigid backs, arms held to their sides like wooden sticks. To one side of the entrance stood an ornate oak table. Behind the table sat a small, thin man with balding hair and small beady eyes. "Governor Omar?" he asked.

"Yes." As Omar showed the man the scroll the doors of the justice hall burst open and the delegation from Calda, led by Kamasar and Marshia, flooded into the lobby with excited chatter and bright faces. Marshia noticed Omar standing by the table.

"Why, if it isn't Governor Prude," she said sarcastically. Omar's face flushed. She turned from him and walked out of the building, her chin held high.

"Good morning, Governor," said Kamasar. "You've come to the right place. The wisdom of Kuman is nothing short of amazing."

JOURNEY TO LIGHT

"Good morning to you, Deputy," replied Omar. The delegation drifted out of the lobby and into the morning sun. The bald man led Omar into the hall-of-justice, then bowed with his forehead to the ground.

"Rise," said Kuman.

The bald man stood and announced, "Governor Omar, from Cormath." Then he turned and left the room.

Omar was stunned by what he saw. On a high marble platform stood a large golden chair. On the chair sat Kuman, dressed in a brilliant white silk robe which was embroidered around the hem, on the sleeves and over the shoulders with fine gold thread. But what took his breath away was the sight of the resplendent golden breastplate hanging over Kuman's chest. He shielded his eyes and gazed in disbelief.

"Welcome, Governor," Kuman said. "It is customary for citizens to kneel with their faces to the floor when they appear before me." Omar didn't move. His heart thumped loudly. "But since you are a governor," Kuman continued. "And an old friend, I will excuse you this time." The guards standing beside the golden chair dropped their hands from the handles of their knives and stepped back. "You seem to be surprised, Governor."

"The breastplate," Omar spoke with forced words. "That's the king's breastplate. My father was killed for it."

"Things have changed in Fabia, Omar. There are people who don't want to defer to Aklavia and its tenacious adherence to outdated customs and traditions any longer. I'm very sorry about what happened to your father. He was a good man and a dear friend. But there are people in Fabia who want me to lead them. They brought the breastplate to me."

"You should have returned it, Kuman. You should have captured the perpetrators and brought them to Aklavia for justice. How could you do this? Assume power for yourself."

"Tell me, Governor. Hasn't Fabia always been a land where the wishes of the people are respected?"

"Yes. But also the traditions and customs of the elders which have been passed down from Elconan."

"Old ideas for another time, Governor. Many of the provinces have come to me. They want me to rule as king. They are very impressed with the progress and changes in Pasidia. They want to bring them to their provinces. Why, just this morning I finalized a covenant with Calda, our neighbour to the east. I will share my wisdom with them, in return their allegiance comes to me. Other provinces are anxious to join me as well."

"But Kuman," Omar interrupted. "This is wrong. The breastplate is conferred by the council-of-elders. My father's murderers were from your province. The council solicits your help in capturing them. And the breastplate must return to Aklavia. The council is the one to decide who wears it."

"Tell the council that the breastplate was brought to me. Tell them that the people want me to rule. I'm open to discussion with the council. But they must come here, to the breastplate." Kuman signalled as he stood from the chair, two attendants rushed up to him and removed the icon. They laid it on a table beside the throne. Kuman walked down the steps off the platform to where Omar stood. He put a hand on Omar's shoulder and looked directly into his eyes. The intense gaze of the deep blue eyes probed deeply into Omar's soul.

"Dear friend," Kuman began. "You and I have known each other all our lives. We've always trusted each other, haven't we?" Omar nodded. "You must trust me now, Omar. I'm doing what's best for the people. The breastplate is safe here with me. You've seen the security we have around here. No one is going to surprise me and steal it. Go and talk to the council. They must get past your father's death and think of the future. Look around you, Omar. Look at our new ways of doing things and the progress you've seen in Pasidia. It can be the same for all of Fabia."

"It's your new ways that concern me, Kuman," said Omar. "What I've seen here flies in the face of what Fabia is all about."

"Precisely," Kuman said sharply. "The old customs of the elders tie us to the past. We'll never be what we can be as long as we're looking behind us. We must look forward to the future. It's new and it's bright. Trust me, Omar." He paused...looked intently into Omar's eyes and continued.

"Tell Sorna to come and see me, or better yet, she can bring the whole council. They should come to Gara and see what the future can be."

"I'll take your message to the council on one condition."

"What's that?"

"You don't make any more alliances with the other provinces until the future of the breastplate has been determined by the council."

"Then it must act quickly. I can't stop the provinces from coming to me." Kuman dropped his hand from Omar's shoulder. He walked over to a table beside the platform and picked up a scroll. "I have an invitation for you, my friend, to a special dedication ceremony of the structure on the hill. You must have seen it." He handed the scroll to Omar.

"I've been meaning to ask, what is that structure?"

"My secret. Come back in six weeks for the dedication and it will be revealed."

"Thank you for the invitation. There's one more thing before I go."

"Speak, my friend."

"The killers. They were recognized as being from Pasidia."

"This is a large province. There are many people here." Kuman said somewhat defensively.

"According to our custom, it's your responsibility to find them. I can give you a description. The council will give you any assistance you need."

"The council's welcome to send men to Pasidia to look for the killers," said Kuman in a brittle voice. "Who knows, they may be hiding in another province. I'm happy to assist them when they search here, but they need to look throughout the rest of the country as well. This is the council's problem, not mine. I'm too busy working for the progress and prosperity of my people."

Kuman placed his right hand on Omar's shoulder and looked

directly into his eyes. "Thank you for coming," he said in a sincere voice. "But I have to go now. I'm late for a meeting."

Omar was disappointed by Kuman's refusal to accept the responsibility to search for the killers. Reluctantly he responded to Kuman. "I'll take your message to the council."

"Thank you, my friend," Kuman replied.

"Will I see you at the burial?"

"Briefly. There is so much to do here that I can't leave Pasidia for long. Of course I will attend, but I'll leave immediately following to return here. Please extend my deepest sympathy to your mother."

"Thank you."

"Will I see you in six weeks?" asked Kuman.

"I must return to Cormath after the burial. But I'll do all I can to come to your event."

"Please let me know. If I know you're coming I'll free up some time to show you around. It would be a great opportunity to see the progress we're making—our new and innovative ideas."

"I'll let you know."

"Thank you, my friend. Safe journey."

Omar's face was clouded as he left the hall-of-justice and walked toward the dock. He was concerned about the change he had seen in Kuman and disappointed that his friend refused to consider the wishes of the council. He hated to return to Aklavia with his mission unfulfilled. He had just stepped on to the pier where Maki, Asher, Raphu and Shaphat were waiting when he sensed the strange feeling as if someone was following him. He turned around and was startled to see two men coming toward him, one of the men had a scar on his right cheek, the other had a red rope around his head. Omar swung around and faced the men. "I want to talk to you," he said, just as Shaphat jumped from the boat unto the pier behind Omar. When the men following Omar saw his friends they turned and hurried away.

"Follow those men," Omar shouted. "Those are the killers. Catch them." His friends leapt forward and ran up the pier. "I'll go tell Kuman, and get some more men." He ran up the steps to the guards at the entrance. "Let me in," he demanded. "I have to see Governor Kuman."

"The governor is busy," said one of the guards as he blocked the doorway.

"But those are the killers." He pointed in the direction of the fleeing men. "Governor Kuman needs to send some help quickly to catch them."

"I told you, the governor's busy. He doesn't want to be disturbed. You can't see him now." Omar was desperate with frustration and moved to push past the guard. Suddenly he was surrounded by several guards with their knives drawn.

"You're not going in there," the guard said sternly. "Now, go and get into your boat and leave, or I'll have to arrest you."

Omar was shocked by the guard's rudeness. He stared at him in disbelief. The guard stared back, fierce hatred poured from his eyes. "Go!" he shouted. "You're not getting in here."

Omar felt anger rising within him. He wanted to attack the guard, but he looked at the knives pointing at him and realized it would be futile. He turned and walked down the steep steps where he met Maki, Asher, Raphu and Shaphat.

"They got away," said Shaphat, gasping for breath. "They disappeared down one of the streets and we didn't see where they went. Sorry, Governor." Omar felt like taking these four men and storming the guards to get into the building. Then he remembered Kuman's indifference.

"Let's go," he said, in a voice ringing with disappointment.

EIGHT

Three days later Omar stood before the council-of-elders and gave a report of his visit to Gara.

"Do you think Governor Kuman was involved in the attack upon your father?" asked Sorna.

Omar reacted immediately. "No. My father was like a second father to him. Kuman may have some strange new ideas, but he wouldn't have killed my father."

Sorna continued with a question. "Are you aware that each of the council members were visited by a messenger of Kuman's while you were away?"

"No." Omar was surprised. "What was their message?"

"Kuman admitted that the breastplate was in his possession. He invited each of the council members to travel to Gara and there proclaim him king."

A cold heaviness settled on Omar's soul. Kuman never told him about this. Why not?

Sorna asked each of the council members to speak in response to Kuman's invitation. The council was divided. Some felt that the authority was in the breastplate. Since Kuman had it, he should be declared king. Others disagreed. There was a longstanding and well established custom in Fabia for selecting the king and vesting the breastplate, they reminded the group. This procedure must be followed. A delegation should be sent to Gara immediately, demanding the breastplate, and to bring it back to Gara.

"But what if Kuman won't release it?" asked Abithar, a tall thin man with a severe face, shaven, except for a long grey goatee. He was the councillor from Pasidia.

"Is that possible?" asked Zegeb, the short fat councillor from Soleb. "Would anyone stand against the wishes of the council?"

The discussion raged on for several hours. There was sharp disagreement. Emotions got heated. Harsh words were spoken. The council had never been this conflicted. Councillors ignored proper procedure. They interrupted one another and all began speaking at the same time. Each trying to shout louder than the other.

Sorna watched in dismay as the councillors railed at one another, ignoring her. Exasperated, she stood up and pounded the table with a heavy wooden mallet. "Order," she cried. "Order, councillors. Order."

Slowly, reluctantly, the room grew quiet

"Councillors," she began. "I see we are in strong disagreement over this issue. Kuman will be passing through here in a few days when he comes for the burial of King Ulis. I recommend that we send a notice to Governor Kuman and ask him to meet with us here the day after the burial. This would give us an opportunity to get our questions answered and remind him of the traditions of our great nation. Do we agree on this?"

"What if he won't come?" Abithar asked.

"Ignore the wishes of the council?" asked Calman, a heavy stocky man from Oso. A buzz started among the group and intensified quickly. Sorna pounded on the table.

"Order," she yelled. Slowly the council chamber became quiet. "We must assume that a request from the council will be honoured. Never, in our entire history, has anyone treated an order from the council lightly."

"Kuman is doing many things in a new way," interjected Abithar.

"If the request is ignored, then we will decide what our next action should be. In the meantime we all need to consider this issue very carefully. Look to Elconan for wisdom. Look deep into your heart for an answer. Are we agreed on this?"

"Agreed," the council responded, although Omar noticed that some members were silent.

***

JOURNEY TO LIGHT

Soft light was breaking the horizon as the long procession began moving out of Aklavia. At the front of the line was Sorna, dressed in a long, flowing, pure white linen robe accented with gold embroidery around the hem, the cuffs and over the shoulder. Her hair was covered by a black headscarf that draped loosely over her shoulders. Around her neck she wore a heavy gold chain from which hung a gem-encrusted pendant of diamonds, rubies and sapphires. She walked slowly, but with assurance, her back straight. Her face, etched with deep lines of sorrow, looked upward, her lips moved in communication with Elconan.

Behind Sorna filed the council members and their families, all wearing black. They walked with their heads bowed, with slow deliberate steps. Musicians, singers and dancers followed the council. Flutes, lyres and psalteries played a solemn background to the songs of sorrow and separation sung by the choir. Dancers in loosely fitting black robes echoed the lyrics with careful, calculated movements that described the agony of a loved one lost.

Twelve muscular men dressed in loosely fitting white robes carried the king's body, which was wrapped in white linen, and lying on a pallet attached to two long poles. They were followed by Miriam, wearing a shimmering white linen robe, her head covered with a long black scarf that draped over her shoulders and down her arms. She wrapped her hands into the ends of the scarf. Miriam was surrounded by her children. Omar on her right, Anna on the left. Behind them walked the two younger brothers, Adriel and Philip. Miriam's married daughter, Tara, and her husband walked beside the boys. They were followed by close relatives, friends and then thousands of mourners who had gathered from all of the regions of Fabia.

The procession wound its way out of the city to the heavy log bridge that crossed the Yoleb River. Across the bridge lay the Plain of Shinar, a large, flat plain studded with clumps of bushes and trees. The north end of the plain was bordered by the sheer rock face of the Aklave Mountain Range into which tombs had been cut for the burial of kings and their spouses.

The city had been flooded by thousands of people who came from all parts of Fabia to attend the king's burial. Many stayed with relatives or friends. Others had quickly crowded the inns. Those unable to find accommodation in Aklavia camped in tents spread across the Plain of Shinar. They joined the procession as it moved onto the plain and wound its way to a large circular seating area cut into a hillside with a high platform at the front.

The king's body was set on a low table in front of the platform. Miriam and her family sat near it and the crowd thronged into the seats behind them. The seating area could not accommodate the huge crowd, so many thousands sat on the grass around it.

Sorna and the council-of-elders moved to the platform along with the provincial governors. All the governors wore black, except Kuman. His robe and head scarf were made of fine white linen. Traditionally, the spouse of a king and the viceroy wore white robes with black headscarves at the burial of a king. All others wore black. Kuman's pure white attire was an insensitive violation of custom; it set him apart from all the other mourners.

The burial ceremony began as Taka, the main choir director, led the musicians, singers and the audience in an extensive ritual of sorrow and passing. Dancers joined the musicians in interpretative dance which expressed the deep mourning of the nation. The people sang, they prayed, they cried. They entered into the emotion articulated by the dancers and allowed their deep pain to find expression, and healing.

The sun was high overhead when Sorna stood to address the crowd. Shouters stood throughout the large throng to repeat her words so that everyone could hear her.

"Beloved people of Fabia," she began. "We've come here today with heavy hearts. We are saddened and dismayed by the events that have brought us to this place." The audience responded with moans and cries. Sorna continued her address, she spoke of the noble character of King Ulis, of his great deeds and of his love for the people and Elconan. She encouraged the family and the nation with her words of comfort and assurance that Fabia would move forward and continue to be a land of love and freedom. And a land where the greatest dreams can be achieved. "As we follow the teaching, traditions and customs handed down to us from Elconan by our ancestors we will move forward from this day to a better day in the future." The audience responded with applause.

"We don't always understand why things happen. Evil has entered some hearts, and their evil deed has saddened all of us. But evil will not prevail. As followers of Elconan we must walk in faith and continue to look to him for a future that is bright, because he is good." The audience applauded.

"Many of us are wearing black today," she continued. "It represents the sorrow that we feel." The audience was very quiet. "But we are also wearing white, a symbol of our hope for the future. Let us move from our sorrow to faith and hope. Because that is what our dear friend, King Ulis, would have wanted us to do." The audience clapped spontaneously.

"Elconan never leaves nor forsakes us. The spirit of our slain king is now in heaven, with him...and we will go to meet them someday. So let's move forward with faith and love and renew our commitment and allegiance to that which is good." The audience applauded as Sorna moved back from the podium. The musicians burst into a triumphant song of praise; as the people sang the king's body was carried from the platform and placed in an open tomb. A cadre of strong men rolled a stone over the mouth of the grave.

People swarmed Omar, Miriam and the rest of the family. They hugged, they kissed, they wept. After some time Omar noticed that his mother was getting weary. He signalled to a group of young men who then moved the crowd back allowing the family to walk to a tent behind the platform. In the centre of the tent stood a round oak table covered with white linen. On it was a bowl of fruit: pears, apples, peaches, tomatoes and figs. Freshly washed carrots, celery sticks, sliced zucchini and mushrooms filled a tray on the table. Beside it was a colourful, small clay bowl filled with a zesty yoghurt and dill dip. A basket filled with a variety of freshly baked breads sat beside a large tray with blocks of different cheeses. Pitchers of fresh fruit juices stood beside delicate clay tumblers.

"Rest here, mother," said Omar as he helped her to a cushion. "I'll get you something to eat." As the family ate in the tent, the Plain of Shinar became a place of quiet remembering as the people shared a meal prepared at the direction of the council.

After Miriam had eaten and rested she entertained visitors. Throughout the afternoon governors, officials and close friends came to her tent to extend their sympathy and love to Miriam and the family.

One of the first was Kuman. An entourage of assistants and servants followed him as he and Tamara came to the tent. He embraced Miriam warmly. "I was deeply grieved when I heard the news about your husband," he said. "Ulis was a good man, and a good friend. My heart goes out to you in your grief. If there is anything I can do to help you, please don't hesitate to ask. Your husband was like a second father to me. I'll miss him greatly."

"Thank you, Kuman," Miriam replied. "You are very kind." Kuman and Tamara chatted with Miriam for a few minutes. They hugged her, then turned to leave.

As they were leaving the tent, Omar said, "I'll see you at the council meeting tomorrow."

Kuman hesitated. "I sent a message to Sorna. I'm not able to stay. I've got some urgent business in Pasidia that I must get back to immediately."

Omar couldn't believe what he had just heard. "But what about the breastplate?" he asked. "And the selection of a new king?"

"I've sent my recommendation to the council. They'll have to deal with it as they see fit. Good day, my friend," Kuman said, nonchalantly. His embrace was stilted and stiff. "I must be off."

Tamara embraced Omar warmly, her eyes filled with tears. "I'm sorry, Omar," she said. "I tried to convince him to stay." After embracing each of the family members and extending their sympathy, Kuman and Tamara left.

Omar was disappointed by Kuman's response. *What had happened to his friend?* He wondered. *Why did he care so little for the welfare of the nation, and disregard its customs and traditions?*

More people streamed into the tent. At first, Omar's greetings were merely cordial, as his mind was troubled by Kuman's response. However, as the steady procession of citizens expressed their love and sympathy, Omar's heart was warmed and thoughts of Kuman faded into the background.

Later, joy surged through Omar's soul as a tall, slender girl that walked with the music of an inner grace and confidence entered the tent. Her bright blue eyes danced with joy as she came toward him. She was accompanied by a large stocky man and a graceful woman whose soft eyes reflected a hidden sadness behind the warmth.

"Ester," he cried. They ran to each other and embraced warmly. "It's so good to see you," he said as they pulled apart. He turned to her father. "Egan, it's good to see you." He embraced the stocky man.

"I'm sorry about what happened to your father," Egan remarked. "He was a good man."

"Thank you for your kind words." Omar turned to the sad-eyed woman. "Deborah, how are you?" He embraced Ester's mother.

"It's good to see you, Omar," she said. "I'm very sorry about your father."

"Thank you. Your thoughtfulness is appreciated." He turned to Ester, his eyes shining with love. "When did you arrive?"

"Last night. We stayed with Aunt Hagar."

"I hope you're staying for a while."

"We have three days," replied Egan. "Then we have to return." The trio turned their attention to Miriam. They embraced her and expressed their sympathy. This was repeated with each of the family members. They spoke for several minutes, words of encouragement, love and support. When Egan noticed the line of people waiting to see the mourners he turned to leave.

"You can stay with us," Omar said. "We have lots of room."

"Your family has enough to deal with," replied Egan. "We'll stay with my sister."

"Ester can return to Aklavia with us," Omar said expectantly. "I'll bring her to Hagar's tonight."

"So be it. Don't be late." Egan and Deborah left the tent.

***

The next morning, when Sorna read the message from Kuman to the council, disbelief hung in the air like a bad omen.

"He can't do this," said one of the members.

"He's just done it," said another. Argument raged back and forth. The council was in confusion and disagreement. Some of the council members favoured acquiescence to Kuman. They recommended that the council travel to Gara immediately and proclaim him king. Foremost among these was Abithar. Others argued that the breastplate must be returned to Aklavia so the council could choose the king according to custom. Kuman must be required to relinquish the breastplate to the council. Since he was not a councillor, Omar did not participate in the discussion. He was dismayed to see the anger and contention of the members.

After much heated debate Sorna pounded on the table to restore order and gain control of the meeting. When the room became quiet, she faced the council and said, "We should hear from Omar. He was in Pasidia recently, and he is a king's son. Let's entertain his wisdom." The council became quiet as Omar stood to his feet.

"Ladies and gentlemen of the council," he began. "It's an honour for me to be here with you. But, as I'm sure you can understand, it's also a very sad time. We're here because of the tragic and untimely death of my father." He paused as he groped for words. "I was surprised and disappointed by Kuman's decision not to attend this meeting. Kuman, as you know, is a long-time friend. We grew up together. Governor Kuman told me that the breastplate was brought to him by others, but he wouldn't identify them. I think we all agree that he should have returned it immediately and brought the killers with him to face you." The council murmured agreement.

"But he didn't. Instead he is forging alliances with the provinces. We're not sure what these alliances are, but I find it a bit strange that he hasn't approached Cormath for an alliance."

"Perhaps he has, Governor. You've been away," said Abithar.

"I spoke to him yesterday," replied Omar. "He never mentioned it to me. Furthermore, on my recent visit to Gara I noticed some very disturbing changes. Governor Kuman has surrounded himself with armed guards and security. He has many servants and forced labour. The people are not free to bring their disputes to him, nor to the king."

"That's not right!" shouted Zegeb.

"Order," demanded Sorna. "Let the governor speak."

"Governor Kuman seems to be consolidating power in Gara while he ignores the customs and traditions of Fabia, as well as the authority of this council."

"So, what do you suggest?" asked Helen of Lowda, a large woman with a warm, friendly face.

"It's not very likely that Kuman will relinquish the breastplate. His guards carry knives and will protect him. To get the breastplate you would need an army of trained fighters with weapons."

"Unheard of," exclaimed Abithar. "Fabia has always been a land of peace."

"Yes," Omar replied. "And I believe we should keep it that way. Brother fighting against brother, sister against sister, that's not the way to resolve a dispute."

"So, what do we do?" asked Tula, a petite, compassionate, female councillor from Ofer.

"I believe the council has to act," Omar replied. "The people are waiting to hear from you. The longer you wait, the more time Kuman will have to consolidate power."

"But we can't act without the breastplate," said Abithar.

"All Fabia knows the breastplate was stolen," said Omar. "And each day more people are learning that it resides with Governor Kuman in Gara. If you don't act, the nation will soon be divided."

"Apparently, it's divided already," said Calman.

"To some extent, yes," Omar acknowledged. "That's why it's critical that you act, before it gets worse."

"So what do you suggest, Governor?" asked Sorna.

"Send a message to the people throughout the land. Tell them that Sorna will rule until the breastplate is returned to Aklavia and a new king is chosen. Also, I suggest you send representatives to the provinces to see what these alliances are and why they are being made."

"You don't think we should go and take the breastplate by force?" asked Tula.

"No. We don't have the army, nor the weapons, nor the tradition. We must look to Elconan and the customs he passed down to us through the elders."

"How will we get the breastplate?" asked Nadia of Aleb.

"We must appeal to Governor Kuman to abide by our traditions," Omar replied.

"But our tradition is not that the viceroy rule indefinitely," interjected Abithar. "But rather that a king is selected immediately following the burial. Your talk about keeping our traditions is pure hypocrisy. We need to select a king, and the breastplate is in Gara," He turned to the council. "I say we go to Gara and anoint Kuman as the king." A buzz erupted.

"Order," Sorna shouted. "Order. One person speaking at a time."

"Let's vote," said Calman.

"Are you prepared to vote?" asked Sorna.

"Yes." The response rippled through the crowd.

"As I see it," Sorna began. "We have two options before us. The one recommended by Governor Omar, the other by Councillor Abithar. Those who vote for Omar's recommendation stand to your feet." The first to stand was Tula. For several minutes she stood alone as the other councillors grappled with the issue in their souls. It was very quiet, some had their eyes closed and faces raised in prayer. Others whispered with those around them. Beads of sweat broke on several foreheads. Sorna waited. Finally, Calman joined Tula. Others followed, standing one by one until only eight councillors remained seated, among them were: Bithar of Calda, Dagmar of Corno, Dan of Vinx, and Abithar. After waiting several more minutes Sorna asked those seated, "Do you wish not to stand?" They nodded.

"It has been decided then. Fifteen are in favour of Governor Omar's recommendation. Eight against. I wish we were united on this issue, but I also agree with Omar, we have to act. I will dictate the letter and instruct the couriers this afternoon. Let's pray to Elconan that this issue will be resolved peacefully."

***

The shadows were growing longer as the heat of the day began to wane. Egan, Deborah and Ester were in Miriam's garden courtyard with Omar and his mother. A fountain gurgled softly in a pool of bright lotus pads. The fresh fragrance of many flowers hung in the air; a gentle breeze rustled the leaves hanging over the garden. Omar and Ester sat close to each other on a small wooden bench. The sweet scent of freshly crushed roses hung around Ester like the radiance of a vibrant flower in the sun.

"Ester, I'm delighted that you will soon be my daughter-in-law," said Miriam. "I can't think of anyone that I'd rather see as Omar's wife."

"Thank you, Miriam. I'm excited about the day as well," Ester replied. She turned her face to Omar and smiled.

"The people of Cormath are anxious to see you," Omar said in a soft, warm tone.

"Will they come to the wedding?" she asked.

"Some will, but it's a long trip. So only a few will come here."

"So, how'll I get to meet them?"

"We'll have a big celebration when we get to Asker. Then people will come from all over the province to see you."

"Sounds exciting," Ester giggled.

"Not as exciting as having you as my wife." He squeezed her hand affectionately. "I hope you get along with Sigmund."

"Who's Sigmund?" asked Egan. "Do you have a roommate?"

Omar laughed. "Oh no, Sigmund is my friendly lion. He lives in the garden."

"Have we settled on a date?" asked Deborah.

"Yes. In two months, I will arrive in Refta with my groomsmen on the twentieth of Mirka. We'll stay overnight, then leave in the morning for Aklavia with my betrothed." He squeezed Ester's hand. "And her family."

"How long is the trip back?" asked Miriam.

"Seven days. We'll travel slowly."

"We'll rest on the Sabbath," said Egan.

"Oh yes, I almost forgot. That'll make the trip a day longer, eight days."

"So you'll arrive here on the twenty eighth," stated Miriam.

"Yes," said Omar. "But let's plan the wedding for the following week. We'll all need to rest from the trip, and Ester will want some time to prepare herself." He looked at her fondly. "My beautiful bride." He kissed her softly on the lips.

"Ehfeeem," grunted Egan. The lovers faces flushed.

"Where will the wedding be held?" asked Deborah.

"At the city centre, by the river," Omar replied.

"Who is performing the marriage?"

"Sorna has agreed to."

"Ulis was looking forward to this wedding," said Miriam sadly. "It's too bad he won't be here...." Her voice broke. A heavy silence hung among them. She closed her eyes but couldn't stop the tears that coursed down her cheeks. Embarrassed, she buried her face in a cloth.

Omar ran to her side. "Mother," he said softly. "Father will be there. He'll be looking down at us from heaven." Egan shifted in his chair self-consciously. Deborah went to Miriam, laid her hand on Miriam's shoulder softly and whispered words of comfort. After a time, Miriam's sobbing stopped. She regained her composure and wiped her face.

They spent the rest of the afternoon discussing the details of the wedding.

Darkness was beginning to shroud the city in its mystery when Anna came to the garden and announced, "Time to eat." She moved quickly to set steaming bowls on a low table in the courtyard. Sweet potato balls, cooked peas, baked beans, roasted peppers, zucchini with a walnut sauce, roasted nuts and fresh bread. Adriel and Philip emerged from their room to join the family and their guests on the cushions around the table.

Omar was eager to speak to Egan about the affairs of government in Vinx. He wanted to know what discussions he had with the delegation from Kuman, but he didn't want to involve the rest of the family in the discussion. *Perhaps later,* he thought. Instead he focused his attention on the charming woman sitting beside him. He was unaware that a formidable force was moving swiftly to thrust itself between him and the woman he loved.

***

Ester and her parents left the next day to return to Refta. Omar stayed with Miriam another week. Then he left for Cormath accompanied by four companions. As he passed through Gathe he returned Oleb's mare and picked up Kaspar.

***

Time passed quickly in Cormath. A steady stream of citizens visited Omar to offer condolences and to inquire about the work and decisions of the council-of-elders. In the midst of their grief and concern about the future the people maintained a solid faith in Elconan. That he was with them, and would help them through the crisis.

Although the people's faith encouraged Omar, and their warm support was balm to his pain, nagging doubts chewed at his spirit. Where was Elconan when his father needed him? And why wasn't he stopping the evil in Pasidia? Whenever he thought about Kuman and what he had seen in Gara a cold heavy depression washed through him. He didn't want to go back there, but he couldn't escape the haunting sense that his questions about Elconan, the breastplate, and his father's death, would somehow be answered in the face of evil.

A few weeks later Omar assembled a small group of friends and left for Gara to attend the dedication of Kuman's hilltop structure.

NINE

The sky blazed with fire as the sun sank in the west when Omar and nine companions arrived at the banks of the Yaseb River, their horses were sweaty and hot from the day's hard ride. The water pulsed with vehement energy as it surged down from the mid-country highlands on its twisted path to the Great Sea. Across the frothing torrent lay Pasidia, a dense mass of tangled forest split by the narrow clay packed road on which they would continue their journey.

Omar was anxious to get to Gara. He wanted to spend some time with Kuman before the dedication of the secret structure. He wanted to discuss his deep concern about the changes in Pasidia that crushed down on his heart like an anvil. A strange uneasiness stirred his soul as he looked across the water. He sensed a strange presence. Foreboding. Eerie.

Fergus, a short swarthy companion with intense dark eyes and a solid muscular body, stopped his horse beside Kaspar and asked, "Do you want to cross tonight? Or camp here?"

"Let's camp here. The horses need rest before we tackle the river." Fergus turned and instructed the riders to dismount and set up camp.

"I'll gather some sticks," said Zared, a bright young man whose beard was little more than patches of fuzz.

"I'll help," said Cedric. Omar watched as the two youngest members of the group began foraging for firewood. Cedric, tall and thin, was only seventeen and Omar didn't want to include him on the trip. But Cedric wanted the adventure and pled with Omar to take him along. Images of Cedric's mother flashed through his mind. Her worried face etched with concern haunted him. Her husband was dead and Cedric was her only child. But still, she agreed that he should go.

Omar could not forget her parting words, however. "Please take care of my baby," she cried as they left.

His contemplation was interrupted by Nadine, a slender athletic woman with shiny black hair cropped at the shoulders. "I'll look after the horses," she said.

Omar slipped off Kaspar's back, then as he rubbed the great animals neck he said softly, "Thanks for the ride, fella. Follow this lady, she'll look after you." Nadine loved horses and was an excellent rider. Omar had chosen her for this trip because of her bright mind, her adventurous spirit and her ability to remain calm under pressure.

"I'll light the fire," said Petrina, a beautiful brunette with a soft oval face and deep brown eyes. She reached into her shoulder bag, took out two pieces of flint and began gathering kindling and soft dry grass. Omar included Petrina on this trip because of her bright, happy spirit, her intense loyalty and her athletic ability. She was also Nadine's closest friend.

"Help me with this bag," grunted a short fat man with balding hair and a shaved face: Morven, the cook.

"Here, I'll help," offered Sol, a stocky man with a full bushy beard. They lifted a heavy bag from Morven's horse and set it on the ground beside Petrina.

Morven pulled carrots, beans and potatoes from the bag and handed them to Sol. "Go to the river and wash these," he said. Morven then placed a clean blanket on the ground and covered it with fresh fruit: apples, bananas and papaya, along with a variety of nuts. He took flour from the sack and prepared dough for flatbread. He would bake this on a hot rock as soon as Petrina heated it in the fire.

The rest of the riders prepared the camp. Setup was simple. Seven blankets on soft, fresh cedar boughs on one side of the fire for the men, three on the other side for the women. Nadine spoke softly to each of the horses, then released them to graze, water and rest. They stayed near their human friends, like they were part of the family.

Each of the riders had a dagger attached to the belt. After Omar's experience on the way to Aklavia, the Provincial Council of Cormath insisted that he take a protective guard with him on the trip to Gara. "A group of people riding with long knives would project an image of fear," he objected. "It will cause apprehension in the hearts of the people. I'll go with faith in Elconan. He will protect me." The council relented only when he agreed to ride with nine companions carrying daggers. Since people often wore short knives to assist them in the garden and in food preparation, Omar felt they would not be conspicuous.

Darkness settled upon the group as they sat on the ground around the fire and enjoyed Morven's culinary delights. He was an excellent cook and specialized in combining herbs that he found in the wild with cultivated vegetables and fruit to produce taste sensations renown throughout Cormath. Omar always relied upon Morven to cook whenever he entertained official visitors in the provincial capital.

After they had finished eating Zared placed fresh logs on the hot coals. Sparks shot up into the darkness as the dry wood ignited and cast warm light over the travellers. Omar turned to Nadine, "Are you going to play for us?"

"Yeah, let's sing," said Damara, the third woman in the group. The others chorused agreement. Nadine, skilled with the lute, reached into a padded bag behind her and gently pulled out the instrument. She plucked each string carefully, listening intently to the sound and adjusted the wooden pegs meticulously until the instrument was properly tuned. Then, plucking the strings with expertise and artistry, she filled the camp with the melodious tunes of songs familiar to the group.

The others joined her, singing with vigour and enthusiasm. They sang the songs of Fabia: song's of creation and beginnings, songs about Elconan and his love for the people, songs of their devotion to him. They clapped their hands with the fast songs.

When Nadine plucked the strings slowly they closed their eyes and raised their hands in worship. The music and the singing was transcendent as well as intense and personal. When the music slowed to a soft melancholy rhythm Petrina stood to her feet. Following the music, she began a slow, artistic dance: bending, twisting, and swaying to the music, playing out in visual form the message of joy and hope the people experienced in their relationship with Elconan. Alix, a young man with sharp, handsome features and olive skin, joined Petrina. As the others sang they spun, twisted and swayed a message of praise and devotion to the deity. Spontaneous joy radiated from the group as they sang, played and danced. Joy in knowing that Elconan was loving, kind and just. And that he participated with them in the high principle of Aoght. Omar's joy, however, was tempered by the gnawing doubt that plagued his heart. His father was dead. *Where were you, Elconan?* The question was a festering sore in his spirit.

The darkness around them deepened and the fire logs reduced to glowing embers. Nadine plucked the lute slowly, then stopped. "Your dance is so beautiful, Petrina," she said. "I could watch you all night, but I'm worn out." Alix looked at Nadine with expectant eyes. "Oh, you're great too, Alix," Nadine chuckled. "Both of you were great."

Alix smiled. "Thanks," he said coyly.

Omar stood up, looked around at his friends, "We better get some sleep. We have a full day ahead tomorrow."

The riders were settling into their blankets around the fire when a horrific scream pierced the air, followed immediately by the frenzied cry of a deer. "What's that?" shouted Zared. Omar's heart beat loud, firm thumps. The hair on his neck bristled.

"It's across the river," said Morven.

"I know, but what was it? I've never heard anything like it."

"It sounded like an angry lion," Omar said gravely. "Only much worse. It was full of hatred."

"What about the deer?" asked Nadine. "It sounded terrified." The riders were suddenly all wide awake.

Fergus rose, picked up some sticks and threw them on the fire. Sparks shot to the sky as the new fuel hit the hot coals. The riders huddled around the fire.

"That was scary," said Petrina, her voice shaking. "What was it?" Nadine went and sat beside Petrina, and put her arms around the frightened girl.

Sol looked at Omar. "Maybe your friend Kuman arranged that as a special welcome for us," he said, trying to ease the tension.

"I'm sleeping with my dagger beside my head," stated Damara. They talked for about an hour until they grew drowsy. No more screams pierced the night, it was quiet. Finally, the riders fell asleep.

***

The leaves on the alder trees shook gently from the breeze off the water as Omar and his companions rode toward the river in the soft early light. Omar would cross first, then the others, one-by-one. Each rider would wait until the previous one was on the Pasidian shore before guiding their horse into the water. The river was narrow but swift. For most of the distance the horses walked, but in the middle it was too deep, and they swam frantically against the current as it pushed them down the river. When the last of the horses' scrambled out of the water, Omar said, "Well done. We've all made it across safely. Praise be Elconan."

They turned the horses onto the roadway and were about to gallop away when Kaspar snorted and jerked to the left. "Whoa, boy. What's the matter?" Omar calmed the horse.

"Over there. What's that?" Nadine pointed to a large lump in the grass on the right side of the road. Omar slipped off his golden mount and walked over to investigate. Cold chills ran through his veins. Lying in the grass was the torn mangled body of a deer. The grass around it was trampled and dishevelled, evidence of the animal's struggle with death. The riders gathered around the carcass and stared in disbelief.

"Lion tracks," Fergus said as he pointed to the soft dirt around the dead animal. "That deer was killed by a lion." Sudden realization struck. "The scream we heard last night. A lion attacked this deer and killed it."

"Unheard of," muttered Alix. "No lion would attack a deer. What for? Lions eat plants, like we do."

The strange uneasiness Omar felt the night before at the river's edge tightened around his heart.

"If he killed a deer, would he kill a man?" asked Sol as his eyes searched the nearby bushes.

Omar faced his riding companions, "Strange things are happening in Pasidia," he began. "When I was here last people were eating animals. Now I see that the animals are eating each other as well. We'll need to be careful that we're not affected by the new way of life in Pasidia." The riders shifted restlessly.

"If any of you wants to return, you have my blessing." He looked around. No one moved. "If you continue with me you may face dangers like we've never known in Cormath." His friends were quiet, solemn. An eagle shrieked in the distance. A soft breeze rustled through the leaves.

"They speak of new ways in Pasidia. New ways contrary to the customs and traditions that came to us from Elconan and have been passed down from generation to generation by our elders. On my last visit I was in Pasidia for only a few hours. Yet I saw many things that disturbed me. Even the relationship between men and women has changed. New ways are practiced that destroy the trust and love we have for one another." Omar remembered Marshia's soft body against his, the richness of her lips.

"I'm sure we'll discover other new ideas and behaviours in Gara. They may shock us, frighten us, but they may also tempt us to veer from the practices and beliefs that have brought happiness, love and security to Fabia."

"Never," cried Fergus.

The others joined in, "Never," they exclaimed in unison. Omar studied his companions' faces carefully. He saw firmness, strength and resolution. He admired their loyalty. Each was a good friend.

Someone he knew he could trust. But then the taste of Marsha's desire flashed though him, and he feared for his comrades.

Had he known what pain lay ahead for his friends in Pasidia, Omar would have sent them all home. But he didn't.

"Okay then. Let's go." He mounted Kaspar and led the group on the road toward Gara. They headed north until they met the main road leading from Calda to the provincial capital. Here they turned west and rode through vast grasslands spread over rolling hills that stretched out before them as far as they could see. The hills were dotted with flowering bougainvillaea, pomegranate and rosemary shrubs.

As the riders crested a hill a herd of deer panicked and dashed away, across the plain. "What's with the animals?" asked Fergus. "They act as if they're afraid of us."

"And each other," replied Omar. "In Pasidia the relationship with animals has been violated. They're killed for food. Wouldn't you be afraid?"

***

The horses were wet with perspiration, the riders throats were parched and dry when they rounded a curve in the road and a line of low buildings from a small village emerged on the horizon.

"That must be Topath," Omar said to Fergus, who was riding beside him on a black mare. "We'll be able to get water there." They slowed their horses and walked them into the village.

"Looks strange. How come these buildings look so neglected and shabby?" Curious eyes studied them from the darkness inside the buildings. Doors hung twisted from broken hinges. Remnants of shutters lay in uncut grass. Yards were barren and dusty. Here and there a few scraggly flowers poked through the crusty soil, faint echoes of a better time. The haunting sound of wailing children rang down the street. Adults quarrelled with one another and yelled at children. Cackling chickens scratched in the dirt, they ignored the strangers. Shaggy dogs ran out to meet them, barking and snipping the horses' feet.

"Whoa boy. Easy." Omar steadied Kaspar. Scared by the dogs, Sol's mount reared into the air. Thud. Sol landed on the hard-packed dusty street. With its rider dislodged the horse galloped down the street followed by the yapping dogs.

Omar jumped off Kaspar and ran over to Sol, lying in the dust, flat on his back, as though dead. Omar placed his ear close to Sol's mouth. "He's still breathing," he exclaimed. The other riders flocked around them.

"Should we move him?" asked Fergus. Omar looked up, then down the street.

"I don't believe this place. Not a blade of grass or the shade of a tree anywhere." A sullen faced child stared at them from a doorway, his finger in one nostril, snot running from the other.

"He's moving," said Alix. Sol's eyes blinked. They opened and he stared at his friends vacantly. He closed his eyes and groaned.

"Sol. It's Omar. Are you okay?" Sol's eyes opened again. Recognition registered. He tried to move. His friends helped him sit up. Sol shook his head.

"Where am I?" he asked with a strained voice.

"We're in Topath," Omar said. "Your horse got spooked by some dogs and dumped you. Are you in pain?"

Sol shook his head. "Guess I blacked out." He started to rise. His friends helped him to his feet. "I'll be okay," he said. A bent-over old man approached them. He had sunken cheeks, dull eyes and walked with a stick.

"Having a problem?" he croaked. "Strangers, aren't ye? Not from around here."

"We're travelling from Asker to Gara, to see the governor," Omar replied. "The dogs spooked this man's horse. It threw him."

"That's what ye get fer comin to ur town unannounced. Strangers aren't welcome here," the old man said curtly.

"We need water. Where can we get some water?"

"No water here fer strangers. Barely enough fer ourselves. Cain't ye see how dry it is?" His arm swept around, pointing to the dusty yards.

"There must be a well."

"Not fer strangers. Nope. No water fer strangers."

"Where is the town overseer?" asked Omar. "I'd like to speak to him." The old man spat into the dirty street.

"Yer speakin to im," he replied. "Ye better be on yer way. As I said, we don't have any water fer strangers here."

"How far is the next village?"

"Bout an hour."

"Is there a stream or a river between here and there?"

"Nope. Dried up."

"We'll pay you for the water." A glint passed behind the old man's eyes.

"Now yer talkin a language I kin understand." They negotiated a price on the water. Omar reached into his sash and pulled out a handful of zorn. He counted the gold coins as he placed them into the overseer's hand.

"Foller me," the old man hobbled down the street toward the village square.

"Pay for water? I've never heard of this," said Fergus. "We share what Elconan has given us freely in Fabia."

"We need water for our horses, and for Sol," Omar replied. "Then we'll get out of here. This place gives me the creeps."

"Me too."

"Give me a hand. Let's put Sol on Kaspar." They helped their friend onto the golden stallion. Then, leading their horses, they followed the old man.

"There's the well," he said as he pointed to a circular pile of stones, open in the centre. A rusty metal bucket attached to a rope lay in the dirt beside the rocks. "Careful now, don't take too much. The village needs water too."

Alix picked up the bucket and dropped it into the well. At the sound of a splash he began pulling on the rope. "You say yer goin to see the governar?" asked the overseer.

"Yes," said Omar. "Governor Kuman is a friend of mine." The old man spat at Omar's feet.

"Tell the governar somethin fer me, will ya?"

"What's that?"

"Tell im the taxes are killin us. Look at this town, will ya? This used to be a pretty place, til the taxes took all we ad. All we ever do now is work fer taxes. Tell that illegitimate pig to back off. Look at what the taxes have done ta us." He spat again.

"If things are so bad why don't you elect someone else to be your governor?"

"Ha," the old man snorted. "Elect? Ee's cancelled elections, that's what ee's done. There won't be any more electing. We're stuck with im."

"No elections? But that's unheard of."

"You've got a lot to learn, sonny. There's lots in Pasidia that's uneard of."

Alix held the bucket up to Sol's mouth. "Yuck," Sol grimaced. "What is that stuff? It's horrible."

"See," exclaimed the overseer. "Even the water's mad. Don't taste like hit used to. Hit don't like those taxes."

"We better fill our water pouches," said Omar. "Even if it tastes awful. It's better than nothing at all." Reluctantly, they filled their pouches. Then Alix used the bucket to offer water to the horses. They snorted their displeasure when they tasted the bitter liquid, drinking only gingerly.

"Be off now," the overseer ordered. "Leave some fer the rest of us." The riders mounted their horses gladly.

"Ride with me, Sol," said Omar.

"Don't fergit to tell yer friend what I told ye. And tell im he ain't welcome here no more. He's taken enough of our people."

"Taken your people? What do you mean?"

"Ee takes the strongest and the best. Put's im to work in Gara. Leaves me nothin but the old and the sick. We can't even look after our gardens anymore. Soon we'll be starvin. But what does ee care?" The old man spat into the dust at Kaspar's feet.

"Thanks for the water." Omar signalled Kaspar with his hand and the group rode out of the village leaving the overseer shrouded in dust.

They found Sol's horse on the outskirts foraging for food in the dry grass at the side of the road. "What are those plants?" asked Sol as he walked to his horse. Small stringy plants with runty yellow flowers bloomed along the side of the road.

"I've never seen those before," said Fergus. "They're killing the grass."

"Another new thing in Pasidia," said Morven. "Maybe we can cook it and eat it."

"Doesn't look like there's much else around here to eat," said Zared.

"Let's leave it," said Omar, cautious of the strange new plants. "There'll be food in the next village." But there wasn't. Not in the next, nor in the one after that. They rode through the rolling hills throughout the day and passed village after village where the same scene was repeated. The buildings, dilapidated and crumbling. The plants, stunted and runty. The people, emaciated, downtrodden and unfriendly. The riders were stunned by what they saw. The love, happiness and prosperity that they were accustomed to was foreign in the countryside through which they rode.

The shadows were long, the riders hungry, and the horses tired when they reached the outskirts of the small city of Octor, several hours from Gara. "Do you want to push on?" asked Fergus.

"No," replied Omar. "It's getting too late. The city will be asleep before we arrive. We better stay here."

"In the city?"

"Yes. Remember the deer? We need to sleep in a building. And we need to find some food." The street was muted, dull, grey. The buildings spoke neglect, the gardens were dry and barren. A few men shuffled down the street, their backs bent, their heads bowed. The riders occasionally passed a woman on the street carrying a heavy load of fruit, vegetables, wool, or other domestic items, in a large bowl on top of her head. Small groups of men sat cross-legged on the ground in front of the homes. They played a game where each man took a turn at throwing a small object into the centre of the circle. The occasional grunt of satisfaction was followed by frequent cursing and disgusted exclamations. Curious eyes turned to the riders as they passed. Curious with a strange longing, with envy, even hatred.

Sleepy-eyed dogs barked at the horses. Sol spoke calming words to his mount to avoid another bucking. The riders rode down the street cautiously with the dogs yipping behind them. Curses spiked the air. The harsh shouts of mothers reprimanding their children collided with the children's screams as they were struck by angry parents.

Suddenly, a circle of men erupted in front of the riders with shouts and cursing. Two of them began striking each other and yelling. Reflected light flashed, a man screamed and crumpled to the ground clutching a knife stuck in his chest. The men began pushing, shoving and hitting one another with loud exclamations and violent curses.

Omar jumped off Kaspar and ran toward the boisterous group. "Brothers," he yelled. "Brothers, stop. Stop this." The men paused and leered at the intruder. Omar dropped to his knees beside the wounded man and put his ear to the man's chest. Nothing. "He's dead," Omar said as he stood up. "Someone needs to get the overseer." He surveyed the group. Empty eyes stared at him out of hard faces. They wore no robes, only dishevelled dirty tunics. Their feet were bare, calloused soles covered with dust.

After a long strained silence, one of the men asked. "Who are you?"

"I am Omar," he replied. "Governor of Cormath. I'm on my way to see Governor Kuman in Gara."

The men grunted derisively. "Take your fancy face to Kuman," said the man whose knife stuck in the silent chest of the dead man. "Leave us alone. We don't need you here."

"Yeah," the others responded. "Get lost, we don't need you."

Omar's body tensed, his riding companions gathered around him. His face was resolute. "Can you tell me where I can find the overseer?"

"Find him yourself," came the sharp retort. Omar looked at the men in disbelief.

"Aren't you concerned about this man?" He pointed to the red stain spreading in the dirt. "What about his family? Someone needs to call his family. And inform the overseer."

"Who made you our judge?" said a short muscular man with beady eyes. "Why don't you get back on your horse and get out of here." Children who heard the commotion came running and gathered around the men. Dirty children, with long, messy hair, tattered tunics and runny noses.

"It's Abe," shouted one of the boys. "He's been stabbed."

"Do you know where this man lives?" Omar asked the boy.

"Over there." He pointed to a small house across the street.

"Go tell his family, they must come quickly."

"He has no family," interjected the beady-eyed man. "He lived alone. He's just a loser anyway. Come on, let's get him out of here." Several men grabbed his arms and feet, and carried Abe to his shack. They dumped him inside, closed the door, then scattered to their shabby homes.

Omar turned to his friends, his face a mask of disbelief. "We better find the overseer."

"Mister, can I ride your horse?" asked one of the children.

"Yeah, give us a ride," the others chimed. Omar looked at the tallest of the bunch, a boy, about twelve, with rumpled, yellow hair, and asked, "Do you know where I can find the overseer?"

The boy eyed him suspiciously. "By the city square," he ventured. Then he turned and walked away. The rest of the children followed him.

The light was fading rapidly as Omar and his companions directed their horses down the dusty street to the city centre. Here the street was wider and paved with stones. High walls of rock surrounded the large masonry homes and hid them from the riders view. The street was neatly swept and verdant grass lined the boulevards along with stately palms, flowering bougainvillaea and brilliant hibiscus. The soft rush of splashing fountains crept over the high walls and caressed the tired riders' ears.

"This is strange," said Fergus. "Why do they have such large walls?"

"Security," Omar replied. "It was the same in Gara."

"Security?" Fergus turned a puzzled face toward Omar. "From what?"

"Didn't you see those people back there?"

"They didn't have much."

"That's the point. Those don't have much while these do. And everyone wants more. So they build walls and hoard it."

"But why? Why don't they follow our custom and share? There should be no poor in Fabia."

"Pasidia is developing new customs. The governor has new ideas. I only got a glimpse of them on my last trip. I hope to learn more about them in the next few days."

"Not to bring them to Cormath," said Fergus, his face aghast.

"Never," Omar exclaimed emphatically. "I'd never bring his ideas to Cormath. What I've seen so far is revolting. But apparently a growing number of provinces are embracing Kuman's ideas. We need to learn about them so we know how to deal with what I fear is a growing problem."

"Doesn't Governor Kuman have the king's breastplate?"

"Yes."

"I wonder how he got it."

"Said someone brought it to him. Apparently, there are some who want him to rule."

"Why didn't he return it, like he should have?"

"He wouldn't answer that question directly. Kept talking about new ways and provinces coming to him."

"To him?" asked Fergus. "But that's not true. Governor Kuman sent representatives to the provinces to convince them to join him. He started with the provinces bordering Pasidia. Then, when they became interested he approached those farther away."

"Where did you get this information, Fergus?"

"I've spoken to the couriers. They know what's going on in the country."

"Have they spoken to you about these walls?" Omar swept his arm, pointing down the side of the street.

"They have. But I didn't understand. Why would anyone need walls? But I'm beginning to see what they were talking about."

"Strange rumours, we ignored them. How could we be so blind?" They reached the edge of the city square and dismounted. The market and the shops were closed for the night. Their windows were covered with shutters, their entries protected by heavy doors.

"It's spooky here," said Zared. "Everything's closed up. No people around." The silence around them was tense, charged.

"I don't like this," said Petrina. "It feels very unfriendly."

"We'll stick together," said Nadine confidently. As they spoke two figures appeared out of the shadows. Large men, their muscles rippling under plain cotton tunics. Long knives hung from their belts.

"Good evening, friends," said Omar.

"Travelling through?" asked one of the men. His black, curly hair stuck out from his head like the quills of an aroused porcupine. Dark, intense eyes peered out from a face with a full, black beard.

"We're on our way to Gara," Omar replied. "We'd like to spend the night here. But first we need to see the overseer. Can you tell me where the overseer lives?"

"He's not interested in people that are just passing through. He's busy."

"But it's about one of his citizens. We need to see him."

"Oh, yeah?"

"Back up the street," Omar pointed behind them. "A man was killed." The bearded man and his clean shaven companion suddenly showed interest.

"Who was killed? Where?"

"Back by the derelict houses. His name was Abe."

"We'll look into it." They marched up the street, their faces grim.

"People here aren't very friendly," said Fergus. "Do you think we'll find a place to stay?"

"The square is deserted," observed Zared.

"Perhaps the citizens will show us hospitality," said Omar.

"Fergus, you and Petrina stay here in case someone comes along to offer us lodging. The rest of us will go and look for an inn. If we're parted we'll meet here at sunrise." Several hours later Omar and his friends returned to the city square. They had found a few small inns, but all were full with travellers bound for Gara. Omar was surprised to see Fergus and Petrina still waiting at the city square.

"Any luck?" asked Fergus.

"No. The inns are all full," Omar replied. "I see you haven't had much luck either."

"Nothing. Nobody came by to speak to us."

"It's too late now, they're going to bed. Guess we're stuck here for the night," said Omar.

"What about food?" asked Morven. "We're all hungry."

Omar looked around at the tired group. "We'll have to wait until morning when the market opens. Guess we'll have to sleep here on the square." Heavy sighs dribbled through the group. Dejectedly, they rolled their blankets out on the grass.

"Guess there'll be no dancing tonight," said Alix sadly. "But how about a little music, Nadine?"

"Great idea," exclaimed Petrina. "I need something to lift my spirits."

"Me too," others chorused. Nadine reached for her lute.

"Let's keep it down," cautioned Omar. "We don't want to wake anyone." Nadine plucked the strings softly; the others joined her in a melancholy song asking Elconan for his presence and protection. Then the tired riders went to sleep.

***

The stars were bright overhead, and the darkness was beginning to soften when Omar was awakened by Kaspar's frightened neighing. In the pale darkness he saw the outline of a man's figure leading Kaspar away from the square. He jumped up. "Friend," he shouted. The man leapt onto Kaspar and kicked the horse's sides. Kaspar lunged forward, but when Omar whistled Kaspar reared, thrashing his front feet in the air. The man clung to his mane, desperately. Omar shouted, "Get up. Everyone, get up," as he ran toward his horse. Kaspar reared again and the man slipped off his back. Suddenly, the fading moonlight glinted off metal. Omar saw the knife in the man's hand and stopped, waiting for his companions to join him.

"What are you doing with my horse," he demanded.

"One more step and I'll kill you," sneered the thief. In the early light Omar saw that his opponent was thin and beardless, barely a man. Images of the knife plunged into Abe flashed through his mind. Omar's companions gathered around him with their knives raised. The thief turned and fled.

"What's going on?" asked Fergus.

"Someone tried to steal Kaspar."

"We can catch him."

"Don't bother. Kaspar's safe. Let him go."

Omar walked over to Kaspar and stroked his neck to steady the great horse. "Good boy," he said softly. "Thanks for waking me." When the frightened animal was calm, Omar led him back to the square.

"Why would anyone want to steal?" asked Fergus. "Don't people share here?"

"It's different in Pasidia," Omar replied with a sigh.

"Close call." Cedric walked toward Omar, rubbing his sleepy eyes. "Glad you didn't lose Kaspar."

"Me too."

The riders were now fully awake and gathered around Omar in excited chatter. After several minutes Petrina said, "Brrrr, it's sure cold. Wish I could light a fire."

"There's no wood here," offered Zared. "Here, this'll help." He picked up Petrina's blanket and draped it over her shoulders.

"Thanks," Petrina glanced at Zared with a smile.

"I'm hungry," growled Morven. "When can we get some food."

"Soon as the market opens," Omar replied. Groans filtered through the group. "Let's stay warm." Reluctantly they wrapped themselves in their blankets and waited for the sun to rise.

"Hey, Nadine. How about some music?" said Alix.

"Yeah, that sounds good," Morven turned to Nadine. "How about it?"

"My fingers are so cold that I don't know if I can play, but I'll try." Nadine picked up her lute and began plucking the strings softly. Petrina began to sing. Then, although sleepy-eyed and cold, the others joined in to welcome the rising sun with the well known songs of Fabia.

An hour later a hunched-over old man wearing a shabby tunic, leading a small donkey laden with fruits and vegetables, approached the market across the street from the city square. He looked at Omar and his friends with suspicion. His eyes revealed a tiredness that coursed deep within his soul.

"Good morning, friend," said Omar. The old man looked away and kept walking. "Friend," Omar tried again. "Can you sell us some food? We're very hungry." No response. The old man led his donkey to an empty stall in the market and began unloading.

"Can we help you?" asked Omar as he and Fergus walked toward the stall.

"Don't need no help," a harsh voice growled. Ignoring the man's harshness, Omar and Fergus lifted bundles of goods from the donkey's back and carried them into the stall. They helped the man arrange and organize the vegetables, making them ready for sale. He showed no appreciation, but as the men helped him his crusty exterior softened and he began to talk to them.

"Not from around here, are you?"

"We're from Cormath, on our way to Gara." Pain flashed behind the tired, old eyes. Omar continued. "My friends and I are very hungry, we'd like to buy some of your food." The old man stood motionless. "Have you been to Gara?" Omar asked.

"Not interested."

"I understand that your governor has many new ideas," Omar continued. "He's building a strong and prosperous province."

The old shopkeeper pursed his lips. "Prosperous for him, perhaps. But not for us. Look at me." He became animated.

Bitterness spilled from his lips. "I'm old and sick. I should be at home enjoying my grandchildren. But no. Governor Kuman comes and takes my sons to Gara. To work on his projects. Then he took my daughters and made them servants in his palace. No one left to work the garden but a sick man and his broken wife." A deep cough shook his body. He spat dirty, brown phlegm.

"But that's not all," he continued. "On top of this, he adds taxes. I work hard in the garden to produce a few vegetables and sell them for a pittance. Can I keep the money? No. First I pay taxes, always more taxes. There's little left for us."

"I'm told that the other provinces are coming to Gara to learn from Governor Kuman," said Omar.

"Learn. Bah. They only learn how to enslave people and build beautiful palaces for themselves. Our children wait on them instead of looking after their old."

"You find life difficult under the new ideas," Omar ventured.

"The ideas are terrible," the old man shouted. "But that's only part of the problem. Our gardens don't grow as well as they used to. Water no longer rises from the ground each morning. We have to draw water from a well and carry it out to the garden."

Omar was puzzled. "You have to water the garden? That must be difficult."

"You said it. But that's not the end. Look at these." He picked up several stunted and runty carrots and cucumbers and held them in front of Omar. "They don't grow like they used to. And they don't taste the same either. Try it." He handed Omar a carrot. Omar bit into the orange flesh, he screwed up his face.

"What is that?"

"Not like it used to be, is it? Yet we have to work hard to produce this garbage. Weeds grow in our gardens."

"Weeds? What do you mean?" asked Omar.

"Weeds and wild grass. They're foul plants that choke the fruit and vegetables. We have to keep pulling them out, but they always grow again. Hard work, gardening has become. Look at me." He showed Omar his gnarled, calloused hands. "My wife and I work long hours in the garden. Our bodies are tired and sick. But there's barely enough to eat. And we have to sell our produce to pay taxes. New ideas." His voice filled with derision. "Governor Kuman can keep his new ideas. Give me back my children, and plants that grow like they should."

"But, I don't understand," said Omar. "What do these new ideas have to do with water and weeds?"

"The new ideas brought a curse. The ground is damned and bitter. It moans and it cries. It is watered by the sweat of men forced into labour and the blood of animals killed and eaten."

"Yesterday we saw a deer killed and eaten by a lion. It seems the animals have turned against one another."

"Yes. The curse has changed them as well. Many have become eaters of meat. They're wild and we can't communicate with them the way we used to. It's like they've entered a different world."

"Do the animals eat people as well?" asked Fergus.

"The lion. The tiger. Yes. Many of the large ones do. But not only large ones. Many small animals, like the snake, even the spider, have a venom that kills. And they strike without warning."

"I've noticed that it's not just the animals that have gone wild," said Omar. "Men kill men as well."

"Yes. They steal and kill. The curse has spread through our bones and into our hearts. Love has been replaced by hatred and greed."

"Don't the citizens protest to Governor Kuman?"

"Protest? Bah! We're not allowed to see him, let alone protest. Some of the overseers have tried to. Those he can't convince to support him are replaced. Some disappear."

"But overseers are elected by the people," said Fergus.

"Not in Pasidia. All has changed here."

"What about the peoples' relationship with Elconan?" asked Omar. "Has that changed as well?"

"Elconan is silent as we suffer," replied the shopkeeper. "His name is seldom mentioned in Pasidia. Some use it as a curse." The old man paused. "You said you wanted to buy food."

"Yes," Omar replied.

"What would you like?"

They stocked up on enough food to last until they got to Gara.

"Thank you, friend," said Omar as he counted out the zorn. "You've been very kind." Omar poured the zorn into the shopkeeper's hand. "May Elconan bless you and keep you."

"There's more blessing and keeping from the zorn," the merchant replied bitterly.

Omar and Fergus carried the produce to the square. Morven prepared a quick meal as the others packed up the camp and attended to the horses. The sun was soft and warm when the riders finished eating. The city was coming to life. Horses and donkeys carried large loads through the streets that smelled of dust, animal dung and urine. Occasionally a colourful litter moved down the street carried by muscular men in short kilts, their muscles rippled and their uncovered bodies glistened in the early sun. The litters were enclosed; the occupants could not be seen. Four large men in animal skin tunics strode in front of and behind each litter. They held grim faces and straight, rigid backs as they walked in unison, their eyes searching the streets. On a belt at each waist hung a long knife with a carved bone handle.

Omar approached the shopkeeper and asked, "What are those men carrying?"

"The rich. Too lazy to walk like the rest of us," the old man spat. "We're not all equal any more. Not like it used to be."

Omar shook his head. Puzzled. "Strange. They call this progress?" The riders bid farewell to the old shopkeeper and thanked him for the food. Then mounted their horses and rode out of the city.

Many hours passed as they travelled in silence. The things they had seen and heard the past twenty-four hours spoke to their souls and left them unsettled and perturbed, but unprepared for the dangers that lay ahead in Gara.

The shadows had moved from west to north, then to the east

when the jagged tops of buildings melted into the horizon. "There it is," yelled Fergus. "Gara at last." Even the horses sensed the excitement and renewed their pace until they came to the edge of the city.

"What are they doing there?" asked Zared. On both sides of the road workmen were building a giant wall. Many horses and donkeys were dragging rocks to the construction area. Large bamboo scaffolding stretched away from the highway in both directions. Men shouted and strained as large rocks were lifted into position by the power of men, levers and beasts.

"That looks like hard work," said Alix.

The men on the scaffolds wore little, only short animal skin kilts. Their sun bronzed bodies glistened with sweat. Their eyes peered out of dirty faces like two bright stones in mud. Large, muscular men in cotton tunics walked among the workers carrying long whips made of animal skin strips embedded with sharp metal and attached to a wooden handle. The whip-men yelled and cursed as they struck the tired workers and the beasts.

Omar and his companions watched in horror as men cried out from the lashes. Some were struck again and again savagely, until they lay moaning in the dust. But the brutality continued, they were kicked and prodded until they struggled up from the blood stained earth. Those who couldn't get up were dragged away to a pile of broken rocks where they lay in silence. They wouldn't move again.

Omar's heart was sick, he jumped off Kaspar and ran toward the cruel men, to wrest their whips from them. But before he got there, Fergus yelled, "Look at that cloud." A heavy dark cloud, black as the deepest ebony moved across the sun. Day became night. The sky boomed a deep throaty rumble that shook the ground. The horses whinnied and reared, throwing their riders. The air pulsed with a mighty crack as a bright light, brighter than a million candles, surged through the sky. It struck a man high on the scaffold and threw him through the air unto a large pile of broken rocks where he landed with such severity that his bones crumpled and his body burst, covering the rocks with intestines and blood. Men scrambled from the scaffolds, their eyes white with fear. The air rumbled again and again, the bright light cracked. The men with whips struck the workers wildly, cursing and shouting for them to get back on the scaffolds. Suddenly, with a mighty roar and a blinding flash of light the sky burst open and balls of ice, the size of hens' eggs, rained down upon them. Men and animals cried out as they were hit by the cold, hard missiles. The whip-men ran to a nearby shelter that had a strong slate roof, but they wouldn't allow any of the workmen to enter.

The frenzied horses ran in circles, jumping and bucking, trying to free themselves of the white rocks pelting down from the sky. Omar looked around for shelter. Flat, barren, emptiness, everywhere. A few blankets had fallen from the horses and lay in clumps on the ground.

"Cover yourself," Omar shouted. "Grab a blanket. Cover yourself. Get down." His mind raced as he dashed about helping his friends. He thought of all the things he wanted to do before he died. He thought of the people of Cormath, their sorrow when they would hear their governor and the other riders had been beaten to death by white rocks from the sky. He thought about his mother, could her heart survive another brutal death of someone she loved? And he thought of Ester, waiting in Refta, and of the future they planned together. "Elconan," he whispered. "Save us." He fell to the ground, shielding his head with his arms.

As suddenly as it appeared, the black cloud moved away. The rain of ice stones stopped and all became very still. Only the moans and cries of the wounded stirred the stillness. Omar shook the mound of wet stones from his back and got up. The earth was white with many layers of ice.

He looked around at his friends. They were beaten and bloody. Their faces contorted with pain. Growing patches of red stained their tunics. One body lay still, twisted and misshapen. "Oh no," Omar groaned as he ran to the broken heap. It was Cedric. Omar dropped to his knees and checked for a heartbeat. There was none.

Gently he rolled the crumpled body unto its back. Cedric's eyes were rolled up. He lay still. A deep sharp pain rattled into Omar's heart. Cedric's mother was now not only a widow, she was also childless. The vibrant spirit of determination and loyalty lay dead amidst the ruins of a violent storm. A heavy blanket of guilt and remorse settled over Omar and crushed his spirit like a cold vice.

"Is he dead?" asked Fergus. Omar glanced at him and nodded. The other riders gathered around them. Unbelief and fear etched their faces.

Omar got up and looked around through blurred eyes. At the construction site men were stirring. Some sat among the destruction holding their heads. Others raised their bruised bodies from the ground. All around the white rocks were stained with blood. A few of the men didn't move. The blow of the ice rocks had been deadly. Their wives had suddenly become widows, their children, fatherless.

The whip-men moved out of the shelter. "All right, men," they shouted. "Time to get your wimpy bodies back to work." They struck the dazed, wounded men with their whips and forced their bruised bodies back to the scaffold.

"We better get the horses," said Fergus sadly. Frenzied by the deluge of white stone, they had scattered across the countryside which now lay as a white desolate waste. Petrina shook with deep, anguished sobs. Nadine placed a hand on her shoulder and wept with her. Dazed and shocked, the others wiped tears as they pulled themselves from their dead friend to find their horses. They whistled and called until gradually, one-by-one, the frightened horses returned. A few had severe bruises, but all the horses survived. Omar caressed Kaspar's neck and rubbed his body carefully around the sore spots. Satisfied that the horse was okay, he mounted and looked for Cedric's horse. It stood by its slain rider, muzzling the swollen face with his nose. His large body quivered as he sensed the darkness of death. Omar calmed the horse with soft words as he rubbed it's neck and face.

"Give me a hand," Omar said. They lifted Cedric's body and laid it across his horse. "We'll take him to an embalmer in Gara."

"What kind of wickedness is this?" asked Fergus as he slipped on the melting hailstones. "I've never seen anything like it. That cloud looked like the heart of evil."

"A sign of the curse we heard about in Octor."

With shouts, curses and lashes of the whip, work resumed on the scaffolds along the wall.

"This is unbelievable! I've never seen men so cruel. How come it's allowed?"

"Underlings gone mad with their thirst for power. I'll speak to Kuman about this, it must be stopped. He can't be aware of what's going on here. Kuman would never allow people to be treated like this."

TEN

"Omar, my dear friend," rang the familiar voice. "It's great to see you." The two old friends embraced warmly in the large lobby of the palace. "Did you have a safe journey?" Kuman asked. He was dressed in a glowing, white robe of fine linen with a purple sash. Gold chains around his neck glistened in the flickering light of many lamps. His bright smile broke the cleanly shaved face. Large, gold earrings hung from his ears, gems sparkled in gold settings on each finger.

"The cloud of white that greeted us killed one of my companions," said Omar sadly.

"Yes, I heard about that. How awful. I'm so terribly sorry. I can't even imagine how upsetting this must be for you. Please be assured that you have my deepest sympathy." He paused, his face a mask of sympathy and sorrow. Then continued, "That was a vicious hailstorm, wasn't it? They seem to be getting worse. Wiped out a lot of gardens." His face brightened. "I'm thankful that we have agreements with the other provinces so that they share their resources with us. The weather has not been kind to the crops in Pasidia."

"But we've always shared equally in Fabia."

"Yes. But this is different. They give to Pasidia whether there is any left for themselves or not." Kuman snickered. "By the way, did you take your friend to the palace embalmer? We have a good one, you know."

"Yes. Leeah directed me to him." Omar's voice was etched with pain.

"Are you all settled into the palace guest-house comfortably?"

"Yes, thank you. Your hospitality is warm. We are well taken care of."

"Good."

"Kuman, what are you building at the edge of the city?"

"A wall. I'm building a large thick wall to protect the residents."

"From what?"

"The provinces that haven't joined with me will envy our progress. I need to speak to you Omar, about Cormath joining the alliance."

"Are you aware of the way men are being treated on the wall?" asked Omar. Their discussion was interrupted as an entourage entered the room. In the lead was a short, dumpy woman whose purple Kuman robe was draped over a large body, misshapen by bulges of fat. Her long, greasy hair fell in rumpled curls around her pudgy face. She was followed by a dozen young men with cleanly shaved eager faces and closely cropped hair, wearing the purple state robes.

"Omar, you know Governor Alaya of Corno, don't you?" asked Kuman.

"Yes, we've met."

"Governor Alaya, how good to see you," Kuman said. "And how is the sweet first lady of Corno?" She extended a fleshy hand toward Kuman. Gemstones sparkled from her fingers.

"Good evening, Governor," she said with a slight bow. Kuman took the fat fingers and kissed them lightly.

"You know Governor Omar, of course."

"Oh, yes. The king's son. I'm so sorry about what happened to your father. How's your dear mother doing?" she asked, her voice dripping with false sincerity.

"My mother is well," Omar replied. "She's devastated, of course, but her faith in the goodness of Elconan gives her strength."

"Oh, yes. And to all of us," Alaya said lightly. "Is Cormath interested in the wonders of Pasidia as well?"

"Governor Kuman is an old friend. I came for the dedication of his structure on the hill."

JOURNEY TO LIGHT

"Of course, the secret structure. The governor will dazzle us all with the magnificence of his project. I can hardly wait."

"I'm glad you were able to come early, Alaya," said Kuman. "Governor Omar has asked me for a tour of our projects. You'll be able to travel together. But that's tomorrow. Tonight we'll dine." Kuman signalled to an attendant waiting in the shadows. Suddenly the doors to the dining hall swung open, musicians burst the air with the sounds of trumpet, flute and lyre. Attendants moved into the lobby and escorted the visitors to tables.

Omar and Alaya were led to a large, round oak table. It's highly polished surface shimmered in the soft light. Alaya was placed to the right of Kuman, while a small, wispy man with beady eyes sat on his left. A tall, full-bodied girl with sleek, black hair, clear, smooth skin and bright eyes placed Omar to the left of the wispy man. "Deputy Cadmus, this is Governor Omar of Cormath," said the girl.

"Good evening, Governor," said the deputy. His face twitched as he spoke. "Aren't you the king's son?"

"Yes...I mean...I was."

"Oh yes. That was a nasty business. You have my sympathy," said the deputy in a flat voice.

"Thank you." Omar glanced around the table. The circle of twelve was completed by a number of male dignitaries from Pasidia. Alaya was the only woman. Omar was disappointed that Tamara was not at the table. She was a good friend and he had hoped to see her again. *Why hadn't Kuman included her?* He wondered.

Alaya's young attendants were seated at a smaller table in the corner of the room. Omar's riding companions sat at a round table next to them. Sobered and saddened by the death of Cedric, they sat in stony silence.

"I understand you'll be touring some of our projects tomorrow," said Cadmus, when they were seated.

"Yes. I've heard a lot about them, but no details. I'm anxious to see what you're doing here in Pasidia."

"It's great, you'll be impressed." Cadmus shifted as he spoke, his hands moved constantly. Omar noticed that his fingernails were chewed to raw flesh.

"What can you tell me about them?" asked Omar.

"Massive. Just wonderful. You'll be impressed. It'll be good to have Cormath in the alliance."

A cold wash swept over Omar. In a cautious voice he said, "Tell me about the alliance."

"Many of the provinces are joining us. It's very exciting."

"But what is the nature of the alliance? And what is its purpose?"

"I must defer to Governor Kuman on that. He's the expert. He's a real genius, you know. Brilliant." While they talked attendants in short, sheer tunics loaded the tables with trays of fruit, blocks of cheese, flatbread, raised bread, vegetables prepared with seasoned sauces, along with the meat of fowl, deer, cattle and pigs. Also with much wine, beer and tekara.

"Is Cormath eating meat?" asked Cadmus.

"No," said Omar firmly. "We respect animals in Cormath. They are our friends. Our responsibility is to protect them, not kill them."

Cadmus laughed with a cackle that sounded like a cluck scared from its nest. "Old fashioned ideas. The animals serve us in Pasidia. We are the masters."

"That's not the way it was from the beginning."

"But things change, Governor. Don't you want Cormath to be progressive? Those old fashioned ideas were for another era. They may have been right for our ancestors. But we must progress."

"I'm concerned about some of the progress I've seen in Pasidia," said Omar softly.

"But wait till you see the projects. And our new ideas. Your concern will wash away." Exasperation swelled through Omar. Cadmus was elusive, his speech empty, and he sat as a wall between him and Kuman. Omar wanted to talk about the poor he had seen in Pasidia. The sad faces and downcast eyes in Topath. The anger in Octor, the murder of Abe and the mistreatment of men and animals at the wall. But both Kuman and Cadmus danced around his questions and could speak only of their new ideas. Never had he felt such frustration. He missed Tamara. At least she spoke to him directly.

"Where is the governor's wife tonight?" he asked. "I was hoping she'd be here."

Cadmus chortled derisively. "She's in her place."

"What do you mean?"

"She spoke out against some of the governor's new ideas, so he's restricted her to their private quarters in the palace. She isn't allowed to have any visitors." A deep and heavy sadness settled over Omar's soul. His heart ached for Tamara. *How could he help her? What was happening to Kuman? To Pasidia?* His thoughts were interrupted by Cadmus.

"We're dividing the roles of men and women."

"What do you mean?"

"This business of equality and shared responsibility—that's old fashioned. In the new Pasidia, leadership is defined more definitely. It's a lot easier this way and it avoids a lot of confusion."

"And how is leadership defined in Pasidia?"

"Men are stronger, so they should be the leaders. It's only natural. The woman's role is to serve the man and look after the family. We're phasing women out of leadership positions."

"Then why is Alaya sitting at Kuman's right. Isn't she a woman, and a leader?"

Cadmus snickered softly. "Oh, yes. We have to work with existing structures. But we're defining the future, you know. And Governor Kuman has a great dream as to what the future should be."

While they were eating Omar noticed Alaya drinking Kuman's tekara freely. Her conversation became more and more animated, her voice shrill. Loud, giddy laughter burst from her heavily painted lips. Her face was flushed, her eyes glazed. Kuman spoke to her continuously, their faces together, his hand frequently around her shoulders, rubbing her back or holding her pudgy hand.

Omar was familiar with Kuman's charm. He had seen it used frequently when they were young. He remembered a time when they went on a hike in the hills around Gara.

***

"I'll be back for the evening meal," he told his mother as he kissed her on his way out the door.

"Where are you going?"

"I'm going for a hike in the forest with Kuman."

"We won't eat until you get back," his mother promised. "So don't be late." Omar picked up the shoulder bag that Miriam had filled with fresh bread, baked beans, boiled eggs, carrots and apples. He wore a light, knee length cotton tunic and heavy rope sandals for the rugged terrain.

The forest vibrated with birds singing, chirping and trilling. Along the trail the boys saw deer, rabbits, tigers, lions and many small creatures that skittered along the ground. They stopped frequently to pet and play with the animals. Man, forest and beast— a stimulating synergy. For the boys it was an exciting adventure.

After they had trekked for several hours Kuman said, "I'm hungry, let's eat." Perspiration dripped from his brow in the midday sun.

Omar pointed to a large oak tree that covered the ground beneath it in deep shade. "Let's sit there," he said. The boys walked to the tree, folded their legs under them and settled onto the ground under the cool canopy. They reached into their shoulder bags and pulled out their lunch.

"Let's go beyond the hills to the next village," said Kuman eagerly. "I've got an uncle who lives there. We can stay with him tonight. Then return tomorrow."

"But I'm expected back for the evening meal," Omar objected. "My family will be waiting for me."

"They know you're with me. You'll be safe," Kuman said, smiling. The boys argued for several minutes but, as usual, Kuman's persuasiveness neutralized Omar's objections. He agreed to go to the village.

JOURNEY TO LIGHT

The next day, as they were returning through the woods they met Ulis and a group of people who had been up all night, combing the woods, looking for the boys. Ulis was furious when he learned what the boys had done. "Your mother is frantic," he said severely. "You told her you'd be back last night. And these people have been up all night, looking for you."

Omar was chagrined. He looked at the grim faces staring at him and shamefacedly, mumbled apologies. Kuman used a different approach. He turned on his charm. He spoke to Ulis and the group with confident respect and thanked them for their concern. Then he humoured them until the grim faces were smiling. Kuman's effect on the tired group was magical. They forgot the long, futile night in the woods and began laughing and sharing jokes.

***

Now, Omar noticed that Kuman's effect on Alaya was just as hypnotic. Her heart and mind were slowly seduced as the meal progressed. Deep in his soul Omar knew that Corno would join Kuman's alliance

A small orchestra of flutes, lyres and harps played softly throughout the meal. As the group ate and drank, their conversations became louder, their laughter boisterous, exaggerated. When they couldn't eat anymore the tables were cleared quickly by the scantily clad servants and Kuman rose to speak. The room became quiet. An expectancy hung in the air. All eyes were focused on the governor. The gold chains hanging around his neck reflected bits of the flickering lamps as they lay on the brilliant white robe. His long, blond hair caught the soft breeze flowing through the room and stirred softly. He stood before them, his intense eyes gleaming with fire, his face glowing in the soft light. His lips formed a warm smile. All eyes in the room were fixed on Kuman.

"Dear friends," he began. "Tonight we stand on the threshold of a bright, new tomorrow." Kuman's effect on the group was mesmeric, it broke into loud sustained applause. Kuman's face radiated pleasure and power. After several minutes he raised his hands and the applause faded. "I'm very happy that you are able to be here with us tonight. We welcome Governor Alaya and the delegation from Corno." Kuman led the group in energetic applause. Then he continued. "We expect that our provinces will soon be joined together in a powerful alliance that will lead us into an exciting, new future." More applause. "Governor Alaya is a brave leader who leads her province with much wisdom, sensitivity and insight." Alaya's face glowed with the adulation. Kuman continued to speak of the glories and strength of the alliance and how it was ushering in a bright future of achievement and accomplishment such as the world has never known.

"We also welcome to our table, Governor Omar of Cormath, and his friends." The group applauded warmly. "I believe that, like his late father, the king, Governor Omar is a leader of great foresight, integrity and compassion." Omar felt embarrassed by the plaudits and by the applause, cheers and whistles from the audience. "Governor Omar, as many of your know, is a long time friend. We grew up together and were both schooled by the noble Kara. He has come to learn of our achievements and progress. Cormath will be a strong and vital member in our alliance." The audience jumped to their feet clapping, shouting, cheering. Omar wished they'd stop. He had no intention of joining the alliance.

"Tomorrow morning," Kuman continued. "We will take Governors' Alaya and Omar to see a few of our projects. Those going on the tour should meet in front of the hall-of-justice at the first light of dawn. A wonderful meal will be ready for you there. Then you'll spend a full day travelling to several exciting construction sites. Unfortunately, I will not be able to travel with you on this tour as I'll be receiving visitors from all regions of Fabia that are coming for the dedication. However, your guide will be the very able and competent Deputy Cadmus." Kuman motioned toward the deputy, then led the group in applause.

"Tomorrow evening we'll all meet here again, with representatives from all of the provinces, for a sumptuous state dinner."

Omar chaffed as Kuman continued. He was disappointed to learn that Kuman would not be with them tomorrow. He had to speak to him about what he saw on his trip to Gara and at the wall. He determined to try and get to him as soon as the speech ended.

"The day following tomorrow, we will all meet on the high hill for the dedication of the great structure." Kuman said in a voice with rising excitement. "You won't want to miss that." The audience applauded. "This will be followed by a celebration such as you've never seen. All the planning has been done under the very able direction of Deputy Cadmus." Kuman once again led the audience in applause.

"Get a good rest tonight. The next two days will be very busy." As Kuman sat down the group jumped to their feet, clapping and cheering.

Suddenly, drums pounded, tambourines rattled and trumpets blared as the orchestra burst into a frantic, driven beat. Young men and women, in short, white sheer tunics swirled into the room. They fanned out among the guests and pulled them onto the dance floor. The tall, full-bodied, girl who had seated Omar earlier moved in his direction. She took his hands.

"Come, dance with me," she crooned.

"I have to see Governor Kuman," he stammered. He looked to his right. The chair was empty. "Where's Kuman?" he asked Cadmus. There was no answer. Cadmus was leading Alaya to the dance floor.

"Come on, let's dance," said the girl. She pulled Omar's hands.

"No," he shouted. "I have to see Kuman." He jerked his hands free and ran toward the door of the palace living quarters. A muscular guard in an animal skin tunic barred his way.

"You can't go in there," he said gruffly.

"But I need to see the governor," Omar blurted.

"The governor has gone to his private quarters. No one can see him."

"But I'm a friend. I need to see him, I came all the way from Cormath to see him."

A second burly guard joined the first. "This guy giving you trouble?" he asked.

"Yeah. Wants to see the governor. Doesn't seem to know what 'no' means."

"But...I need to see...Kuman," Omar stammered as the guards grabbed his arms and dragged him out of the room.

Outside, the fresh air in the dark night hit his face, he breathed deeply and calmed his spirit. "What's the big deal?" he asked his brawny captors. "Governor Kuman and I have been friends since childhood. I have to talk to him. It's very important."

"If he wanted to talk to you, we'd know about it," said the first guard. "To see the governor you have to make an appointment with Secretary Shobal. You can see him in the morning."

"But the governor said he'd be busy tomorrow receiving visitors."

"You make the appointment with the secretary tomorrow," barked the guard. "Now, where are you staying?"

"In the guest quarters."

The guard whistled and two more guards with long knives attached to their waists appeared out of the darkness. "Take this man to his room," said the first guard. "And place a watch at the door. Make sure he doesn't leave the room until further orders. I'll check with Deputy Cadmus when the party's over as to what we're supposed to do with him."

ELEVEN

The sun was breaking the eastern horizon as Omar, Fergus and Nadine walked toward the hall-of-justice. Cadmus had instructed Omar that only two companions were allowed to ride with him. The others would be taken on a city tour.

The trio was followed closely by a muscular guard. Omar turned to him, annoyed. "You don't need to follow me. I won't do anything I'm not supposed to."

"Orders," grunted the guard.

Birds trilled and sang from the trees and bushes. A pleasant fragrance of many flowers opening to the sun filled their nostrils. The sky was clear and blue, a promise of a beautiful day. They rounded the corner of the building and saw several tables laden with fresh fruit, cheese and bread. Tired faces and red eyes greeted them as they walked toward the people standing around the tables, eating.

Cadmus flitted among the crowd, greeting people and giving directions to the servants. "Good morning, Governor," he said brightly, when he noticed Omar and his friends. "Did you rest well? I'm sorry about that business last night, but the guards were just trying to protect you. They have their orders." He nodded to the guard, who then turned and left the group. "Governor Kuman insists that every guest at the palace be well taken care of."

"I didn't feel very well taken care of last night. How can I get to see him?"

"He's very busy today with new guests arriving. And tomorrow there's the dedication. He'll be tied up with that. But since you're an old friend I'll do a special favour for you. I'll talk to Secretary Shobal about arranging a meeting. But I won't be seeing him for the next couple of days. Details, details, details. So many details," he shook his head as he spoke. "Good morning," he said brightly to Fergus with a bow. "Did you enjoy the banquet?"

"That tekara really made my head spin," Fergus replied with an amused voice. "That's dangerous stuff."

"Welcome to Gara," Cadmus chuckled. "You'll enjoy today's tour. We have many wonderful things to show you. I'm very glad that Cormath is interested in what we're doing. Please," he pointed to the table. "Enjoy some food." He slipped away to greet another arriving guest.

As they were finishing the meal Cadmus addressed the group. "Ladies and gentlemen, we're so happy that you are here with us in Gara this morning. I believe most of you met last night. Wasn't that some party?" His questions got several tired grunts of approval. He continued. "We're really excited that Corno and Cormath are here to see the wonders of the new Pasidia."

Cadmus outlined the travel plans for the day. They would be riding to several construction sites around Gara, getting back in time for the lavish evening celebration with representatives from every province.

***

Cadmus and his entourage were accompanied by an escort of sixteen riders dressed in animal skin tunics over which they wore a heavy metal mesh that protected their bodies and their legs. On their heads they wore heavy metal helmets. Shiny, long knives with looped metal handles hung from their waists.

"It must be hot under there," Fergus said to Omar. "What are they wearing that for?"

"I don't know, maybe we'll find out on this tour."

Two groups of four of the uniformed riders rode in front of Cadmus, while another two groups of four followed the entourage out of the palace grounds and down the dusty street that led to the edge of the city. Omar was dismayed to see metal bridles in the horses mouths. The uniformed riders spoke to their mounts with harsh words and controlled them by pulling on the bridles and kicking their sides with the ends of the hard, wooden soles of their boots, in which sharp, pointed metal was embedded. Omar was happy he was riding Kaspar. He directed his horse with soft words and gentle hand signals to the neck.

The city was coming to life in the early light. The air was pungent with dust, animal sweat and dung. Cadmus rode at the front of the group on a large chestnut mare with black mane and stockings. "I hate these loathsome creatures," he muttered. He rode with distaste etched upon his face, sitting on the horse gingerly, as though he was afraid the animal carried a fierce contagious disease. Alaya followed Cadmus in a chariot. Her massive body prevented her from mounting a horse. One of her attendants, a tall, thin man with beady eyes and claw-like hands, drove the chariot while two more followed on horseback. Next rode Omar, with Fergus on his left and Nadine on his right. Three male officials from Kuman's administration rode among the group.

The uniformed riders in front of the entourage shouted, "Make way...Make way," as they rode with stern faces, their backs straight and rigid. The traffic on the street parted in front of the advancing host. Those who didn't move aside fast enough faced a barrage of curses and bitter words, and had to jump out of the way of swinging knives.

Omar felt embarrassed and ashamed to be part of a group demanding its right to the street in such a rude, harsh manner. His spirit cringed, his heart ached with sympathy and compassion for the frightened citizens on the street. As the riders passed, the people stared at them with vacant eyes, their shoulders stooped in resignation. A few stood defiant and erect, their eyes shining hatred.

When they reached the edge of the city the horses were prodded into a gallop. They rode toward the highlands southwest of the capital for about an hour. The horses were wet with sweat and the riders were caked with dust when a large scaffold on top of a high hill loomed ahead of them. As they approached, men became visible moving all over the scaffold. Dust was rising from their work amidst shouts and curses.

"On that hill we are building a large ziggurat," said Cadmus. His face twitched as he spoke. "It will be a giant tower reaching up into the heavens." Behind the tower smoke poured to the sky from many ovens that baked the clay brick with which the tower was being built. The base was a large, rectangular shape that reached across the top of the hill. From there it tapered upward to the sky. The men working at the top looked like ants climbing around on a giant ant hill. "Steps wind all the way up to the top inside the tower," said Cadmus. "At the top there will be a large observation deck and an altar."

"What's it for?" asked Omar.

"From it we'll observe and study the movement of the stars. We'll also be able to communicate clearly with the spirits of the sky. It will be a bond between heaven and earth."

"What's the altar for?" asked Nadine. Cadmus looked at her and grinned. "You'll find out tomorrow, at the dedication," he said.

"That's amazing," said Alaya. "Whose idea was that?"

"Governor Kuman's. He outlined the plans and then hired skilled draftsmen to draw up the details. We have ten thousand men working on the project."

"Who is looking after their gardens?" asked Omar. "And their families?"

"Most of the men are young. Taken from their homes before they had gardens to tend, or families," replied Cadmus.

"Taken?" Omar questioned.

"The vision of our great governor is so exciting that all Pasidian's bow to it gladly. The men are happy to be working for the future glory of Pasidia."

When they approached the construction site dirty, vacant faces stared at them. Behind their eyes Omar saw hatred, fear and resignation.

"Oh look," said Nadine. "Why are some men chained to the scaffold?"

"Lazy scoffers. They don't want to work for the greatness of our future," replied Cadmus. "They don't yet understand the privilege they enjoy, working on the governor's dream." A whip cracked, followed by a deep, agonized moan.

"He's beating him," cried Nadine. "Stop." She jumped from her horse, but before she could run toward the man holding the whip, she was surrounded by four of the armed escorts.

"Don't get involved," Cadmus twitched. "The lazy must be taught how to participate in the governor's vision. He'll be okay," he added coldly.

"I think your idea is marvellous," piped Alaya. "Governor Kuman told me about this ziggurat last night. I can hardly wait to see it finished. I'd love to communicate with the stars."

"We must move on," ordered Cadmus. Nadine looked at Omar, her eyes pleading.

"We'll speak to the governor about it," Omar said quietly. "That's the only way to change it."

Nadine shook her head in disbelief. "Just like at the wall. I don't believe what I'm seeing in this province." Reluctantly, she tore herself away from the brutal scene and mounted her horse. Omar's heart felt like a cold piece of jagged rock as they followed a packed dirt road heading northwest from the ziggurat. He rode in deep silence and contemplation, his thoughts troubled.

The sun was high in the sky when they stopped beside a noisy stream cascading over rocks; its spray reflected the bright sun in diamonds of brilliant light. The chariot driver spread a large, brightly coloured cotton blanket on the ground. He placed bowls of fruit, mounds of raisin cakes, chunks of cheese, cold sausage, sliced duck breast and bread on the blanket along with two clay jugs of wine.

"I'm glad to get off that animal," Cadmus muttered as he limped toward the blanket. "Should have taken a chariot, like you, Alaya."

"But of course," said Alaya, in a fruity voice. "It's the only way to travel."

"Come on," Cadmus urged. "I'm hungry. Let's eat."

Omar spoke softly to Kaspar, then released him to drink from the stream and graze while he joined the others for the meal. The riders folded their legs under themselves around the edge of the blanket and ate eagerly.

After the meal, as they were mounting their horses, Omar overheard Cadmus quietly instruct one of the armed escorts. "Ride ahead and tell them, 'no whips while we're there.' I don't want another scene." The escort nodded, mounted his horse and rode away.

***

An hour later the road broke out of the highland trees and the riders saw a large valley stretch out ahead of them. It was a flat plain with few trees bounded on the northwest by the Yoho River.

"What's that?" exclaimed Nadine. The riders stopped to look at a large structure under construction in the middle of the valley. Men, donkeys and horses swarmed the valley floor moving rocks toward the construction site. In the midst of the dust and the noise rose a large, stone building as high as twenty men and at least twice that distance on each side.

"We call this the embryo," said Cadmus. "Twenty thousand men are at work here."

"Embryo?" Omar questioned.

"Yes. The symbol of life. From this valley a new breed of people will arise that will help us take over the world. The rulers of tomorrow. See that building over there?" He pointed to the west side of the valley where a low, clay brick structure stood. "Temporary housing for the infants who are the beginning of a new race. When this building is finished large numbers of babies will be produced here that will grow up to be giants."

Omar was puzzled by the deputy's words. "What are you talking about?"

"Come. See for yourself." They rode across the valley to the low, windowless building. They stopped in front of a large door in the centre of the side facing northeast, toward the construction site. "Leave the horses here," said Cadmus. "The men will look after them." He nodded toward the armed escort. "Follow me, and stay close. What you see may startle you, so let's stay together." Two armed guards stood at the door. They bowed as Cadmus approached. Then they swung the door open. The group stepped into a roofless entryway that faced a second door. Cadmus waited until all were in the lobby and the door closed behind them.

"What is this place?" Nadine whispered to Omar. "It feels spooky."

Cadmus knocked on the inner door. A small window in the door opened, revealing a woman's face. It was sad, weary and deeply lined. Her vacant eyes sparked recognition, she opened the door and bowed.

"Good day, Semira," Cadmus said, as he stepped through the doorway.

"Good day, Deputy Cadmus," Semira replied blandly. "More visitors, I see."

"Yes. Corno and Cormath. There is a growing interest in what you are doing here." Cadmus turned to his entourage. "Semira oversees this nursery. It's the key to the future of Pasidia. These children are the offspring of the gods and choice women that have been carefully selected by Governor Kuman for this very important task."

Fergus looked at Omar. "Offspring of the gods? What's he talking about?"

"Sounds strange," said Omar in a grave voice. "I guess we're about to find out."

"Come," continued Cadmus. They stepped into an open courtyard in the centre of the building. It was bare and dull. Grotesque, naked children played on the hard, packed dirt. Their oversized bodies, hands, feet, arms and legs were too large for their years and sprouted hair like animals. Their movements were exaggerated and clumsy. Their play was loud, boisterous and rough, with the intensity of combat. Pushing. Shoving. Fighting. They chortled with sadistic laughter when one triumphed over the other. Large, muscular women supervised the children.

"What are those creatures?" Nadine whispered. Cadmus overheard. He turned to her with a sardonic grin.

"Those aren't creatures," he said firmly. "They're superchildren who will help us rule the future once they've grown up and are trained."

"All boys?" asked Alaya.

"Yes. Girls are not given life."

"What do you mean?" asked Omar.

Cadmus just looked at him. He didn't answer. He turned to the children and continued. "As you'll notice, the children are well taken care of. Each has his own nurse, twenty four hours per day."

"Are the nurses their mothers?" asked Fergus.

"No," replied Cadmus bluntly. "The children are separated from their mothers at birth and placed with the nurse. It's better that way. They stay here until the age of eight. Then they are moved to another facility to begin their formal training in the art of war. We'll visit that this afternoon."

Omar was puzzled. "War? What's that?"

"When other provinces see our success they may become envious and attack us. These young supermen will be a great asset to our army to protect our nation. You'll learn more about this at the next stop. We must move on."

As they prepared to leave one of the children lumbered over to look at the visitors. Omar looked into his eyes. He saw a thirsty evil that thrust a penetrating coldness through his blood. As he stared into the child's eyes a deep depression settled over him like a blanket of lead. A heavy sadness that he could not shake.

"We must move on," Cadmus intoned. "We've got more riding to do." They left the building and mounted their horses. Then they took a northeast path along the Yoho river past the construction site.

"That's a large building," Omar said.

"Just wait until it's finished," Cadmus said with pride. "It'll be a pyramid of giants, where the gods will help us establish a generation of great and powerful men. The building must symbolize its noble purpose. Nothing like this has ever been built before. It's a joint project we're doing with the help of the gods."

"Is this guy crazy?" Fergus whispered to Omar. "What's all this stuff about the gods?"

"I'm not sure," Omar replied quietly. "But you saw those children back there. What do you make of them?"

Fergus shuddered. "I feel devoid of the presence of Elconan around here."

"Me too. I've never felt so cold and empty."

"What you're showing us is very fascinating," chirped Alaya. "Did you say there was more?"

"Yes," replied the deputy. "There's one more stop on this tour. But we must hurry." Cadmus whipped his horse. It lunged forward, its nostrils flared, its eyes wild.

"Let's go, Kaspar," Omar urged the golden stallion. Kaspar's hooves dug into the packed soil as the horse sprang to life. The horses ran with their heads pushed forward and low, the sharp hooves tore into the packed road, the ground rumbled and shook as they sped across the plain.

It was late in the afternoon when they arrived at a construction site, surrounded by bamboo scaffolding, where walls of dressed stone were being raised by workmen that swarmed the structure like honey bees. The walls were as high as four men and filled a rectangular space as wide as twenty men and as long as forty.

"This is the first in a series of buildings that we will construct here," Cadmus informed the group. "Here we are teaching young men the art of war." Behind the building a row of low, clay structures stretched back toward Gara. Acrid clouds rose from clay chimneys and stung the nostrils of the riders.

"We're burning coal over there," Cadmus pointed to the dark smoke.

"What's that?" asked Omar.

"It's a hard, black substance that we dig from the ground. It produces more heat than wood."

"Amazing," gushed Alaya.

Shouts and curses pierced the air along with the sharp clang of metal banging metal.

"What are they doing in those buildings?" asked Omar.

"Let's go see," said Cadmus gleefully. He slid from his horse. "I'm always glad to get off this beast." He threw the reins to one of the escorts. Fierce fires burned in stone stoves throughout the compound. Large, muscular men worked in short skirts, their naked chests glistened with sweat which ran down the grime covered bodies in black rivers. The group watched as red hot metal was taken from the fires and pounded into long, sharp knives.

"So, this is where you get those long knives," exclaimed Fergus.

"We call them swords," said Cadmus. "We have thousands stored in these buildings."

"Whew," Omar whistled. "What will you use them all for?"

"Defence," came the sharp reply. "We're training soldiers how to use them to fight. They will defend our borders against invaders."

"Why would anyone invade Pasidia?" asked Omar. "Wouldn't you share your resources with those in need?"

Cadmus laughed. His face twitched. "We're not thinking about need. Rather greed. When others see the wonders of Pasidia they will become greedy and want to take them from us."

"The only province that has soldiers is Pasidia," said Omar. "You have nothing to fear."

"But, perhaps the other provinces should fear us," said Cadmus. The coldness in his voice sent a shiver through Omar. In the distance men were marching in formation, turning, stopping, dropping to the ground, running with their swords drawn—to the loud barks of a short, fat but pugnacious commander.

"What are they doing?" Fergus pointed to marchers.

"Battle training. Our soldiers are being trained to defeat any enemy."

"But we have no enemies," Omar protested. "Fabia is a land of peace and caring for one another."

"But, Governor," Cadmus said flatly, his face twitched as he spoke. "Wasn't your father killed by evil men? Wouldn't armed guards have been able to protect him?"

A sharp pain stabbed through Omar. In a quiet voice he asked, "Where did the killers come from?" Cadmus didn't respond.

"I think you're being very wise," said Alaya. "I would like to send some men here to be trained to protect me. Who knows when the killers will strike again."

"Many of the provinces see things as you do, Governor Alaya," said Cadmus. "We have agreements for mutual benefit with a number of our neighbours. But this is not the place for that discussion. We must leave. It's a hard ride back to Gara. I'm sure you don't want to miss tonight's banquet."

TWELVE

Omar shifted restlessly at the banquet table. He was distracted. Distant. Fergus sat to his right, Nadine to his left. His other Cormath friends were scattered throughout the huge crowd. All day long delegations had arrived from every province. They were seated with Kuman's advisors, administrators, their wives and a large group of carefully selected admirers of Kuman. The tables filled the room and swept out onto the lawn surrounding the palace. Torches, mounted on posts spread across the lawn, cast flickering, eerie light on those seated at the tables.

The air was full of noise, conversations, laughter and the excited buzz of a celebrant crowd. Harps and lyres played a soft backdrop to the friendly, festive clamour.

Male and female servants in short, sheer tunics moved among the tables and loaded them with bowls of fresh fruit, plates of cheese, fresh flatbread, dishes of pickles, stuffed artichokes, mushrooms roasted with pine nuts along with plates of butter-fried shrimp and grilled scallops.

"There is no modesty in Pasidia," said Fergus, in a dull, critical tone, as he observed the servant's attire.

Omar turned to Nadine. She blushed. Her eyes were fixed on a stocky servant placing a tray on their table. "I've never seen a man with so little on," she mumbled. "This is embarrassing."

"Keep our eyes on your plate," he encouraged her. "They'll be done serving soon." The servants kept the wine goblets full, and for those who preferred it, tekara and beer was readily available.

Kuman required all of the guests to wear a purple robe secured with a yellow sash. He stood out in the crowd wearing a white robe of gossamer linen, tied with a purple sash. Ample gold chains hung around his neck and wrists. Exquisite gems glistened in elegant gold settings on each finger. The governor sat at a raised table at the end of the room, facing the crowd.

Omar was pleased to see Tamara sitting at Kuman's left. She sat with her shoulders slumped, a dark pain etched on her face. Omar wanted to run to her, to encourage her and share her agony, but the tables were arranged so that no one could reach the dais. On her left sat a dark, gloomy man who Omar recognized as one of Kuman's advisors.

On Kuman's right sat a thin drawn man with shaved head and face. He wore a dark green robe with a yellow sash. Omar didn't recognize the man and wondered about the green robe since it was the only one, except Kuman's, that wasn't purple. To the right of the green robe sat Cadmus. His face twitched as he surveyed the crowd.

Kuman greeted his guests with a warm smile and spoke to them with grace and charm, welcoming them to Pasidia and to the great dedication celebration. With their veins warmed with wine, beer and tekara, the audience responded with loud applause, shouts and cheers.

After Kuman's welcome, the servants moved among the tables quickly with trays of food. Each guest was served an elegant strawberry and shrimp salad. This was followed with bowls of vegetables and trays of meat: barbecued beef steaks, rack of lamb and roast pork. Each dish was served with a delicious sauce and constantly refilled by the attentive servants.

Omar watched the guests eat the piles of meat with a sinking heart. Pictures of the animals that were killed to feed this gluttonous crowd plagued his mind and made his stomach sick. He picked at the vegetables, but couldn't eat. He felt Nadine nudge his ribs.

"I feel sorry for the person that had to kill all the animals," she said.

"I feel sorry for the animals. They've always been our friends, but here they're killed and eaten."

The crowd became boisterous as it consumed the food, wine,

beer and tekara. Hilarious laughter punctured the air as people became drunk and animated. Suggestive, rude and lewd remarks were flung at the scantily clad servers as they carried trays of cakes, tarts and other sweets to the tables.

When the guests finished eating, Kuman stood to his feet. The crowd hushed. Shouters were stationed out on the lawn to convey Kuman's words to all of the guests.

"Dear friends," he began. "On behalf of all of us in Pasidia, I'm happy to take this opportunity to welcome the delegates from all of the provinces of Fabia. You are among friends. Welcome." The audience applauded spontaneously. When the applause slowed Kuman continued. "I'm delighted that you have come here for our celebration and the dedication of a monument that will define the future of both Pasidia, and all of the provinces that are allied with us." Omar noticed Marshia staring at him from a table across the room. Her eyes were cold, her face hostile. A cold shiver ran through him in the hot room.

"Tomorrow morning," Kuman continued, "We will dedicate a landmark for the future on the high hill. I know you've all been waiting for this." The guests applauded boisterously. Kuman waited for the applause to die, then he continued. "Tomorrow morning we will reveal what you've all been waiting for, our giant structure on the hill." More applause. "Our future is full of potential, dreams, visions. Yes, they can all come true. At the dedication you will get a glimpse into the future glory of Pasidia and its alliance of provinces." Cheers and applause.

"I want to introduce you to someone who will be very important in our future." Kuman motioned for the man in the green robe to stand. He put his arm around the thin man's shoulders. "Ladies and gentlemen, please welcome our new high priest, Jahaz of Pasidia." The audience stood to their feet as they applauded, cheered and whistled. The man in green bowed, then waved a bony hand at the throng.

Jahaz and Kuman stood proudly as the people exalted them. They drank in the praise with broad smiles, their faces shining. After several minutes the noise slowly subsided. Kuman motioned for the diners to sit down. Then he addressed them. "Tomorrow morning, Jahaz will welcome a glorious future to Pasidia on the high hill. You must be there before sunrise." A groan rippled through the room and out across the lawn. "Trumpets will blow all over the city before dawn. When you hear the call of the trumpet, rush to the top of the hill and you will see a spectacular sight, such as has never been seen anywhere in Fabia." The crowd listened attentively as Kuman spoke. "The music and dancing will be short tonight. Go to sleep early. We will dance on the hilltop at sunrise. Thank you all for coming.... Before I close I'm excited to report that our alliance is growing. Governor Alaya of Corno has joined the confederation of provinces."

"Long live the alliance!" shouted a pitched voice in the audience. The crowd broke into applause. A large drum began beating vigorously. Trumpets joined in. Flutes and lyres broke forth. Scantily clad dancers in sheer tunics moved through the people pulling them to their feet. Soon the crowd was dancing on the floor, on the grass, wherever they were, they began to shake, twist and twirl to the beat of the music.

Omar wanted to speak to Kuman. He got up to push his way through the crowd to the head table, but Kuman and all those on the dais had slipped away. They were gone. Omar pounded the table with his fist. Two armed guards moved next to him. "I need to see the governor," he exclaimed.

"The governor has gone to rest," said one of the guards. "You will see him on the high hill tomorrow morning." Omar groaned. Deeply frustrated. But as memories of the previous night flashed through his mind he realized he'd have to wait to see Kuman.

"Okay. Tomorrow." As he turned to leave he was surprised to see Marshia speaking to Fergus. He pushed his way through the crowd toward them but before he reached them they moved to the side of the room and started dancing.

"Poor Fergus," Omar said to Nadine when he reached their table. "In the hands of the temptress."

Nadine wrinkled her forehead. "You know her?"

"Yes, Marshia will try to seduce Fergus. She's a dangerous fire, and difficult to resist."

"We better keep an eye on him then."

"Where's the rest of our group?"

"There's Alix," said Nadine as she nodded toward the end of the room. "Looks like a dangerous fire may have reached him as well." A slender girl with dark hair and kohled eyes was swaying sensuously as she danced with Alix.

"Let's get him out of here." They began to push through the crowd toward Alix, but before they reached him he had disappeared through an exit. Omar pushed to the doorway, stepped out and looked around. There was no sign of Alix.

"They're gone," Omar said as Nadine stepped beside him.

"I'll see if I can find him. You better go rescue Fergus."

Omar pushed back into the crowded room. Fergus was gone. So was Marshia. Omar's heart sank. In the noisy crowd he prayed. "Elconan, please protect my comrades. Fill them with your strength." He looked around the room and noticed Zared standing by himself. He pushed his way through to him.

"Are you having a good evening, Zared?" he asked. Relief spilled across the young man's face when he saw Omar.

"What kind of place is this? I've had two different women come after me." He paused. "Wanted me to go behind some bushes with them." He grimaced. "Then a man."

"Welcome to the exciting new Pasidia. Let's get out of here." They pushed their way out of the room and stepped into the cool fresh air of the night. Wispy clouds travelled across the sky casting a haze over the full moon. A dog barked in the distance. From behind the bushes scattered across the courtyard came the sounds of giddy laughter, soft voices, cries of ecstasy and soft moans. The sight of Fergus dancing with Marshia flashed through Omar's mind and his heart sank. Was he behind one of these bushes?

Suddenly, the music stopped in the banquet hall. The drummer spoke, "As Governor Kuman mentioned, we are quitting early tonight so you can all be on the high hill before sunrise. This will be our last song."

"Have you seen any of the others?" Omar asked.

"I saw Sol dancing with an incredibly beautiful blonde lady," replied Zared. "Then they left the room. This place is like a whirlwind, with sex coming at you from all directions."

"What about the others?"

"I haven't seen any of them since the banquet started. We were separated and placed at different tables."

Omar groaned. "Let's see if we can find them, but be careful. I don't think we want to go searching around behind those bushes." Nadine approached them in the dim light of the flickering lamps. Her pale, drawn face brightened when she saw Omar.

"Thank Elconan I found you," she gasped.

"You look like a ghost. What happened?"

"I was looking for Alix. A man approached me and said, 'Come behind the bushes with me.' When I refused he grabbed me and began tearing off my robe as he pulled me toward a bush. I had to hit him. He was so drunk I was able to shake him off and get away. But such cursing. I've never heard the kind of names he called me as I ran away."

"Thank Elconan you're safe. I'm concerned about the others," said Omar.

"Damara wasn't feeling well tonight," said Nadine. "She left the banquet early."

"Maybe she's safe then. What about Petrina?"

"I haven't seen her since we sat down. I think she was seated at one of the tables on the lawn."

"Let's go check the rooms," said Omar. They were walking across the courtyard toward the guest-house when they heard pitiful crying behind a low bush. Nadine ran behind the bush and gasped.

"What is it?" asked Omar, as he and Zared rushed to her. A searing pain shot through Omar's heart, for sitting on the ground was Petrina. Her hair dishevelled, her face bleeding and a torn tunic hanging from her young athletic body.

"Petrina, what happened?" Nadine asked as she knelt beside her, putting her arm around the distraught girl's shoulders.

"There were three of them," she sobbed. "They grabbed me and dragged me here." She laid her head on Nadine's shoulder and wept bitterly.

"Did they hurt you?" asked Nadine softly. Petrina nodded. Through her sobs she told them that a man approached her when the dancing started and asked her to go behind the bushes with him. When she refused he cursed and belittled her. She left the banquet to go to her room but as she was crossing the courtyard the man met her with two friends. They dragged her behind the bush, tore her clothes from her and then took turns, two holding her while the third violated her.

"They stuffed a cloth in my mouth so I couldn't scream," she wept. "I fought as hard as I could, but three were too many!" Zared found Petrina's robe lying on the other side of the bush. He draped it around her gently.

"I was a virgin," she said tearfully. "Now, what man will want me?" Barely able to conceal his rage, Omar put his arms around the distraught girl and held her tenderly while she sobbed, deep, heart-wrenching cries from the depth of her soul.

"I'm terribly sorry about this, Petrina," he whispered softly. "I'm so sorry this happened. You are a wonderful person. I'll always love and respect you." He held her as Petrina's body shook and tears poured down her face. He held her until the sobbing stopped. She leaned her head against his chest and wiped at the tears. He kissed her softly on the forehead. "You're a very special person. I'll do whatever I can to help you....I'll pray that Elconan will give you strength and healing from this terrible pain."

He released her slowly. The courtyard was quiet. The crowd had dispersed. "Zared and Nadine will take you to your room. I'm going to speak to the guards."

A few minutes later he met one of the burly guards standing at the palace entrance. "I need your assistance," Omar said. The guard came to life.

"What can I do for you."

"Three men violated a woman in the courtyard. I need help to find them." The guard laughed derisively.

"With all that was going on here tonight? She probably asked for it."

"No. She didn't!" Omar retorted. "She fought them. If you won't help me, let me through to Governor Kuman."

"Sure," the guard said with mockery in his voice. "See the governor. Everybody wants to see the governor. But he's not available. Big day tomorrow. You can see him at the dedication."

"Okay then. Can you tell me where I can find Deputy Cadmus?"

"Not tonight. You can see him in his office tomorrow after the dedication."

"But you don't understand!" Omar shouted. "A guest from Cormath was raped by three men in this courtyard. As Governor of Cormath I demand that these men be found and arrested." His voice rang across the empty courtyard. Two armed guards approached him.

"This guy giving you a problem?" one of them asked the guard at the entrance.

"Some story about a woman being raped," he replied. "Look." He turned to Omar. "There's nothing you can do about this tonight. Tomorrow you can come and discuss it with Remus."

"Who is Remus?"

"He's the captain of the palace guards. He'll know what to do. So, for now, better go to your room, or these men will have to help you." He nodded toward the two guards approaching.

Omar shook his head in disbelief. "I appreciate your concern," he said in a voice filled with derision. He stared at the guards coming toward him. They pulled their swords and pointed them at Omar. The guard at the entrance drew his sword as well. Omar was surrounded. He realized that there was nothing he could do tonight. He'd have to wait until tomorrow. With anger burning deep within him like a hot furnace, Omar turned from the entrance and made his way across the courtyard to the guest-house. When he saw a light in Fergus's room he walked to the door and knocked. The door swung open.

"Omar," the swarthy one exclaimed. "It's good to see you. Come in."

"How are you?" asked Omar blankly as he stepped into the room. They embraced.

Fergus looked at his friend. "What's wrong?" he asked. "What is it?"

"I guess you haven't heard about Petrina."

"No. What happened?" When Omar described Petrina's catastrophe, Fergus slammed his fist against the wall. He looked at Omar with deep agony in his eyes. "This place is evil. Poor Petrina. We're to blame. We should have protected her."

"No one expected anything like this. We've never had to protect women in Fabia. To take a woman by force and tear her virginity from her...", his voice trailed off, he shook his head. The friends were silent, each deep in his own thoughts and entering into Petrina's pain. After several minutes Fergus spoke.

"I've never experienced anything like this. What's with this place?"

"Guess I didn't prepare you for how bad it is, did I? But it seems to have gotten worse, even since I was here last." Omar looked at his friend with concern. "How did it go with Marshia?"

"Nothing could have prepared me for that woman—she came after me like a mare in heat."

Omar was afraid to hear the rest.

"A delicious body," Fergus continued. "I've never been so tempted in my life." Omar waited, expecting to hear that his friend had fallen. "But I prayed to Elconan. Never have I prayed like that. And he gave me the strength to resist."

A smile crossed Omar's face. "You did?"

"Yes. I can go home and be with my wife honourably. With a clear conscience."

"Praise be Elconan," Omar exclaimed.

"What about the others?" asked Fergus.

"Damara left the banquet early. Nadine and Zared were with Petrina."

"That leaves Morven, Alix and Sol."

"Let's go check on them," said Omar. They left the room and hurried to the guest-house.

They found Morven asleep. He woke when his friends entered and told them that after he ate so much strange food his stomach hurt, so he left the banquet before the dancing started. He was unaware of his friends' experiences.

"Alix and Sol are staying together," said Omar. "Let's check their room." When they got there the room was dark and empty.

THIRTEEN

Omar was awake before the blasting trumpets woke the city. The room was dark. He pulled on his robe and lit a candle. Then he stepped out into the predawn darkness to check on the others. He was disturbed when he discovered that Alix and Sol were not in their room. He checked with the women. Nadine said the she and Damara would stay with Petrina. They had no desire to attend the dedication.

Omar's heart ached for Petrina as Fergus, Zared and Morven joined him in the courtyard for the walk to the high hill.

"Have you seen Sol or Alix?" he asked.

"No," Fergus replied. The others shook their heads.

"I'm concerned about them."

"Maybe we'll meet them on the hill," offered Fergus.

"I hope you're right." Omar looked at his friends. "Ready?" They nodded. "Let's go."

The streets pulsed with people rushing toward the hill. Young mothers and fathers carrying infants, grey-haired grandparents struggling to keep up, obstreperous teens, unhappy to be dragged out into the predawn darkness, all swarmed toward the high hill like a gigantic army of ants. Dogs barked. Neighbours grunted sleepy greetings. Children cried. The city pushed itself toward the hill, eager to reach the top before sunrise.

It was the first day of spring, when the hours of sunlight defeated the hours of darkness and began their ascendance to the long days of summer. The stars that had danced in the sky all night were growing tired and dim as the darkness began to soften. The faint remains of a crescent moon hung low on the western horizon.

When they reached the top the crowd gathered around the

base of the huge rock structure in the semi-darkness. With the gathering light it became a silhouette in the form of a man, but as high as four men. Hugh rocks had been skilfully carved and then raised up on top of one another to form a gigantic statue.

"What is it?" asked Fergus.

"It looks like a very large man," said Morven.

"Look carefully," said Omar. The light was increasing. "It's a statue of Governor Kuman."

"You're right," exclaimed Fergus. "It is a likeness of Kuman. But it's so huge. How did they get those rocks up there?" The statue stood on a large, square base that was the height of a man. It provided a platform around the bottom of the statue. At the centre of the base, in front of the statue, a stairway led up from the ground to the top of the platform. Two figures began moving up the steps. One was wearing the unmistakable white robe of Governor Kuman, the other was wearing green.

"Kuman and the high priest," said Fergus. "Wonder what he's high priest of?"

"Guess we're about to find out," Omar commented. The men reached the top of the platform and turned toward the sea of faces stretched out before them. The crowd forced a sleepy cheer and applauded.

"What's on his chest?" asked Fergus.

"I don't believe this," remarked Omar. "He's wearing the golden breastplate of the king."

"People of Fabia," Kuman began, using the common greeting of the king. "Welcome to this great event. This morning we're standing on the threshold of a new tomorrow. It's not just new for Gara. Nor is it just for Pasidia, but it's a new day for all of the provinces in Fabia that have joined our alliance." Shouters, stationed at strategic locations throughout the crowd, relayed Kuman's words to all.

"This morning we've come to dedicate this great monument," he pointed to the statue behind him. "It is the greatest marvel of engineering and construction in all the world." The crowd murmured assent. "It stands here to commemorate a joint effort between our most skilled craftsmen and the spiritual forces that have enabled us to accomplish this superhuman feat."

"Spiritual forces. What's he talking about?" growled Fergus.

"I have no idea," replied Omar. "Maybe they're related to the gods Cadmus talked about yesterday."

"Scary," Fergus grunted.

The crowd listened attentively, with puzzled faces. Kuman continued: "It is with the help of the spiritual forces that we have been able to introduce progressive, new ideas to our land that will free us from the bondage of old customs and traditions....This is a new day for Fabia....The beginning of a new tomorrow....With the help of the spiritual forces we are building a great army that will allow us to take our message of emancipation throughout the farthest reaches of Fabia."

A cold dread shivered through Omar. "That sounds a lot like a threat," he said to Fergus.

"Thought his army was just for defence."

"Throughout the farthest reaches of Fabia. Sounds pretty aggressive, if you ask me."

"You're right," exclaimed Fergus. "His spiritual forces are related to the gods."

Kuman spoke again, "Watch as the sun rises. Look across the top of this mountain." He pointed to his left where two large stone pillars stood. As the sun broke the horizon it sent a beam of light in perfect alignment between the pillars and across the front of the platform. Jahaz stood beside Kuman with his hands raised, looking toward the sun. The crowd cheered and applauded.

When the noise subsided Kuman continued: "On the other side of those pillars we are building a great temple. Here, on the first day of every spring the sun will light the altar as it rises to usher in another season of fertility, growth and prosperity."

Jahaz signalled to several men in green robes standing at the base of the platform. They moved up the steps. A goat bleated pitifully in the early light.

"They're carrying a goat up there," Fergus exclaimed. The green robed men moved up the steps to the top of the platform. Here a raised, stone altar covered with wood was bathed in the sun's first light.

"Until the temple is built," Kuman intoned. "We will use this altar to dedicate ourselves in thanksgiving to the spiritual forces that control the fertility of our land." A knife flashed, the goat struggled briefly, then ceased as life drained from it. A bucket was held under the goat's throat to collect the blood gushing from a wound in its neck.

"Gruesome," muttered Zared.

"People of Fabia," Kuman spoke again. "This morning we are establishing a new institution." The crowd was hushed, expectant. "Let us welcome the priests of the Temple of the Shadow to Fabia. The are led by our high priest, Jahaz." Spotted applause rippled through the crowd. "As the sun returns from its sleep each spring and pushes back the shadows of winter, we must welcome it and offer our devotion to it, so that it will bring growth and prosperity to our land."

"Sacrilege," said Omar gravely. "He's replacing Elconan with his own ideas. He's raised up a high priest to his own gods."

"Who's the shadow?" asked Fergus.

"Kuman's new god, I guess."

As the priests lifted the goat onto the wood, Jahaz dipped his fingers in the blood of the dead animal. He touched his forehead with the blood, then dipping his fingers again he placed blood on Kuman's forehead. After this, he placed blood on the forehead of each priest. Jahaz then reached into the bucket and sprinkled blood over the crowd.

"To commemorate this day," Kuman shouted. "My craftsmen have prepared something very special for you." He raised his right hand, the sun reflected off a small golden replica of the giant Kuman monument, as he held it above his head. "We have designed and produced a representation of this great statue. It will be for sale throughout the shops of Gara later today. It will be available in gold, like this one." He waved the statue. "Or silver. Or carved from stone. Or even from wood. All good citizens of our alliance will buy them. Put them into your homes, your places of business, the schools. Any place where people gather." He paused....Then continued. "Everyday you must take some time to remember and reflect before the statue. Remember this great day. Reflect upon what the priests of the Temple of the Shadow will teach you. Temples will be built throughout the provinces in our alliance. You must attend at least once each week for devotion and instruction in the ways of the spiritual forces that we now acknowledge. Failure to do so will result in bad crops, misfortunes in business, sickness and unhappiness. Even death."

As he spoke a large shadow appeared in the sky above the monument. It was shaped like two plates put together facing each other. The crowd screamed in terror.

"There it is," cried Fergus. "The shadow."

Brilliant beams of light flashed from the apparition. It spun up and down, over the crowd. It zigged and zagged. It spun, it whirled, it flashed. Then it hovered over the giant statue.

A voice thundered from the shadow and rumbled across the people. "Kuman is the great leader. Listen to what he says. Do it with all your strength."

A bright light burst around the shadow and flashed to the altar. Then it vanished, leaving only a smoky haze drifting in the sky. The wood on the altar blazed and the acrid smell of burning hair, skin and flesh assaulted Omar's nostrils.

"Wow," Zared exclaimed. He turned to Omar. "What do you make of that?"

Omar's voice was brittle. "Kuman has aligned himself with some very disturbing forces."

The crowd began to chant. "Kuman, Kuman, Kuman...." The governor stood facing the horde. His face showed pleasure in the adulation. After several minutes he raised his arms with his palms turned down. The crowd hushed.

"Thank you for your loyalty," he said. "This day is a new day for our land. A day to remember. A day to celebrate." The crowd cheered agreement. "In honour of today, to celebrate our dedication to the shadow, I have prepared a banquet for you." Hundreds of servants swarmed out from behind the altar. They carried large trays of food through the mob. The people pushed and shoved to get at the food. They ate greedily. They also drank much wine, beer and tekara as the sun slowly moved up in the sky.

As the people feasted, drums around the platform began a hard, rhythmic beat. They were joined by tambourines, trumpets and stringed instruments. Male and female dancers in scanty, sheer tunics ascended the steps to the top of the platform where they began a slow, sensuous dance around the altar. As they twisted and turned their young, athletic bodies they began pulling off their tunics with slow, deliberate movements. The people watched in amazement as the dancers removed their clothes until they danced naked around the smoke that rose from the cremating goat.

With their stomachs full and their veins inflamed by the strong drink, the people joined the altar dancers in their frolic. Robes were dropped. Tunics were pulled off, soon thousands were dancing naked, celebrating their new god.

Omar turned to his friends. "Let's get out of here. I've seen enough." They pushed their way through the crowd and hurried back to the palace guest-house.

***

"Remus is hopeless," said Omar as he met with his travelling companions later in the afternoon. "There is no concern here that a woman has been violated. The captain's position is that the woman must have initiated it. That she is accusing the men of something she started. So he won't help us. And I can't reach Kuman, his guards won't let anyone near him."

"What do we do?" asked Fergus.

"I guess we have two choices."

"Which are?"

"We can get some swords and take a run at the guards. Maybe we can get through them to Kuman."

Fergus looked at Omar in disbelief. "The only way past those guards is to kill them," he said gravely.

"I know. So we won't do that."

"What's the other choice?"

"We can take this matter to Aklavia. Have Sorna enter an official protest, demanding action."

"Will Kuman heed the council?"

"I don't know, but that's our custom. We'll begin there. I have to speak to Sorna anyway, to let her know what's going on here. Has anyone seen Alix or Sol?"

Fergus looked at Omar with a blank face. "They're back," he said. "They're in their room sleeping. I don't think either of them got much sleep last night."

"Where were they?"

"They left the banquet with two women and ended up at the home of Edolf. He's one of Kuman's top aides and owns a large house not far from here. There was a big party there after the banquet."

"Where did they spend the night?" Fergus shrugged. "Were they at the dedication?"

"It seems they were," replied Fergus. "But their recollection is rather sketchy. Maybe after they wakeup they'll be more coherent."

"We must leave for Aklavia immediately. Wake them up and tell everyone to get packed."

"But the day is half over. Do you want to leave now?"

"Yes. We must get to Aklavia as quickly as possible"

***

"I need a quick bath, Georgie," said Omar as he entered the bathhouse. "I've got a long ride ahead of me."

"Are you leaving, Governor?"

"Yes. But I want one of your good baths before I go."

"Step right in." The bathhouse attendants poured hot scented water over Omar.

"Aaaah, that feels good," he said, as they scrubbed his hair and body until his skin tingled. Then, using soft cotton towels, they rubbed him dry. "You want to know something, Georgie?"

"What's that?"

"I could get used to this. Your baths are definitely one of my favourite parts of the trip to Gara."

"Your women are very shy," said Georgie.

Omar's brow wrinkled. "Yes?"

"They wouldn't let us wash them. We had to leave and they washed themselves."

"That's because there's a different standard of modesty in Gara than elsewhere," said Omar.

"What's the big deal?"

"One of my companions was deeply wounded by Gara's immodesty last night."

"You mean the woman that was raped?"

"You know about it?" asked Omar, surprised.

"Everybody does. It's all over the palace. The guys are bragging about it."

"So you know who the men are?"

"I know who's bragging about it."

"Could you give me their names?"

Georgie paused. "You won't get me into trouble?"

"Georgie, I promise. I won't tell anyone who told me. If the news of the deed is so common then no one should be surprised that I know who did it."

"Okay, Governor. But if I get into trouble I'll pour scalding water over you next time you come here."

"My word of honour, Georgie, with Elconan as my witness."

"The guy that's bragging is Jalam. I don't know who the others are."

"Thanks, Georgie," said Omar as he slipped on his robe and tied the sash. "You're a good man."

Omar returned to his room and packed his travelling bag. Before leaving the room he folded his legs under him and sat on the soft rug for a few moments of meditation and prayer. This habit had always been a source of inspiration and strength, but since his father's murder Omar found meditation difficult. Instead of being encouraged, his spirit reeled with questions, disappointment and anger. *Where was Elconan when his father needed him?* He was deep in thought when he heard a knock on the door. "Come in," he said as he arose. The door opened and Sol's stocky frame filled the space. "Sol! It's good to see you. Come in, my friend." Sol stepped into the room with a clouded face and downcast eyes. Omar put his hands on Sol's shoulders, looked intently at his friend and said, "I've been worried about you. You didn't return to your room last night. Are you okay? What happened?" The room became quiet. A heaviness hung in the air. Sol drew in breath, sighed deeply, then began to speak.

"I messed up," he said quietly. "It was a woman." He stopped, looked at the floor, fidgeted with his hands. "They're different here...I didn't heed your warning." He paused. Omar waited for his friend to continue. "I yielded to temptation...and spent the night with her...I know I've disappointed you, and I've disappointed Elconan." He hesitated, looked into Omar's eyes. "I'm sorry." His head dropped.

Heaviness pressed Omar's heart. He felt responsible for what had happened. Omar placed his right hand on Sol's shoulder. "Elconan is strong on forgiveness to those who ask him," he encouraged his friend. "Ask him for forgiveness, and you have mine as well."

Sol looked at Omar. Relief flashed across his face. "Thank you, Omar." The friends embraced.

***

"I've made arrangements with the embalmer to return Cedric's body to Asker," Omar told his companions as they gathered in the courtyard. "We must get to Aklavia as quickly as our horses can get us there. They're rested and ready to go. How about you, are you up for it?"

"We're ready," said Fergus.

"Petrina, are you ready to ride?"

"I'm fine," she replied blankly. Others nodded agreement. Alix didn't respond. He scowled and turned his sullen face away from the group.

Birds trilled, twittered and chirped as they left the lush courtyard with the splashing pool. The horses were ready and waiting at the palace stable. On their backs hung food and water Omar had requested from the palace kitchen.

"We'll follow the Yaseb River into the highlands," Omar informed the riders once they were mounted. "The river is narrow near Otta. We'll cross there, then ride through the forest to the capital. If we ride fast we should be there in three days."

FOURTEEN

Alix was quiet and kept to himself as the group camped beside the river that evening. He held his face in a heavy scowl and his eyes distant as they ate the meal Morven prepared. When they finished eating Omar approached his friend and said, "You're very quiet tonight, Alix. Is something wrong?"

"Who are you to judge Governor Kuman," Alix spat. "Isn't he allowed to have his own opinions?"

Omar was surprised at his friend's fierce response. "Opinions, yes," he replied calmly. "We're all free to have our own opinions. But in regard to Kuman, we're talking about more than opinions. In Pasidia we've seen forced labour, greed, poverty of many so a few can live in extravagant luxury. We've seen the violation of a woman, with no recourse. And if one, how many others?"

"So you're going to judge the whole country because of the deeds of three men?"

"I'm not judging the country. I'm merely stating the facts. Governor Kuman retains the golden breastplate that belongs in Aklavia. He's forming alliances with other provinces. He has also formed an alliance with spiritual forces that promote war and whose plan seems to be to dominate Fabia."

"Maybe these forces are good. They're offering the people a new kind of freedom."

Alix's words shocked Omar. Petrina's stricken face flashed through his mind. "Yes," he said sadly. "Freedom from the traditions and customs of Elconan. Freedom for one man to enslave another. Freedom for people to be greedy and hoard so that many become poor. Freedom for people to forsake the positive relations between men and women for every kind of immorality. Alix, that's not freedom at all, but the worst kind of bondage. Why even the animals and all nature has been affected."

"I just don't see how you can say you're so much better. I'd say that's very arrogant."

A deep sadness settled over Omar's heart as he listened to his friend rant. Alix had been affected by the evil in Gara, and Omar felt responsible. "I'm sorry you feel that way," he said quietly.

Fergus interrupted their conversation. "Are you taking the first watch?" Earlier they had agreed that as long as they were in Pasidia one of them should be awake at all times, to keep the fire burning and to watch for any signs of danger.

"Yes," replied Omar. "Here's the roster." He handed a papyrus scroll to Fergus. "I've left Petrina off the list. And Alix and Sol as well since they didn't get any sleep last night. Morven will take the last watch and use it to prepare the morning meal." As Omar and Fergus spoke Alix slipped away and curled up by the fire with the others to sleep. Fergus joined them, leaving Omar alone in the night. In the distance the whoo...whoo...whoo of an owl broke the stillness. The crescent moon shone brightly overhead among the twinkling stars. *What was that flying shadow?* Omar wondered. *And where did the fire come from?*

***

"Wake up! Wake up!" Omar stirred in his sleep to the sound of Morven's urgent pleading. He opened his eyes. Weak early morning light was creeping into the darkness. The morning chorus of the birds was about to begin. "Alix is leaving."

Omar got up quickly. "Where?" he asked.

"Over there, by the horses." Alix was mounted and ready to ride.

"Wait," Omar shouted, as he ran toward him. "Where are you going?"

Alix looked at him coldly. "I'm going back to Gara. I have a friend there."

"No, Alix. Don't. Come with us. Elconan forgives, and heals."

"You can keep your Elconan," Alix retorted. "I've tasted new life and freedom. I'm going to Gara." He kicked the horse, it lunged forward and covered Omar with dust torn up by frantic feet.

The others heard the commotion and awoke. "What's going on?" Fergus cried.

"Alix has gone back," Omar replied sadly.

Fergus was on his feet. "Back where?"

"To freedom—in Gara."

A puzzled look crossed Fergus's face. "Should I go after him?"

"No." Omar shook his head. He sighed deeply. "Alix has made a choice. We must honour that. Let's pray that Elconan will protect him and bring him back to us."

***

"The council must act," insisted Omar in frustration when he met with the elders in Aklavia. "No provincial governor can ignore the council."

"But Governor Kuman has ignored this council," replied Sorna. "What makes you think it would be any different now?" The rest of the council members listened quietly, waiting for Omar's reply.

"This entire council must go to Gara, and meet with Governor Kuman. He can't ignore you if you're in Gara."

"And what would that look like?" asked Councillor Calman. "The council deferring to Governor Kuman. It would appear as if we're going there to make him king."

"And what do we do if Governor Kuman refuses our demands?" shouted Councillor Zegeb. "We would leave Gara humiliated, and lose the respect of the people." Chaos erupted. Councillors shouted at one another. Everyone speaking at once.

"Order!" shouted Sorna as she pounded on the table. "Order!" Slowly the heated discussion died down. "One person speaking at a time," she said firmly. "We don't accomplish anything by shouting at one another. Let's keep our discussion orderly. Now, what other options are there?"

"I suggest we send a group of armed men to Gara to take the

breastplate by force and bring it back to Aklavia," said Helen of Lowda.

A large-framed man with a warm, friendly face rose to his feet. Abby of Hoso was one of the councillors that had glimpsed the king's killers. "But, according to Governor Omar," he began. "Pasidia has weapons and a well-trained army. How do we raise a force against that?"

"We can't," interjected Dagmar. "Talk of retrieving the breastplate is foolish. We should anoint Governor Kuman as King of Fabia as quickly as possible to resolve the issue." Omar groaned loudly. The council erupted.

"Order!" Sorna banged the table. "Order, councillors!" Sorna hammered the table until the arguments subsided and the council chamber became orderly.

"Three options have been suggested to deal with this very critical issue. We must choose our course of action carefully. Let me review the options suggested. First, the entire council travels to Gara to demand the return of the breastplate. Second, we select a large group of strong men, arm them and send them to Gara to take the breastplate by force. This option would most certainly result in fighting and bloodshed. That's something we've not familiar with. The third option, is to crown Governor Kuman as king. This would violate the normal process of the customs and traditions handed down to us from our ancestors."

Sorna looked around at the council members. Her eyes were intense, focused. "Now, I want you to pray sincerely about these issues and to consider the options earnestly."

She paused...then continued. "Perhaps there is another course of action that we have not yet considered. Pray to Elconan for wisdom." The council chambers grew quiet as each member reflected on Sorna's words.

"There's another issue involved here as well," continued the viceroy. The councillors all looked at her—waiting. "We must remember the violation of Petrina. Whichever option we choose will have a direct effect on how we deal with that crime." She looked at each councillor directly, then continued. "This is a critical issue. I ask you to consider this very carefully. We'll meet tomorrow morning to make our choice. Councillors, you are dismissed."

A buzz erupted among the councillors. Some huddled in small groups where they argued with loud voices and animated gesticulations. Others gathered around Omar to ask questions. A few left quietly. After several hours the council chamber became quiet. Omar was left alone.

He walked along the tree lined streets to his mother's house. Fountains splashed in the verdant gardens. Flowers blossomed, birds chirruped and trilled. The air was fresh and fragrant, but Omar was oblivious to the beauty around him, he was deep in thought, his spirit troubled.

Ester's face flashed through his mind. It was etched with pain and stained with tears. Panic seized his heart.

FIFTEEN

Miriam rose from her chair as Omar entered the garden. She was weeping and her face was twisted with pain. "Mother, what's wrong? What's happened?" He rushed to her and held her in his arms.

"It's terrible, Omar," she sobbed. "It's Ester."

"What is it, Mother?" His voice filled with alarm. "What happened to Ester?" He became frantic. "Mother, what is it?"

Miriam picked up a scroll lying on a small table and handed it to him.

It was a letter from Egan. Fear, anger and pain shot through him as he read. *"Dearest Miriam,"* it began. *"I regret to have to inform you that the betrothal of my daughter, Ester and your son, Omar must be broken.* "What?" exclaimed Omar. His hands shook as he continued to read. *Ester has been chosen for a great and noble purpose for the people of Vinx and of the Alliance.* Beads of sweat broke out on Omar's forehead. "What's he talking about?" he gasped. *To seal the covenant with Pasidia, our province is privileged to provide choice virgins to be given to the gods for sexual relations to produce the future supermen who will be the strength of our alliance.* Omar's body started convulsing. Fear, disbelief and anger swept over him. He fell into a chair. The message continued.

Please convey my regrets to your son, Governor Omar. The gifts given as tokens of our children's pledge are hereby returned. May you rest in the blessing of the Shadow.

Sincerely written by, Egan—Governor of Vinx

"No. No," Omar groaned, his voice twisted with agony. "This is crazy—it can't be—when did you get this?"

"A courier brought it this afternoon. About two hours ago."

A cold dread numbed Omar's brain and seeped down through his body. Ester. Gone. The gods. He shuddered as his memory relived the nursery near Gara. The rapacious evil in the eyes of the monstrous children. His dream of a life together with Ester smashed with a cold blow of cruelty. He had to do something. He had to rescue Ester. What could he do? He sat in numb silence, his mind reeling, his heart hammered staccato against his chest.

"This is terrible, Omar," Miriam said tearfully.

Omar got up from the chair and gathered his mother into his arms tenderly. Pathetic sobs shook her body as he held her. After several minutes he loosened his embrace and spoke. "I must speak to Councillor Dan. I wonder what he knows about this?"

He led his mother to a chair and gently lowered her into it. "I'll be back as soon as I have some answers." He kissed Miriam on the forehead and rushed out of the garden.

***

The councillor from Vinx lived in a spacious cedar and rock house a short walk from Miriam's. Dan was relaxing in the garden when Omar walked up the stone path that led from the street. "Governor Omar," said Dan with false sincerity. "How good to see you. What brings you to my humble home?"

Omar gasped for breath as he stood in front of the councillor. He looked at Dan intensely and shook the parchment in front of him. "What's this? What's going on in Vinx?"

Dan reached for the scroll and read quietly. He looked at Omar with sympathy. "I guess you've lost your girl," he said softly.

"But this is unheard of! We had an agreement! And who are these gods anyway, that they should have the woman I love?"

"Your agreement was superseded by an alliance agreement," said Dan gently. "Governor Egan had no choice in the matter."

"So, whose idea was it?"

"The order came from Governor Kuman."

"Kuman?" Omar cried incredulously.

"Yes, he requested the most beautiful virgins in Vinx, and specifically asked for Ester."

"That's preposterous. Kuman wouldn't do that. He knew we were pledged to each other. Didn't Egan remind him of that?"

"Yes, but that didn't change anything. Kuman insisted on Ester." Strange emotions tore Omar's heart. Kuman was supposed to be his friend, why would he do this? Anger. Frustration. Denial. Panic. Fear...pierced his soul and numbed his senses.

"When did you hear about this?"

"This morning, before the council meeting," replied Dan.

"Where is Ester now?"

"In Pasidia."

"And given to the gods? I saw the brutish offspring of such union." He shuddered.

"There is a preparation time," said Dan soberly. "Ester is in seclusion in Gara with virgins from Corno and Calda. They will be prepared for three months before they are given to the gods." Three months. A sliver of hope touched Omar's heart. He fought against the dark cloud of reality that was wrapping its loathsome tentacles around him, and the despair that settled over him like a heavy vapour.

What could he do? The rule of law in Fabia was the council-of-elders. "I'll take it to the council," he said with new determination. "The council will require Egan to uphold the agreement."

"You're free to do so, of course," replied Dan. "But the alliance places its laws above the council."

"What? Above the council? There is no one above the council but Elconan," he stated emphatically.

"Omar," Dan began gravely. "You were at the dedication in Gara, weren't you?"

"Yes."

"Didn't you see fire flash from heaven?"

"Yes, from some kind of flying shadow. I've been trying to figure out how Kuman did that."

"The Temple of the Shadow guides the alliance. The ways of Elconan are old and outdated, Omar."

"There are many of us who don't believe that. This will tear our nation apart."

"Governor Kuman's vision is that all of Fabia join the alliance. As one complete and united nation we will all follow the same spiritual guides once again."

"Are you in agreement with this?" asked Omar bluntly. "Do you worship the shadow?" Dan didn't respond for several long seconds. His eyes were far away. His voice forced.

"I'm a councillor from Vinx. I must represent the wishes of Governor Egan."

"That's not true," countered Omar. "Your duty is to the people of Vinx. The people who elected you."

"Things have changed in the alliance. I now represent the governor."

"And who does he represent?" asked Omar with accusation. "Kuman? Kuman is responsible to no one. He's cancelled elections by the people. So Kuman has become the god of the alliance. Can't you see what's happening?"

"It would be in the best interest of all for Cormath to join the alliance. And for your interest as well."

"Never."

"Would you do it for Ester?"

"What do you mean?"

"Perhaps Governor Kuman would agree to release Ester if Cormath joined the alliance." Dan's words shook Omar with cruel intensity. He gasped. His mind went numb. He stared at Dan for several minutes. Unbelieving. Finally, words moved from his mouth in a cold chopped accent.

"I'll have to think about that," he said.

***

Early the next morning Omar was in Sorna's office. He told her about the events of the previous evening. "Are you willing to sacrifice the freedom and future of Cormath for Ester?" asked the viceroy.

"I can't allow her to be consumed by Kuman's gods."

"But he'll demand virgins from Cormath to seal the agreement. To save Ester you'll condemn others."

"But his plan is to take over all of Fabia eventually anyway. With his army, his weapons and his supermen. We don't have a force that can stand against him. So, if it's inevitable anyway, I might as well save Ester."

"How would the people of Cormath feel?" asked the viceroy. A cloud passed over Omar's face. He studied the floor. "Could you face them if you sacrificed their daughters to save your beloved?" A heavy silence hung between them. Birds trilled outside the window. A rooster crowed in the distance.

"No," Omar replied with a strained voice. "But how can I save Ester?" He paused, turned to Sorna, his eyes pooled with pain. "And how do we save Fabia? Kuman's a blight to the entire nation."

"We must trust in Elconan, Omar. We can't acquiesce to evil."

"But how do we stand against it? We don't have a force strong enough to oppose Kuman's army."

"We cannot let this evil prevail!"

"Elconan seems to be distant...and very silent."

"But he requires us to act, nonetheless. Tell me, Omar, what kind of future would Fabia have with Kuman as king?"

"We would see war, poverty and greed. Our choice daughters given to the gods to produce a race of monsters. Hatred, crime and every kind of immortality."

"And Kuman is just beginning. What horrors would we see if this scourge is allowed to grow, gain power and spread?"

"I can't imagine it; not the kind of world I want to live in. I could hardly wait to get out of Pasidia."

"You must return, Omar. You must go and get the breastplate. It's the only way you can save Fabia...and Ester."

"But what about the council? You're meeting in a few minutes. What if they capitulate?"

"Last night, as I was in meditation, I was reminded of principles your father lived by. I saw him act upon those principles many times."

"My father lived by many principles. Which are you thinking of?"

"Never fear. Always stand for what's in the best interest of all. And a deep and abiding confidence in Elconan."

"My father never faced the kind of foe that we're facing."

"He did," Sorna said softly. Omar looked at her in surprise. "It took his life."

"Are you saying that Kuman killed my father? Never. He's a friend of our family."

"Would a friend steal your fiancé? What kind of friend is he?"

A heavy hammer of realization struck Omar. He dropped his head into his hands. His head throbbed each heartbeat. He closed his eyes and allowed the painful truth to seep into his soul. After several minutes he looked at Sorna, his eyes stabbed with pain. "You may be right. I guess I was blinded by our friendship." He paused. "And then he tried to kill me too?"

Sorna nodded quietly. "That's the way it appears," she replied. "Who else would kill the king and take the breastplate to Kuman? Your father was loved by all."

"Why don't the provinces stand up to Kuman? How come his alliance keeps growing?"

"Could it be fear? Intimidation? You see what kind of pressure he's putting on you. Not everyone has the resolve to stand against that."

"So what do you suggest?"

"I'm going to delay the council decision. We must have more information and input from the provinces. I'm going to call all of the provincial governors to a meeting in Aklavia to meet with the council. I'll call for the meeting to convene four weeks from today. Omar, you must bring the breastplate to that meeting, or we cannot save Ester."

Omar sighed deeply. The stillness that hung between them was broken only by his heavy breathing. After a long pause he asked with a hollow voice. "How?"

"I have faith in you, Omar. And faith in Elconan. He will give you wisdom as you stand for the customs and traditions he handed down to us through our ancestors and which were exemplified so vividly in your father."

SIXTEEN

Nadine was the first to arrive at Miriam's house for the meeting. Stars shimmered overhead as Omar greeted her at the door. "Come in, Nadine. I'm glad you were able to make it tonight."

"What's so urgent?"

"I'll tell you when the others get here."

"Others? Who else is coming?"

"Fergus and Morven. They should be here soon. Can I offer you something to drink?"

"I've heard about the excellent drinks from the orchards of King Ulis, but I've never had the opportunity to validate the rumour." Omar reached for an intricately decorated clay jug standing on a low table and poured bright liquid into a delicate goblet.

"Please sit down," he said as he handed it to her.

"Thank you." Nadine folded her legs under her and sat on a cushion beside the table.

"How's your mother?" she asked.

"She's grieving deeply. I've never seen my mother so sad."

"Your parents were such lovers. My heart goes out to her."

Voices were heard in the garden. "Here come the others," said Omar, as he walked to the door. After the customary greetings Fergus and Morven joined Nadine on cushions around the table. Omar handed each a goblet of the robust drink.

"So what's up?" asked Fergus once Omar was seated with them.

"I have to return to Gara. And I'd like you three to accompany me."

"To Gara?" asked Nadine. "That hideous place." She shuddered. "Why?"

"It's some very urgent business for the council. It could be extremely dangerous. You don't have to come if you don't want to. I'll understand. But you three are my first choice."

"Is that it?" asked Morven. "Just the four of us?"

"Yes," said Omar. "Zared is leaving for Cormath with Damara, Petrina and Sol in the morning. You can return with them if you want to. Or you can come with me."

"What's the mission?" asked Fergus. "Can we know what this is all about?"

"You must promise absolute secrecy."

"You've got my word," said Fergus.

"Mine too," said Morven.

Omar looked at Nadine. Her face was an expression of puzzled curiosity. "Of course, Omar. My lips are tied with threads of steel," she said.

"Good. Our mission to Gara is to retrieve the king's golden breastplate." Omar's guests froze. They stared at him, surprise registered on their faces.

Fergus broke the silence. "But Governor Kuman doesn't seem to want to release it."

"That's the challenge. We must get the breastplate, whether Kuman releases it or not."

"You mean, steal it?" asked Fergus. "But we don't do that!"

"Return it," Omar corrected. "There's something else." The trio waited expectantly. Omar spoke with a strained voice. "Egan has broken my betrothal to Ester."

"Oh no," exclaimed Nadine. "That's awful. Why?"

"Vinx joined Kuman's alliance. To seal their covenant Vinx must provide Kuman with virgins for the gods. Remember the embryo?"

"How can I forget," said Nadine sadly. "Those poor women. Those grotesque children. What does this have to do with Ester?"

"Kuman requested that Ester be one of the virgins provided by Vinx to be given to the gods to produce the super race."

"Ooooooh...noooooo," Nadine uttered a long agonized cry. "This is horrible. What are you going to do?"

"I'm going to Gara, and I'm going to return with the breastplate...and with Ester."

"She'll be heavily guarded," said Fergus. "Are you planning to put an army together? We don't have any swords. Our people don't know how to fight."

"No. There'll be no army," replied Omar. "We'd just end up killing people. And I'm not interested in that."

"So how will we sneak the breastplate and Ester from Kuman's armed guards?" asked Morven.

"I'm not sure yet. But we'll find a way to save, not only Ester, but all of Fabia from Kuman's malevolent thirst. We must be brave, but we'll find a way."

Omar studied the faces of his friends intently. "It could be very dangerous. I know I'm asking a lot, but I can't think of anyone that I would rather undertake this mission with than you three trusted friends."

"I'm in," said Fergus. "I saw enough in Pasidia to make me want to rid the world of that curse. I don't know how we'll do it, but I trust you, Omar."

"I'd be happy to join you, Omar," said Nadine. "I can't imagine Ester in that horrible embryo."

"Guess you'll need a cook," said Morven. "You won't find a better one than right here." He slapped both hands to his chest. He reached into his sash, jumped up and slashed the air repeatedly with his dagger. "I've been practising with this," he exclaimed. "Kuman's guards better watch out." The others burst into laughter.

"Put it away, Morven," said Omar, smiling. "There are no Pasidians here."

"We'll get Ester and the breastplate," said Morven firmly as he sat down on the cushion.

"When do we leave?" asked Fergus.

"Tomorrow we'll prepare and pack. We'll leave the day after."

"Which route are you planning to take?"

"We'll ride through the highlands to Otta, then we'll take a boat down the Yaseb River. This way we'll avoid that depressing ride through lower Pasidia."

"Good," Nadine interjected.

"I've sent a courier to Kuman's secretary requesting a meeting with him."

"How will you approach the governor?" asked Fergus. "Just walk in and say, 'give me the breastplate and the girl'?"

"We'll pray for wisdom, and put together a plan as we travel."

SEVENTEEN

Secretary Shobal greeted Omar and his friends with the cool crispness of an insecure man who enjoyed his position of authority from which he could feed his insatiable appetite for dominance. He held his fat, squat body straight and rigid beneath the purple robe as they entered his office. He bowed his small, balding head perfunctorily with a slight motion of his short, thick neck. A large brass statue of Kuman stood in the corner of the room behind the secretary's desk. Smoke from a small incense burner, standing on the floor in front of the statue, filled the room with its sweet, pungent aroma and stung the visitors' nostrils.

Omar and his friends were amazed how Gara had been transformed since their last visit. Kuman statues were everywhere. Life-sized, expertly carved, stone copies of the image stood at major street corners. On the lawn in front of the hall-of-justice a scaffold teemed with workmen chipping at a huge rock, the height of two men, which was slowly taking the form of Governor Kuman. Small wooden versions of the statue stood in the windows or at the front entrance of homes. Wood carvers, stone sculptors, gold and silver smiths were frantically working to produce more statues for the insatiable demand.

"Welcome to Pasidia," Shobal said flatly. "Please be seated." He motioned to several cushions in front of his elegant, hand-carved oak desk. Omar and his friends folded their legs beneath them and sat down. A shapely, young female attendant entered the office carrying a tray and offered them goblets of wine, water and fruit juice.

"Your appointment with Governor Kuman, Great Leader of the Alliance, is tomorrow morning, two hours before midday," Shobal continued. "You must report to Phelan, the schedule-keeper at the entrance to the hall-of-justice no later than one half hour before your appointment. Is the time clear?"

"Yes. I understand," replied Omar.

"If you arrive late, your appointment will be cancelled and you will have to reapply for permission to see our great leader." As he spoke Shobal paced with his hands clasped behind his back. He spoke deliberately and appeared to be drawing each word out of a reservoir buried deep in his soul.

"Phelan, the schedule-keeper will assist you in your entrance to the hall." He paused, as if in deep thought. Then he continued. "I understand that the last time you were here, Governor, due to your long relationship with our leader you were allowed to appear before him without proper protocol." He looked at Omar directly, waiting for an answer.

"Yes," Omar replied flatly.

"This must never happen again. The rules have been tightened. The guards have strict orders. Anyone who fails to show proper reverence for our great leader will be struck dead immediately." A cold chill flashed through Omar's veins.

"Is it understood?" Shobal's eyes scanned the group. They nodded. "That's good," said the secretary.

"Now, since you are barbaric and uncultured, it is my responsibility to teach you how to approach the Great Leader of the Alliance properly so you will not be killed in his presence." Shobal sat behind his desk and rang a small bell. "Watch," he said.

The door opened and as a young man entered he immediately fell to his knees and bent forward until his forehead touched the floor. His arms were stretched out along the floor above his head with the palms turned upward. Shobal rose from his chair and began pacing.

"Notice the position. On your knees, forehead to the floor, hands stretched out, palms up. It's important that the palms be turned up, it symbolizes your complete dependence upon the good will of Governor Kuman. He may choose to allow you to make your request, or he may choose to ignore your plea. If that's the case our great leader will signal to the guards and you will be executed immediately. Do you understand?" He studied the four faces which were frozen by incredulity.

"If you should be so fortunate as to have the governor's favour," Shobal continued. "He will say, 'You may state your plea'. At this signal you may raise your face from the floor, but remain on your knees with your hands in front of you with the palms turned up. Watch."

Shobal said to the young man whose face was on the floor. "You may state your plea." The young man raised his face until his back was upright, keeping his palms turned up in front of him.

"Great and noble Kuman," the young man intoned. "Your humble servant is filled with gratitude that in your great wisdom you have chosen to hear my plea."

"You must use those precise words," said Shobal, with emphasis. "Or you will be executed. You must remain on your knees as long as you are before our leader in the hall-of-justice." He paused...then continued. "Only in rare exceptional circumstances, if you are highly favoured, he may give you permission to rise. Either way, you may now state your plea. I understand that you wish to discuss interprovincial matters, is that correct?"

"Yes, it is," Omar replied.

"It is then Governor Kuman's choice as to whether or not he will discuss your plea with you. If not, you must leave immediately. If he left you kneeling before him, you must back out of the door on your knees with your head bowed. If you were privileged to stand, you must bow from the waist, turn and walk out quietly. We will now demonstrate. Watch carefully." Shobal had the young man enter several times to demonstrate each of the possible alternatives. Finally, after several demonstrations, he turned to the four seated on the cushions and said, "Okay. Now it's your turn to practice. Oh, by the way, I've noticed that you are wearing daggers. Visitors to the hall-of-justice are not allowed to carry weapons. So please place your daggers on the desk before we begin."

***

"Are you going to approach Kuman as his 'humble servant'?" asked Fergus as they walked back to the guest-house.

"No. We're not his servants," Omar said indignantly. "We're his equals."

"But we could get killed," exclaimed Fergus.

"We'll trust that the force of love and justice is greater than the force of evil. But if any of you fear for your life you do not have to accompany me tomorrow."

"I'm with you, Omar," said Nadine. "I believe our cause is just and am willing to risk Kuman's wrath to stand for it."

"Me too," said Fergus. "We knew this was risky when we got into it. I'll trust Elconan."

"I have a wife and two children back home," Morven said with a strained voice. "I have to think about them as well."

Omar put his hand on Morven's shoulder. "Dear friend," he said. "Don't feel any pressure to come with us. We'll pray that Elconan gives you wisdom to make the right decision, and the courage to stick to it."

***

The sun was warm and soft as Omar and his friends gathered beside the courtyard pool for the morning meal. The splashing fountain caught the sun's rays and projected them onto the rocks around the pool in kaleidoscopes of prismatic rainbows. Birds twittered and chirped as they flitted around in the trees and revelled in the fresh, clear water of the fountain.

"Good morning," Omar greeted the others in a bright voice. He embraced each one warmly. "Did you sleep well?"

"I couldn't stand that Kuman statue beside my bed," Fergus exclaimed. "So I set it outside."

"I covered it with my robe," Morven laughed.

"That thing gave me the creeps," said Nadine.

"Making these statues sure puts a lot of people to work," Fergus mused.

"Forced work," said Nadine coldly.

"And Kuman gets a percentage of each one that's sold," said Omar. "Helps him pay for his army."

"Good morning," a friendly voice rang across the courtyard.

"Good morning, Leeah," they chorused.

"Did you sleep well?" she asked with a warm smile. She was wearing a short, purple robe with a yellow sash. Her soft, yellow curls bounced over her shoulders as she walked toward them briskly. Three attendants in short, purple tunics followed her carrying large trays of food.

"It was difficult sleeping with Governor Kuman standing beside my bed," Omar replied with a smile.

Leeah laughed. "I know what you mean." She turned to her attendants and said. "Over there, on the table." She looked at Omar, "I brought everything you asked for."

"Thank you, Leeah," said Omar. "You are a great hostess." Bowls of fruit, plates of cheese, flatbread and a large pitcher of freshly squeezed orange juice were placed on a low table.

"That looks good," exclaimed Fergus. "I'm hungry."

"Please let me know if there is anything else you need," said Leeah.

"This looks great. Thank you," said Omar. He turned to his friends. "Let's eat."

They folded their legs and sat on plush cushions around the table. As they were eating Omar turned to Morven and asked, "Have you decided what you're going to do?"

"Yes. To back away from danger is unthinkable. What would that speak of my confidence and trust in Elconan? I'll go with you."

"My father also trusted in Elconan, yet he was killed," Omar stated softly. "Our trust in him does not mean we cannot be touched by evil."

"I know, but it calls me to stand against evil, no matter the cost."

"You are very brave, Morven. I'm privileged to have you as a friend."

After they finished eating the friends took scrolls that contained the words of Elconan, read them and spent some time in quiet prayer and meditation. Omar was careful to watch the play of the sun on the gnomon; when he noticed that their time was approaching he said, "It's time to go." They put on the purple robes supplied by Kuman, tied them with yellow sashes and walked toward the hall-of-justice.

***

Omar used the scroll Shobal had given him to get past the guards at the entrance. Then the group stood in front of Phelan's elegant oak table.

"Yes," said the keeper as his beady eyes flashed. "You're next. You will be given permission to appeal to the great leader of the alliance shortly. Be seated." A plain oak bench stood along the wall behind the schedule-keeper's desk. The four friends sat down and waited.

A few minutes later the door to the hall-of-justice opened and they watched in tense amazement as a heavy-set, grey-haired man backed out through the door on his knees. When the door closed the man stood to his feet, his face a mask of anger and disappointment. Omar recognized him.

"That's Edolf," Omar whispered. "It was his house where the party was that Alix and Sol attended. Obviously fallen from grace. I wonder what he's done wrong?"

Phelan waited for several minutes after Edolf bristled out of the building before he entered the hall-of-justice. Omar noticed that he fell to his knees when he entered.

"Things sure have changed around here," Omar said to his friends quietly. "Looks like Kuman has tightened up the protocol for anyone who goes before him."

"Powertrip," whispered Nadine. "Why is he so insecure?"

"People hate him," said Morven. "Remember the man in Octor?"

"Wish we could wear our own clothes," said Fergus "I feel uncomfortable in these". He tugged at the purple robe.

The door opened and Phelan returned. "The great leader has given permission for you to approach him." Omar and his friends rose from the bench. "You know the protocol?" Omar nodded. Phelan stepped back into the room and announced, "Governor Omar of Cormath, your majesty. With assistants Fergus and Morven and under-assistant Nadine".

As Omar and his friends stepped into the room they fell to their knees and pressed their foreheads against the cold marble floor with their arms stretched out, palms up. They waited in the harsh silence for what seemed like several minutes. What's he waiting for, Omar wondered. This floor is cold and smells bad. They waited until Kuman spoke.

"You may state your plea," he said coldly.

Omar and his friends raised their bodies upright, but kept their palms turned up in front of them, as they remained on their knees. On the floor, on each side of the platform, stood a large stone Kuman statue with incense pots burning around the base. Omar squinted to shield his eyes from the bright light reflected from the breastplate.

"Great and noble Kuman," he began. "Your humble friend is filled with gratitude..."

"Halt!" shouted Kuman to the four guards rushing toward Omar with swords drawn. The guards stepped back. The room echoed with electric silence. After several minutes Kuman spoke in a strong tone. "You are very brave, Governor. But also very foolish. You impose upon our friendship to flaunt the customs of the alliance. I'm surprised, Governor. You make such an issue about the customs and traditions of Fabia, yet have so little regard for our new protocol. It's only because you are my friend that you are still alive. Remember that I saved your life today. Had I not stopped the guards they would have thrust swords through you and your friends." Omar and his companions waited with their knees on the floor as Kuman berated them. Finally, after his anger was satisfied, he said, "Continue."

"I am filled with gratitude that in your great wisdom you have chosen to hear my plea."

Kuman glared in icy silence at the group kneeling before him.

"Noble Kuman," Omar continued. "I understand that an agreement has been made between Pasidia and Vinx that involves the woman to whom I am engaged. I would like to discuss the requirements for this girl's release."

Kuman laughed ebulliently. He stood and looked at Omar with warm intensity. "Stand, dear friend," he said. Omar and the other three stood to their feet but held their hands out, palms up. Kuman signalled and two attendants hurried up the steps to the throne, removed the breastplate and laid it on the table beside the great chair. Kuman descended the steps from the throne and, ignoring Omar's request, said, "Relax, you're with a friend." He embraced Omar warmly. "I'm glad you're here. Come with me, friend. Let me show you some of the plans I have for our future. You can play an important part in what I have planned—if you want to, that is." As they turned to leave the hall-of-justice Kuman said, "The woman will stay here. My attendants will look after her." Visions of Petrina's pain etched face flashed through Omar's mind.

"But she's with me," he said.

"Women aren't allowed where we're going." Kuman's voice was hard.

"I'll stay with her," said Morven.

"I'll be okay," said Nadine confidently.

Omar looked at Morven. "Don't let her out of your sight."

The men walked down a long hallway to a large room where many scribes were working at tilted tables. "These are the plans for the Temple of the Shadow," Kuman said as they approached a table in the centre of the room. "This is Lothar, my chief scribe."

A tall, thin man with a wispy beard wearing a plain, purple tunic bowed and said, "Good morning, Great Leader."

"Show us the drawings for the temple," Kuman instructed.

"Of course," Lothar replied. As he unrolled several large scrolls on the table Kuman continued to talk. "It will be a large building. The largest ever built in all of Fabia. Built of dressed stone. We have thirty thousand workmen on the site now. It will be the pride of all who join the alliance and the envy of anyone stupid enough not to."

"What will take place in the temple?" asked Omar.

"The central image will be the large statue of myself that we recently dedicated. The temple is being built around it. Here the people will come to pray and to make their requests before their great leader."

"But a carved rock can't hear."

Kuman laughed. "Now you're getting it. I don't have time to listen to all their petty gripes. They can talk to the rock and they'll believe they've been heard. They can access the temple any time of the day or night. So, you see, I'm doing them a great favour. If they were all to come to me they'd have to line up and wait. Some would have to wait months to see me. But this way, I'm providing access whenever they want it."

"But it's not real access. You aren't there," protested Omar.

"The spiritual forces that are everywhere will carry the intent of the peoples' pleas to my spirit and will guide me to rule accordingly," said Kuman.

"Why not just ask Elconan for wisdom?"

Kuman's face clouded. He spoke with a brittle voice. "My source of wisdom guides me to greatness. The intelligent people are coming to me from all over Fabia to learn of it. I'm glad you've finally come as well."

"I came to talk to you about Ester." Omar was feeling more relaxed and bold now that he was speaking to Kuman face to face.

"But it all hangs together, my friend," Kuman replied. "The future of the girl is bound to your response. Let me show you more. Show us the harem," he said to Lothar. The chief scribe quickly unrolled more scrolls. "Here, look at this, at the side of the temple we'll have a large residence for the temple priestesses."

"What are they for?"

"In order to intercede before the gods of abundance, provision and plenty, the men will be encouraged to come to the temple priestesses to celebrate fertility rites before the great altar."

"Fertility rites?"

"Yes. The sexual intercourse between the men and the priestesses will encourage the gods to rain fertility down from heaven on the crops, the fields and the womb. We'll charge a fee, of course. It costs a lot to build and maintain a temple like this."

Omar was shocked by Kuman's ideas. He groped for words to respond. "But that's prostitution, sanctioned and encouraged by the temple."

"That's right. It's time for new ideas. We've been held in darkness by the old customs and traditions. The spiritual forces that I'm in contact with are showing us a new way."

"Pardon my ignorance, Governor," Omar replied. "But what are these spiritual forces you're talking about?"

"Hah!" Kuman exclaimed. "That's my secret. This information is reserved for members of the alliance. I can't tell you more until you join with us." A tense silence vibrated between them. Finally, after several minutes Omar spoke.

"Kuman, there's something I've wanted to talk to you about for some time."

"Yes."

"Your workmen, they're being mistreated. Beaten with whips and kicked brutally."

"Don't worry about my workmen," Kuman interrupted coldly. "I thought you came to talk about the girl."

"I did, but..."

"Let's keep it at that. You won't get her back by pointing fingers at me." The air crackled with tension.

Fergus changed the subject by pointing to a large drawing of a pyramid shaped structure. "What's that?" he asked.

"The embryo," replied Kuman. "I believe you visited the site on your last visit."

"We did," Fergus replied.

"That's where the gods come to the women to give us the giant offspring who will be our army of the future. Did you see the children?"

Omar shuddered. "Yes, we did."

"Our army will be unstoppable. An army of giants that will take over the world."

"What does this have to do with Ester?" Omar asked, somewhat exasperated.

"The women chosen for this task must be exceptional in beauty, strength and intelligence."

"Do they volunteer to marry the gods?" asked Fergus.

"Volunteer? Some do. The gods prefer willing partners. Others are chosen."

"Forced," escaped Omar's lips.

"It's not force," said Kuman coldly. "They're given the privilege to radically change our future. They should welcome it. Should be thankful."

"Ester didn't choose it. She's being forced against her will and the engagement agreement," said Omar.

"You wanted to speak to me about her."

"Yes. I speak to you as a friend. Ester and I are planning to be married. I ask that you release her to me."

"Sure, Omar. You can have her, there's only one condition."

"What's that?"

"Join the alliance, and seal our covenant by providing one hundred of your finest virgins for the embryo."

Omar was stunned. "Your price is very high," he said with a strained voice.

"Consider it. I understand you're here for a few days. Let Shobal know when you're ready. He'll arrange another meeting. I must go now. Lothar will show you the rest of our plans. Good day, my friend." Kuman left the room.

EIGHTEEN

Later that afternoon Omar and his friends met around the courtyard pool of the palace guest-house. Leaves on the trees rustled softly in the gentle breeze. Birds chirped and bees buzzed from flower to flower gathering nectar. The quiet garden, however, did little to ease the anxiety Omar felt in his heart. "Kuman is building immense buildings," he told the group. "The engineering of these buildings is beyond anything we've seen in Fabia. And he's getting his ideas from contact with spirits."

"What spirits?" asked Nadine.

"I'm not sure, but it's obvious that they don't follow the teaching of Elconan."

"What do they teach?" asked Morven.

"Kuman was pretty guarded in what he told us. But Lothar was more open after Kuman left."

Fergus interjected: "The spirits have taught him the art of war. How to make weapons and conquer others. They've also instructed him to build the embryo and provide virgins for the gods."

"That doesn't sound like Elconan's wisdom," reflected Morven.

Omar turned to the cook. "You're right. They've also given him great ideas in engineering and construction. They've been able to accomplish things here we haven't even dreamt of. The size of the statue on the hill, for instance. How did they move those giant rocks? And now he's building a massive temple around it."

"Any word about Ester?" asked Nadine.

"He's willing to release her, but at a great price." Omar spelled out Kuman's condition. Nadine groaned.

"You can't do that," she exclaimed. "You can't sacrifice one hundred girls to Kuman's evil spirits."

"I know. I'd never do it."

"So, how'll we get her out of there?" asked Nadine.

"I don't know, yet. First we have to find out where she is."

"She's being held here at the palace," offered Morven.

"How do you know that?" Omar's voice rang with pleasant surprise.

"The attendants that entertained us were quite talkative. They know where Ester is. There's a special building right here on the palace compound where a number of virgins are being prepared. They call it the harem of the gods."

"Here?" Omar's heart skipped.

"Yes. But it's heavily guarded at all times."

"Do you know where it is?"

"Yes, I was able to locate it. But all you can see is a blank wall with a few very small windows, high off the ground. The only entrance is guarded by men with swords."

"We have to get in there," said Omar.

"How?" asked Fergus, perplexed.

"We'll find a way. What about the breastplate? Did you find out where he keeps that?"

"It stays in the hall-of-justice," said Morven. "But that's also heavily guarded. No one is allowed in there unless Kuman's present."

"No one?" asked Fergus. "How do they clean it?"

"Shobal controls entry. Perhaps there are exceptions."

"We'll be one of them," said Omar.

***

The next few days passed quickly for Omar and his friends. They explored the palace grounds very carefully so no one would become suspicious of their activity. They also befriended the servants and frequently engaged them in casual conversations. In this way they learned the routines of the palace and developed a comprehensive outline of all its activities.

One hot, bright morning Omar and his friends sat around the

low table beside the courtyard pool where servants had placed a variety of breads, figs, dates, bananas, raisin cakes, cheese and boiled eggs for the morning meal. Birds chirped in the trees and splashed in the fountain as the soft fragrance of many flowers floated through the air.

"How long can we stay here in the guest-house?" asked Fergus as he reached for a fig. "Does Kuman mind us being here?"

"Not as long as he thinks we might consider joining the alliance," Omar replied. "By the way, did you know that Tamara is expecting to give birth to their first child any day."

"How exciting," exclaimed Nadine. "Have you been able to see her?"

"No. Kuman keeps her hidden." Omar chewed slowly on a piece of cheese. "Hmmm. Considering we're in Gara, this cheese is actually quite good."

"Could we see Tamara?"

"No. Only the palace servants, and they're not allowed to speak to anyone about her."

"Do you think she might be sick with the pregnancy?"

"I don't think that's it. She's being punished for disagreeing with Kuman about his new policies. And he's also changing the role of women."

"In what way?" asked Nadine, gravely.

"He's putting them down," Omar replied. "They're not equal with men. Women are being forced from all areas of leadership in Pasidia. And in the home they are subservient to their husbands."

"That's awful."

"Remember how he treated you when we went to see him?" asked Fergus.

"How can I forget? *Under-assistant.* And then I had to stay behind while he showed you his great plans," her voice dripped with sarcasm.

"That's typical of what women face here," said Omar.

"Yeah," interjected Morven. "At the market yesterday, there was a line-up at one of the stalls. The women had to wait until all the men were served, even though some had been there much longer."

"Why do they put up with it?" Nadine's voice was filled with consternation.

"Kuman enforces his rules with his armed soldiers. The people have no choice," said Fergus.

"And the other provinces are attracted to this? Why would anyone join this alliance?"

"They fear the threat of Kuman's army coming against them and taking them by force," said Omar. "Better to join than be destroyed, they think."

"This fruit is awful," Morven interjected as he chewed on a fig. "The curse must have killed the flavour."

"What about that curse?" asked Nadine. "Is it spreading to other provinces?"

"The degeneration of a society takes time," replied Omar thoughtfully. "Pasidia has had several years of the curse, so it's the worst, but apparently Calda and Corno are beginning to change. Vinx will be next."

"What are we going to do?" Nadine's voice was urgent. "We can't let this sickness take over Fabia. What about Cormath? How can we protect it?"

"We have to get the breastplate. It's our only hope."

"And Ester," added Nadine.

"Of course." Omar spoke with determination.

"I'm missing Elita and the children," signed Morven. "Can't wait to get out of here. Wish we could go home now."

"Soon, Morven," Omar chuckled. "You and Elita will be at my wedding. We just have to find the bride."

"Yeah, I know," Morven's voice was dry. "You don't think he's getting suspicious?"

"Kuman? He could be. We must assume that he has people watching us to see what we're up to. But he's invited us to stay until Tamara has the baby."

"Good, do you think we'll be able to see her?" asked Nadine.

"I hope so. Apparently he's planning a special dedication for the infant. But I think he'll be expecting us to give him some kind of answer after that."

Two female servants in purple tunics approached them. "Did you enjoy your meal?" asked one.

"The food was sufficient," said Omar. "Thank you. But it seems to have little flavour."

"Ever since the curse," replied the servant. "Everything has changed." The servants cleared the table, then left the courtyard.

Omar looked at his friends. "Let's review our assignments for the day. We need to work quickly."

***

The next morning incessant chirping and trilling of the birds greeted the first rays of the sun as it broke the horizon. Omar stirred in his sleep, then awoke when he heard the cry of the courier in the palace courtyard.

"Good news," he proclaimed. "A son has been born to Governor Kuman, great leader of the alliance. A prince in Pasidia. A servant of the people."

"Prince?" Omar muttered. "He's no prince. Kuman isn't king." He threw the covers aside and got out of bed. The courier's voice continued.

"All of Pasidia is invited to a special dedication of the new child on the high hill on the sixth day. This day is declared as a special holiday by edict of the governor. No work will be done, nor business transacted, so that all citizens can attend the dedication."

Omar threw on his robe and walked to the steaming bathhouse. "Good morning, Georgie," he said. "You're here early."

"Got special orders from the palace. We were ordered to be here before the courier. Guess they knew he'd wake people up."

"That guy has a good voice," said Omar as he stepped into the stall. The boys poured hot scented water over his head and began scrubbing his body.

***

"Isn't that exciting?" exclaimed Nadine, as Omar and his friends gathered by the pool for the morning meal. "Tamara has a baby boy."

"I'm concerned about Tamara," said Omar.

"Why? Did you hear something we didn't?"

"No. But that's just the point. Nothing was said about Tamara. Not a word."

"You're right." Nadine's face was clouded. "That's strange. I hope she's okay. How can we find out?"

"I've heard that childbearing has become difficult in Pasidia," said Fergus. "Women go through great pain and many die."

Nadine gasped. "In childbirth? Why?"

"It's part of the curse," offered Morven. "Just like the plants and animals, even childbearing is cursed."

"How awful."

"Let's inquire among the servants," urged Omar. "They usually know what's going on."

"Six more days," Morven reflected. "Then I get to go home. Can't wait to see my kids." Soft longing passed behind his eyes. "Seth is ready to learn to ride. I'll teach him as soon as I get back."

"Stop whining," chided Fergus. "At least here we don't have to eat your cooking."

"You can cook your own. You'll starve."

"Ha!"

***

Six days later, Gara lay in dark morning stillness when Omar awoke. The candle flickered on the small oak table and cast soft, wavering shadows along the wall. Omar threw back the blanket and swung his legs over the edge of the bed. As he sat there his mind projected to the day ahead. Kuman's newborn son would be dedicated at sunrise. Omar's repeated requests to see Kuman were denied by Shobal, but yesterday a courier brought an invitation for Omar and his friends to attend the dedication. Special seating was reserved for them near the large statue on the high hill.

JOURNEY TO LIGHT

Omar's attempts to see Tamara had also been blocked by the palace guards. No one was allowed to see her but the midwife, but she came and went with sealed lips. The servants, however, were more forthcoming. Nadine had succeeded in befriending them, and in penetrating their silence.

Tamara was weak, they said. She lost a great deal of blood giving birth, and was confined to bed. Due to her weakened condition the baby was being nursed by another. Tamara would attend the dedication, they said. She would be carried on a bed by servants. Omar's heart was heavy as he thought about his friend. *Perhaps he would see her on the high hill. In her weakness, how would she handle the crush of all the people? Why couldn't the ceremony wait until the boy's mother was stronger?* Many thoughts raced through Omar's mind, but it was time to check on the others.

He slipped on a robe and left the room. Fergus and Nadine were awake. Morven didn't answer when Omar knocked, so he walked into the room. "Wake up." Omar shook his friend. Morven grunted and opened his eyes.

"Go away," he growled. Morven rolled over and pulled the blanket over his head.

"Come on, sleepy head." Omar pulled the blanket off. "Time to go."

"Aaawwww, all right," Morven groaned. He sat up, dropped his legs over the side of the bed, placed his elbows on his knees and held his head between his hands.

"I was having a wonderful dream about Elita," he sighed. "We were walking in the garden under soft moonlight...Now you've ruined it."

Omar chuckled. "You'll have lots of time to walk in your garden soon. Now, get up. It's time to leave for the dedication."

"Oh that," Morven groaned. He got up and slipped a tunic over his head. "It was a beautiful dream..."

***

The four friends from Cormath arrived on the high hill early, before the crush of people filled the streets. When they reached the top, Omar looked back, the early light revealed a moving mass of people swarming up the hill like a formidable army of giant ants.

"Good morning." They were greeted by a tall, bright-eyed, athletic girl wearing a green, knee-length tunic. A fresh rose was perched in her glossy, black hair that was carefully braided and rolled into a bun at the back of her neck.

"Good morning. I'm Governor Omar, of Cormath."

"Oh yes," replied the girl. "Right over here. We have a spot reserved for you." She led them to an area near the platform where the ground was covered by colourful rugs and soft cushions. Omar noticed that a large metal pillar, the height of a large man, stood on the platform beside the huge stone Kuman statue.

As the light increased, details of the pillar were revealed. It resembled the body of a serpent that curled upward with a fierce hideous head at the top. Its fangs thrust from the large open mouth like a pugnacious threat. The serpent pillar was hollow and a huge fire roared in its innards, spewing sparks and smoke out of the mouth.

"What an ugly statue," observed Nadine.

"I wonder what the fire's for," Fergus remarked.

"Maybe they'll cook some food for us in the fire," muttered Morven. "I'm starved."

"I have a bad feeling about this," said Omar. The seats around them filled quickly and the crowd moving up the hill soon formed a huge mass of people all around the statue.

"Make way. Make way," gruff voices shouted. The throng parted as brusque, muscular soldiers pushed through, waving their swords and brutally pushing aside the people that couldn't get out of the way. Four large men with rippling muscles followed the soldiers carrying a covered litter.

"That must be Tamara," exclaimed Omar.

Nadine's eyes were on the litter. "I hope they bring her close to us." The procession stopped at the base of the statue, beside the steps that led unto the platform. The men lowered the litter to the ground; the soldiers stood around it.

"I'm going to see if I can get there." Omar got up and moved toward the litter. Nadine followed. When he reached the soldiers he called out, "Tamara." The soldiers turned toward him, raised their swords and pushed him back.

"Go sit down," a gruff voice shouted. "Before I thrust this sword through your wretched body." Omar stepped back, bumping into Nadine.

"Easy, easy." Omar raised his hands. "I just wanted to greet a friend."

The guard pushed him away. "Get out of here."

Omar turned to Nadine. "These guys sure are unfriendly." Embarrassment flushed his face when he noticed the people watching the altercation. "Let's leave it. Maybe we can see her later." They returned to their seats.

Soft light was breaking the eastern sky when a figure clad in white moved out of the shadows at the base of the statue. "There's Kuman," said Omar. The white figure was followed by another man wearing a dark robe. "That'll be Jahaz." Omar watched as the two men moved around the front of the platform and walked toward the steps. When he got to the litter Kuman paused, pushed back the curtain, reached in and picked up the baby from Tamara's arms. Then he and Jahaz slowly ascended the steps to the statue. The baby woke and began to squirm and whimper.

At the top of the platform Kuman handed the baby to Jahaz, then turned to address the crowd. In the gathering light Omar noticed the golden breastplate shining on Kuman's chest. Silence settled over the huge crowd. They looked toward Kuman and waited expectantly.

"People of Fabia," he began in a strong voice. "Welcome to this great and noble event. We're gathered here to celebrate the birth of my son, Zuriah, Prince of Fabia."

"He's just declared himself King of Fabia," Fergus whispered to Omar.

"Not for long."

"The birth of a firstborn is always an exciting event," Kuman continued. "The opening of the womb and the promise of things yet to come." The crowd cheered.

"This morning I am going to express my thankfulness to the gods who bless our land. The gods of the sun, the moon, the stars, and of the Shadow. The gods we can see and that sustain life on the earth." Jahaz tried to comfort the frightened child in his arms, but Zuriah's screams grew louder.

"These gods must be honoured and obeyed," Kuman shouted louder. "If we don't obey the gods they will withhold blessing from the land and we will not prosper."

The crowd nodded. A few muffled, "Yes."

"To honour the gods I am going to do something this morning that has never been done in Fabia before." An uneasy hush filtered over the hilltop. "I'm going to show the gods that I appreciate the blessing of new life they have given to me by returning it to them." Omar felt his stomach tighten. He noticed that armed soldiers had moved to the base of the steps.

"What I do this morning will be an example for all of you to follow. Every firstborn child must be returned to the gods as a thank offering."

"Oh no," exclaimed Nadine. "What's he going to do?"

"As we honour the gods and offer them gifts of thanksgiving for what they have given to us they will continue to bless and prosper Fabia. And so this morning I am going to offer my new son as a thank offering to the gods." The sun broke the horizon as Kuman took Zuriah from Jahaz's arms and walked toward the serpent pillar.

"No," shouted Omar as he jumped up and ran toward the steps. He was grabbed by the guards and thrown to the ground. A sword pointed at his throat.

Jahaz stood by the statue with his arms raised toward the rising sun as Kuman lifted Zuriah above his head and flung the baby into the mouth of the fiery serpent. Zuriah's piercing cry shattered the morning air as his tender body hit the flames. Mothers gasped. A pitiful scream broke from the litter, then grew quiet.

JOURNEY TO LIGHT

Tension and incredulity rippled through the crowd. Many of the mothers standing close to the platform fainted. Others wept. The crowd began moving. Those close to the platform pushed to get away from the statue. Those in the distance pushed to get closer, curious to see if what they'd seen was really true. Had the baby really been thrown into the flames? Or was it some trick? They pushed. They shoved and they cursed. The women who fainted, and many small children, got trampled by the frantic feet. Distraught husbands and fathers screamed as they saw their wives and children crushed. Nadine rushed toward Tamara. The soldiers, distracted by the commotion, didn't stop her. She pulled back the curtains. Tamara lay slumped on the cot.

"She's dead," Nadine gasped.

A soldier heard her gasp, rushed over and pushed her away. "Get away from here," he bellowed.

"Tamara's dead!" Nadine shouted at the soldier. Two more soldiers grabbed her and pushed her back. The crowd roiled in confusion and fear as the foul smell of burning flesh filled their nostrils.

Musicians appeared from behind the platform and scrambled up the steps. Rhythmic drums began to pound. They were joined by trumpets, flutes and lyres. Male and female dancers clad in sheer, white tunics ran up the stairs and began a sensuous dance on the platform. "Join the dancers," Kuman shouted. "We have much to be thankful for. Let's show the gods that we appreciate what they've done for us. Let's show them!"

The frenzied hypnotic throbbing of the drums slowly drew the throng into its spell and the frantic pushing and shoving ceased as the music and the dancers calmed the crowd. A chant started in the reserved seating where Cadmus and other top aides sat. "Kuman, Kuman, Kuman...," they repeated as they filed out of their seats and began dancing around the statue. Gradually, more people joined the dancers, and the high hill became a moving mass of celebration as they danced unto the gods.

Others, not entranced by the performers, began to push their way down the hill toward the city, the cries of the baby still ringing in their ears, their nostrils stung by the stench of burning flesh.

All over the hilltop the shocked and broken-hearted wailed beside the crushed remains of their loved ones. The hill became a throbbing mass of frenzied celebration, anguished cries, and wild-eyed panic.

Omar turned to his friends. "Let's get out of here."

"That man's a barbarian," exclaimed Nadine, as they joined the exodus moving down the hill back to the city.

"A fiend," Fergus growled.

"We have to get the breastplate," said Omar. "The longer he has it the more people he'll deceive."

As they rushed down the hill they passed people in many stages of shock, fear and denial. "I won't burn my baby. I won't burn my baby...," one young mother kept repeating as she clutched a newborn infant to her breast, her face stained with tears. Her young husband walked beside her resolutely, his eyes distant, his face drawn.

"Look at those clouds," exclaimed Fergus. He pointed back toward the hill where huge black clouds boiled across the sky. The sun was blocked. Darkness descended. Dust swirled through the throng as wind swept down the hill. Their robes flapped and whipped as the wind grew stronger. Dust and debris struck their faces.

Omar remembered the white rocks that killed Cedric. "Find shelter," he yelled. The crowd rushed toward the city. Dogs barked. Horses neighed. Eagles screeched from the sky. Then, suddenly...as quickly as the storm began...all was quiet. The air grew thick and heavy, expectant. Electric. The rushing crowd slowed, as if suspended.

"Keep going," yelled Omar. "Get to shelter."

"Can we make it to the palace?" gasped Fergus.

"We must." As they passed the first houses on the street Omar shouted, "We'll leave these buildings for others." Streaks of fierce light cracked across the sky. The black clouds rumbled and shook the city. More flashes of light. Rumbling. Thundering.

JOURNEY TO LIGHT

Suddenly, a light brighter than the sun flashed down the sky to the earth, followed immediately by a horrific crash. People screamed as bodies on the hilltop flew through the air. The clouds broke and water poured down like a swollen river. Morven stumbled when the water struck, and nearly fell, but he regained his footing and caught up with the others. The panicked crowd crushed into every available building. Brown, muddy water poured down the streets and flooded into the homes. The river from the sky became a flood on the earth. Soon every street was a raging torrent of debris, trees torn out by the roots, pieces of buildings, bodies of dead animals, men, women and children caught in the fatal deluge.

"Let's hang on to each other," cried Omar. The friends each grabbed the hands of another. They struggled down the street that was an angry vortex filled with the casualties of its rage.

"There's the palace," shouted Fergus.

"It's on high ground," said Omar. "We'll be safe there." The guards at the entrance had fled from the fierce storm. Omar and his friends rushed through the gate and into the guest-house.

"Thank Elconan, we made it," exclaimed Omar as they collapsed on the floor.

"What vicious weather," panted Morven. "We've never seen anything like this before."

"The new Pasidia," Omar said sarcastically. "Fortunately, there weren't any white rocks, or we would've been killed."

"I keep seeing those dead children floating down the street," groaned Nadine. "I can't get those images out of my mind. I wish we could have done something to help them."

"The storm with the white rocks ended quickly," Omar reflected. "Let's hope this one is short as well." But it wasn't. The storm continued all day. In the afternoon Omar faced the tempest and made his way to Shobal's office. After several hours he returned in the driving rain and knocked on his friends' doors. He invited them to meet in his room for the report on his meeting with Shobal.

"The sky is crying because of the brutal death of Zuriah," wept

Nadine as they gathered in Omar's room. "And the horrible death of his mother." She shook the rain from her robe. "What a way to die. I just can't get the sound of her anguished scream out of my ears. And I keep seeing her face, full of pain. Just lying there. Dead. I just can't believe it."

Omar put his arms around Nadine and held her gently. "There's no heart like a mother's heart. And none can feel the pain as deeply."

"Killed by the pain of watching her baby thrown into a fire," Nadine sobbed. "I just can't stop crying. It's so awful."

"It's good to grieve when our friends suffer," said Omar softly. "It allows us to identify with their pain. But Tamara and Zuriah are with Elconan now. They'll never suffer again." He led her to a chair and gently lowered her into it.

"How'd you make out with Shobal?" asked Fergus.

"Not good. I had to wait a long time to see him. He was at a big meeting with Kuman and his top people. When I finally got to him he was very evasive. Said there'd be an announcement later this afternoon that would be of interest to us."

"Did he say anything about the burning?" asked Morven.

"No. He wasn't interested in discussing anything. Everyone is pretty tight-lipped around the palace right now."

"What a way to run a country," muttered Fergus.

"Has it ever rained like this before?" asked Morven.

"Apparently not. There seems to be more concern about the rain than about Zuriah right now."

"The rain is symbolic of the tears of Elconan," offered Nadine. "He's crying over his wayward children."

As they were speaking the voice of a courier was heard in the courtyard.

"Quick. Open the door," said Omar "That might be the announcement." Fergus jumped up and jerked the door open. A gust of wind drove rain into the room. "We better go out there. We won't hear him in here."

"I'll go," said Fergus. He stepped out into the storm. Omar followed him. A few minutes later they were back. Drenched.

"Here, you can dry with these." Nadine handed them towels.

"So, what's the news?" asked Morven.

"Apparently Kuman's gods are angry because of Tamara's behaviour at the dedication," replied Omar, as he shook the water from his robe.

"What?" exclaimed Nadine.

Omar towelled his hair as he continued, "She was supposed to be happy to return the life in sacrifice to the gods. Instead, she offended them by dying. They're very angry, and sent this fierce storm as a punishment." He paused. "Apparently many people died when their houses slid down the hillsides. Low lying areas flooded and hundreds of people drowned. To appease the wrath of the gods Tamara is to be offered to them in the city square tomorrow morning at sunrise. All residents are ordered to attend, in honour of the gods. Failure to do so will result in immediate death and burning. According to Kuman, we must show the gods we are grieved over Tamara's behaviour."

"That man's insane!" Nadine cried. "He caused Tamara's death. If anyone should be offered, it should be him!"

"He's blaming Tamara for the death of all the people who died," said Fergus.

"No one'll dare to stand up against him," Morven remarked. "For fear they'll get burned."

Omar's face was grim. "Out of respect for our friend Tamara, we'll attend the offering, whatever he means by that. But not out of respect for his gods. They're vengeful and sadistic."

"Will Elconan understand?" asked Nadine.

"Yes, Elconan always looks at motives. Our motive is to respect Tamara. He will understand. Then tomorrow night we'll act."

"The sooner the better," Fergus chipped. "I can hardly wait to get out of this creepy place."

"I can't wait to see Elita and the children," sighed Morven.

***

It was dark outside when Omar awoke the next morning. He

heard the rain drubbing the roof. He got out of bed and looked out the window. The rain, which had been driven at a sharp angle yesterday, was now falling in straight, vertical lines. The flooded courtyard reflected the light from a few sheltered torches that were still burning.

"Yuck," he muttered. "It's going to be wet." He slipped on his robe, wrapped a blanket over it, gritted his teeth and stepped out into the rain to wake his friends. He could use a hot bath this morning, but he noticed that the bathhouse was cold and empty. *Guess Georgie's afraid of the storm*, he thought. After waking his friends he returned to his room, hung the wet blanket on a peg and washed his face. Then he folded his legs under him and sat on a cushion to meditate and to pray. He grappled with the deity. "Why are you allowing this evil to continue? Where are you? Don't you care?" He was confused and angry at Elconan's silence. He felt abandoned, and very much alone as the storm of evil raged around him.

Omar had never seen a storm like this. The climate in Fabia had always been warm and pleasant. The gardens were watered by a mist that rose from the ground each morning. Rainstorms were unknown. Much had changed in Pasidia since Kuman began following his new ideas. This destructive storm was only one of them. He grieved for the people who died yesterday. The rape of Petrina also lay heavily on Kuman's heart. He wondered how many other women had suffered like that. And what about the women being offered to the gods for sexual encounters? He thought of Ester. Pain rattled through his heart. He must rescue her. "Elconan, what's happening to Fabia?" he prayed. "How can your goodness be restored?" Quietly, he asked Elconan for wisdom, strength and courage.

Omar's meditation was so intense that he didn't hear the knock on the door. It was only when Fergus yelled, "Omar, are you in there?" that his reverie broke. He got up and opened the door. Fergus, Nadine and Morven stood in the rain. Their hair was plastered to their heads and water ran down their faces; rain soaked robes clung to their bodies like heavy skin. "Were you sleeping?" asked Fergus.

"Just meditating."

He stepped into the rain and joined the others for the short walk to the city square.

"I'm glad we don't have to go all the way to the top of the hill in this mess," said Morven.

"It's too dangerous in the storm. That's why it's down here." The streets throbbed as people hurried toward the large open area in the centre of the city. They were wet, cold and irritable. Men cursed. Children cried. Mothers cuddled infants in their robes and cuffed the heads of laggards.

Suddenly, Nadine stopped. "Oh no. It can't be." Ahead of them people crowded around a large pile of wood set in the middle of the open square. Standing upright on top of the wood was a large pole with a beam across it near the top. Tamara's naked body hung on the cross. Her arms were outstretched along the horizontal beam. Her head was strapped to the upright by a band around her forehead so that it appeared as if she was looking out across the crowd that was transfixed by the naked corpse.

"He doesn't even respect the dead," gasped Omar. "Tamara was a good person. She shouldn't be treated like this."

"This is horrible," cried Nadine.

"True to form," growled Fergus. "Yesterday morning he threw her live infant into the fire. Today he hangs the dead mother on a cross, naked. This guy's a lunatic!"

The rain slowed to a drizzle as the crowd pushed into the square. Their sandals sank into the wet turf and crushed the elegant lawn into soggy muck. Soft light pushed at the heavy, dark clouds and the sky was beginning to brighten when a commotion erupted at the main street leading into the square. "Make way...make way...," a gruff voice shouted. A phalanx of fierce, bearded soldiers on horses pushed their way through the crowd toward the square. The soldiers slashed their swords at the crowd madly to push them aside. Women screamed, men cursed, as the crowd jammed together to create an opening in the mass.

Behind the soldiers trudged a large group of priests in green robes. They walked with their freshly shaven heads bowed, chanting in a low, monotonous drone. Ahead of them marched Jahaz, his head held high, his face grim. A large, white horse pulling an elegant chariot followed the priests.

"There's Kuman," Omar announced. He recognized the familiar white robe. Poles ran up each corner of the chariot and held a cover of animal skin over the governor to protect him from the rain.

"Beast," muttered Fergus. The chariot stopped at the pile of wood. Kuman stepped off and mounted a set of stairs to the top of a covered platform that stood beside the pyre. He stood on the platform and gazed over the crowd. A heavy silence hung in the soggy air. The people were wet, tired and impatient.

"Burn her," someone shouted.

"Burn her. Burn her. Burn her...." the crowd began to chant. Kuman stretched his arms toward the people. They grew quiet. The priests stopped their chant and formed a circle around the woodpile. They gazed up at Tamara's body with cold, severe faces.

"People of Fabia," Kuman began. "We're gathered here this morning to appease the gods who were offended by an attitude of ingratitude and rebellion." A murmur rippled through the crowd. Omar noticed that the horizon was clearing. The rain stopped.

"Yesterday, when this woman's infant was offered to the spiritual forces as an offering of thanksgiving this mother grieved the gods by her outcry."

"This woman, he calls her," said Nadine with cold disdain. "She was his wife."

Kuman continued, "Instead of being thankful that she had a gift to offer to the forces of life and death, she chose grief, remorse and rebellion. We have all suffered in this terrible storm, many have died in our province. Some have lost their gardens and their homes. Others their lives. All because of the bitter attitude of this woman." He pointed to Tamara's naked corpse.

"We cannot allow this in our province, nor in the alliance. Let all citizens hereby understand that when an infant is offered to the spiritual forces in the fire, it must be with a heart of gratefulness and thanksgiving. Let no one show remorse, or who knows what further punishment the gods will afflict upon us. Let it hereby be known that anyone who fails to obey this edict will be treated as this woman."

An attendant rushed up the steps with a torch. The priests, led by Jahaz, raised their hands and began a penitent chant to the shadow god, begging for forgiveness; begging the shadow to accept the offering as restitution for the violation. Kuman took the torch and held it to the wood.

"It won't burn," grunted Fergus. "It's too wet."

"Apparently they kept the wood dry all night," Omar explained. "And they've poured the fat of animals over it. It'll burn." The flames flickered, almost died, then slowly began licking the wood.

"Offer thanks to the gods," Kuman shouted. "Offer thanks to the shadow, who gives us the sun to sustain life on earth."

A loud cheer erupted from the crowd as the sun broke the horizon and shot the fleeing clouds with blazing patches of red. The chant began slowly among the people close to the fire. "Kuman. Kuman. Kuman..." It spread throughout the square and out into the streets crammed with people. "Kuman. Kuman. Kuman..." they shouted. The governor stood on the platform and waved to the crowd as they chanted. His face beamed with the adulation as the flames reached Tamara's body and spread the acrid smell of burning flesh through the crowd.

"Let's go," said Nadine with disgust. "I've seen enough."

NINETEEN

Later that day, as darkness settled over the palace complex, Nadine carefully rumpled her hair and smudged her face with cosmetics until it appeared drawn and weary. When she was satisfied that she was prepared for the task ahead she slipped out of the guest-house and shuffled across the palace courtyard, with shoulders drooped and her head bent low, like one dejected by forced servitude. She noticed the remains of the storm all over the courtyard. Pools of water, broken branches and uprooted trees lay everywhere. The flower gardens were crushed by the rain, their stalks bent and broken, blossoms ripped away and scattered. The splashing pool was quiet. A few pole lamps cast eerie, flickering light across the courtyard.

Nadine was wearing the simple, purple tunic of the palace servants. The cold metal of the dagger strapped to the side of her left thigh bit into her soft flesh. She walked with assumed confidence, her stomach was tense and her heart beat high in her chest. Once across the courtyard she followed a path between several buildings that passed behind the hall-of-justice and led to the far north of the complex toward the servants' quarters.

Nadine had been successful in befriending the administrator of the servants that worked in the harem of the gods. A bag of zorn had convinced her to allow Nadine to enter the harem with the servants as they went in for the night duties. "I want to visit a friend," Nadine told her. "Once she goes to the gods I'll never see her again. She was taken quickly and I didn't have the opportunity to say goodbye."

The administrator was a tall, thin woman with cold, hollow eyes. "This is Zelda," she said to the twenty women gathered in front of the servants' quarters preparing for their evening assignment. "She'll be part of our crew tonight. There'll be additional work because of the storm." Tired, dispassionate faces turned toward her. Several nodded. A few forced weary smiles. "Talga, you work with Zelda tonight and show her what she needs to do." A flash of panic shot through Nadine. She had not expected this. Talga would interfere with what she had to do. But it was too late. She had no option. She'd have to go with Talga and find a solution once she got inside. After a few announcements and instructions the administrator dismissed the servants to move to the harem.

They slouched in pairs toward the entrance which was guarded by four fierce, muscular men, each with a sword hanging on his left hip and a dagger tucked into his sash. The leader of the first pair of women handed a scroll to one of the guards. He studied the scroll and the faces of each servant carefully as they walked past him through the entrance. Nadine breathed deeply and tried to relax. She was afraid that her nervousness might betray her. The guard looked at her and shouted, "You!" He pointed his finger menacingly. "You're new. Where are you from?" Nadine's heart froze, her mind whirled. She hadn't expected this. She must answer quickly, truthfully. Her tongue felt thick and dry. She knew that the wrong answer could have her killed, her friends endangered and Ester would remain imprisoned.

"Gara," she said. After all, she had been here two weeks. The guard made a note on the scroll, waved her through. Once inside, Nadine noticed that the palms of her hands were wet and perspiration covered her body. But she was in.

When all the servants were inside, the guards closed the door and bolted it from the outside. Nadine realized that no one could escape from this building. *How would she get Ester out?* She wondered. The entrance led onto a large, square, open air lobby with polished marble floor and wooden benches along the walls. Large landscape murals were painted on the white plaster walls. To the right of the entrance was a heavy, black, wooden door with a small opening cut at eye level. Nadine noticed a cold eye watching them through the opening. After the guard bolted the entrance, the black door swung open. A short, skinny man stood in the doorway. He had a sharp, pointed nose like a bird's beak, and a short neck so that his head appeared to be attached directly to his shoulders. His narrow, pinched face was hard and cold, and his eyes shifted constantly as he faced the group.

"That's Sacar," whispered Talga. "He's the harem keeper." Sacar wore a short, black, tunic made of rough cotton. His skinny legs stuck out the bottom of the tunic like two small sticks attached to bony feet. His face was etched by disdain as he surveyed the group. Beside him stood a small, thin girl with sad, sunken eyes. She was wearing a similar black cotton tunic. She held a papyrus scroll on which she wrote the name of each of the women as they entered. Then they moved into a crowded dressing room where they began removing their purple tunics by slipping them over their heads. Nadine hesitated, embarrassed by the naked bodies around her.

Sacar entered the room and began examining each woman carefully. He examined their hands, their fingernails and every part of their bodies. Nadine noticed that he seemed to take pleasure in stroking the women's hair and running his bony hands over the fresh young bodies. Nadine cringed with embarrassment for each of the women as they endured the humiliation.

Then, cold fear surged through her heart as she remembered the dagger strapped to her thigh. How could she hide it?

Some of the women failed the examination. Sacar barked curses at them and ordered the guilty into the bathhouse. Here eager, young, naked boys scrubbed the offensive bodies with sponges and hot scented water. "I always come here clean," whispered Talga. "I hate being scrubbed by those boys." Once purged, the women returned to the keeper for another inspection.

When a woman passed Sacar's scrutiny she was handed a coarse, black, cotton tunic. No sandals were worn in the harem. The keeper was moving closer to Nadine. Most of the women were undressed. Nadine realized she had to act. She sat on a rough bench and pointing through the doorway that led to a large open courtyard, where a fountain splashed, she asked Talga, "What's that?" When Talga looked to see what she had pointed at Nadine reached under her tunic and tore the dagger loose, then with one quick move she stood and pulled off her tunic and wrapped it around the dagger.

"That's the courtyard where the women bathe and receive their beauty treatments." She turned to Nadine, who was standing self-consciously naked. "That was fast. You seemed hesitant to get undressed."

Nadine shrugged. "I'm not used to this, but it had to be done. So I did it quickly. What do I do with this?" She held up her purple tunic.

"Over there." Talga pointed to a row of shelves and pegs along the wall. "You can hang it on a peg."

"I like to leave it wrapped up," Nadine replied as she placed the bundle on a shelf.

"So, what do we have here?" Sacar squeaked. "A new recruit." His eyes shone with pleasure as they roved over Nadine's well-formed body. "Turn around," he murmured. As Nadine turned she understood Sacar's vulnerability and a plan flashed through her mind. She grimaced inwardly as she reached into herself for strength to do what she knew she must. Suppressing her embarrassment, she moved slowly and sensuously. A faint smile broke Sacar's stark face.

"Very nice," said the keeper. His shifty eyes bulged and glowed intensely. He handed Nadine a black tunic without touching her. Then he threw a tunic at Talga and scurried out of the room.

"What was that all about?" asked Talga. "You like him?" Nadine's face flushed red. She noticed several of the servants staring at her with disdain.

Nadine shrugged. "Well, at least he didn't fondle me. And he left you alone."

"There's something you should know about Sacar," said Talga. "He often calls for new girls to come to his room where he forces them. The way you acted, he'll definitely call for you."

"How was I supposed to know that?"

"I'll bet you did," Talga's voice clipped sarcastically. "You wanted him to notice you."

Nadine ignored the accusation. "What do we do now?" she asked. "What's our job here?"

"We clean the area around the pool. The storm made a big mess so we have a lot of work to do. Take this bucket and scrub brush. You can wash the tile floor."

The courtyard was a large rectangle of carefully manicured grass open to the sky. Trees, flowering shrubs and flowers had been carefully placed throughout the courtyard to provide beauty and a relaxing atmosphere. Signs of the storm's devastation were everywhere. Branches torn from trees were scattered over the plush grass. Flowers had been beaten into the earth by the rain. Petals, torn by the wind, lay scattered around on the ground and floated on the large, kidney-shaped pool in the centre of the courtyard. Chairs and cushions had been blown around, ripped by the storm and drenched by the rain. A layer of mud covered the tile floor where the downpour washed through flowerbeds and carried the dirt throughout the courtyard. At the far end of the pool a splashing fountain gushed and gurgled vigorously. To the right of the fountain bubbled a large mineral bath. A cushion, from a lounge chair, rocked gently in the bubbly suds. The storm had not erased the sweet scent of fragrant oils that hung in the night air as echoes of the beautiful women to whom they had been applied.

"What's that?" Nadine pointed to several stalls at the left end of the pool, each as high as a man.

"The bathhouse," Talga replied. "That's where the ladies are scrubbed clean of all their impurities by young boys eager to get their hands on their naked bodies." Nadine shuddered. A wide tiled border ran around the pools and the bathhouse. Massage tables and lounge chairs with soft cushions were scattered on the tile. Around the outside of the courtyard stretched two stories of small rooms. The upper level had a balcony that ran along the front and led to a stairway at each end.

"Who lives here?" asked Nadine. Talga looked at her with arched eyebrows.

"You don't know?" she asked. "The future harem of the gods.

The women are prepared here for three months, then taken out to the embryo."

"To be given to the gods?"

"Yes. And to mother a future race of giants that will allow Pasidia to rule the world." Pictures of the grotesque children at the embryo flashed through Nadine's mind. She shuddered. "Guess we better get to work," said Talga. "I'll move the furniture. You scrub the floor," she ordered. Nadine dropped to her knees on the cold tile and began scrubbing with a fine bamboo brush. As she worked she prayed quietly to Elconan for wisdom and strength.

They had worked for about an hour when a young boy, about ten years old, walked across the courtyard toward Nadine. His oiled hair was brushed back from his face and his cheeks were reddened with pigment. He was naked. When Nadine saw him she turned away quickly, embarrassed.

"Oh, oh," said Talga. "Sacar's errand boy." He walked to where Nadine was kneeling on the tile and tapped her on the shoulder.

"Servant Zelda," he said. Nadine straightened her body and looked at his face.

"Yes."

"Keeper Sacar desires your company. Come with me."

Nadine looked at Talga, who shrugged and said, "Guess you're his plaything tonight. Have fun." Nadine dropped the brush into the bucket, stood to her feet and followed the boy across the courtyard. Her heart was pounding with fear and embarrassment as the servant girls watched her follow the boy.

TWENTY

Omar and Morven crouched low in the darkness of a small storeroom in the hall-of-justice. A few days earlier Morven had discovered an unguarded back door to the building. He hid in a patch of thick shrubs and watched the door carefully for several days to learn the routines of the people who used it.

"It's only used by servants," he told Omar. "And they only use it in the morning to carry supplies into the building. It's not used in the afternoon."

"Doesn't it get locked for the night?" asked Omar.

"A cleaning crew enters the building late in the evening, after the governor has left for the night. They lock it when they leave."

"Good work, we'll use it. It's the only way in that we've found."

Earlier in the afternoon Omar and Morven had slipped into the building through the unguarded door and hid in a small storeroom that contained shelves of parchment scrolls. Working quickly, they rearranged the shelves and hid in a small cramped space behind the scrolls.

"These parchments give me the creeps," whispered Morven, after they were settled. "Animals were killed to make these scrolls. It feels like we're hiding behind them."

"The animals are dead," replied Omar quietly.

"I know. But it seems we should have more respect."

They waited quietly in the storeroom for the rest of the afternoon and into the evening, until they heard the cleaning crew enter the building. Omar and Morven barely breathed as the cleaners walked down the hallway past the storeroom. Several minutes later Morven whispered, "It won't be long now. It doesn't take them long to do the cleaning."

"Good," Omar replied. "I'm thinking about Nadine. I hope she's okay. It's going to be a tough job, getting Ester out of there."

"If anybody can do it, Nadine can," whispered Morven confidently. "She's a courageous woman...And also very capable."

"Agreed. I'm sure glad she came with us."

The soft thud of guard's boots moved down the hallway toward them. It stopped in front of the storeroom. In the darkness Omar's fingers closed around the wooden handle of the dagger hidden in his sash. He breathed very quietly but feared that his thumping heart might be heard through the door. The guard grunted, then moved back down the hallway.

"Wheeww," Morven whistled softly.

"Thank you, Elconan," Omar whispered.

The two friends waited in the storeroom until they heard the cleaning crew in the hallway. As the cleaners walked past the storeroom Omar heard a high pitched voice say, "I wonder if Aklavia will ever get the breastplate back."

"Never," replied a husky voice. "Governor Kuman will never give it up."

"You're probably right there." squeaked the first voice. "Hear he's got a harem."

"Yes, that's what I've heard too. Since his wife died, he's ordered virgins to be brought to the palace. Guess he has a different one every night."

"Lucky dog..." Their voices trailed off as the crew moved down the hallway and out of the building. A bolt slid and locked the door securely behind them.

"A harem?" asked Morven, surprised.

"Torn from their homes and forced to submit to Kuman against their wills," replied Omar sadly. "Just like Ester." New resolve surged through his soul. "It's imperative that we get the breastplate."

Morven sighed deeply. "I can't wait to get out of here."

***

Fergus paced in his room nervously, his mind was on the evening ahead. "Elconan, be with us," he prayed quietly. "Protect my friends...Give us success..." His reverie was interrupted by a knock on the door.

"Good evening, Fergus. Your evening meal," said Leeah when he opened the door. She stepped into the room and set a tray on the small oak table. "Where are your friends?" Leeah asked as she stepped back.

"Enjoying the night life in Gara," he replied simply. He was in no mood for conversation. "Thank you for the food," he said as he remained standing by the door, expecting her to leave.

"You didn't want to go with them?"

"No. I had some things to do," he said flatly.

"Breakfast as usual tomorrow?" she asked. He nodded.

"We'll be eating together." *But not here*, flashed through his mind.

"If you set the tray outside I'll pick it up later without disturbing you."

"Okay," he nodded. "Thank you Leeah. That'll be all for now." She left the room. He closed the door and turned to the tray. It contained a bowl of steaming peas and carrots. A plate of grilled eggplant, baked beans, freshly baked bread, roasted potatoes, fresh pears, a bowl of grapes and a jug of wine. After several requests the kitchen finally stopped sending meat. His mind went over the details of the evening ahead as he ate. *Would their plans work? Would he see his friends again?* He ate slowly. He wasn't hungry. His stomach was tense and his mind distracted. But he knew that he needed energy for the night and so he forced himself to eat.

When he couldn't eat any more he set the tray outside. Then he folded his legs under him and sat on a cushion to pray and meditate. Late in the evening he got up from the cushion, slipped his dagger into his sash and left the room.

TWENTY ONE

Nadine followed the boy until they stopped in front of a freshly oiled cedar door beside the lobby. It was elaborately carved with a scene of two naked bodies locked in a sensuous embrace. The boy knocked on the door. "Who is it?" asked a squeaky voice.

"Servant Zelda," the boy replied.

"Enter." The boy pushed back the door and motioned for Nadine to move forward. When she stepped into the room the door closed behind her. Nadine felt her heart throbbing in her throat. The room was dimly lit, with only a small candle flickering on a table beside a large bed in the centre of the room. As her eyes adjusted to the darkness she noticed that the bed was covered by a blanket of elaborately embroidered silk and large, soft pillows. On the table, beside the candle, stood a finely crafted bronze Kuman statue. In one corner of the room she saw a chair and a large desk. Above the desk, high in the wall, was a small window. The wall beside the desk was covered by a series of shelves filled with papyrus scrolls.

"Welcome," said a thin, scratchy voice in the darkness to her left. A figure moved, Sacar shuffled out of the darkness. He reached behind Nadine and bolted the door. "Come." His cold, bony hand clasped Nadine's arm and he led her into the candlelight. A cold chill rattled through Nadine's body as the keeper's shifty eyes studied her intensely. She noticed that he had changed his tunic. He was now wearing an elegant, blue, silk garment with bright embroidery around the neck and over the shoulders. His hair was slicked back with aromatic grease and his body radiated a strong, musky fragrance that permeated the room. "Here, change," he said abruptly, as he handed Nadine a sheer, white linen tunic.

"Where...," she stammered. He pointed into the dark corner of the room. Nadine stepped into the darkness, pulled off her coarse tunic and slipped on the sheer linen garment. Embarrassed and self-conscious, she stepped back into the light.

"That's much better," Sacar cackled. "Come." As he reached for her hand, Nadine's nostrils were struck by the strong odour of tekara on his breath. He led her to a cushion beside the bed. "Sit down," he ordered blankly. As Nadine folded her legs and sat on the cushion the keeper asked, "Would you like some tekara, or wine?"

"Tekara's too strong for me."

Sacar giggled. "I prefer it. Helps me forget about this miserable place."

"You don't like it here?" asked Nadine, as she accepted a tumbler of wine from him.

"Oh, the women are beautiful...and I like that. It's just this whole city...I don't like it."

"I thought Governor Kuman was building a beautiful city. What don't you like about it?"

"Beautiful." Sacar's voice dripped sarcasm. "Aren't you naive." His cold eyes stared at her—mocking. Nadine felt a heaviness settle over her. "This city reeks with political manoeuvring, betrayal and lies." He reached for the jug of tekara and poured into his tumbler.

"So, why do you stay here?"

Sacar's face brightened. A sardonic smile crossed his lips. "I get to be with beautiful women—like you."

Nadine felt a cold jerk in her soul, followed by a spreading numbness.

Sacar held up his tumbler. "To the strength and future of Gara," he said, with false sincerity.

"And to all of us," said Nadine, as she clinked his tumbler. She took a sip. "This wine is very good."

"Supplied by the palace. One of the few things they do well over there."

They discussed the affairs of the palace briefly, and the alliance Kuman was building. Sacar refilled his tumbler several times as they spoke. His speech became slurred and his eyes glassy. Finally, he set his tumbler on the table and stood to his feet. "Come," he beckoned with a thick tongue as he wobbled in front of her. Nadine stood up. Sacar reached for her tunic with both hands and tore it from her. She cringed, embarrassed.

"Come on," he ordered, as he pushed her onto the bed. "Let's have some fun."

TWENTY TWO

Earlier in the day Fergus had purchased a boat large enough to carry five people. He had also stored food on board in back packs for easy carrying. During the past several days Fergus and his friends had studied the movements of the guards on the pier. They found that the guards spent the late watches of the night gambling with dice and drinking wine, beer and tekara until they grew tired and fell into a drunken stupor. This is when Fergus and the others planned to escape. *If all goes well,* he thought.

"No friends tonight?" asked one of the guards at the entrance to the palace compound.

"No. They're occupied."

"Have a good night," said the guard as Fergus passed the sentries.

"Thank you. I'm sure I will. Pasidian nightlife is very interesting." The guards laughed gruffly. Fergus walked away from the palace along the boulevard that bordered the palace complex. The stately palm trees that lined this street had been ripped and shredded by the storm and their tattered remnants now hung in the darkness like disembodied monsters. Flickering torches on poles cast an eerie light in the darkness. He walked past the end of the palace compound and the torches into the darkness of the Pasidian night. Lights quivered in the windows of the elegant homes along the boulevard where Kuman's army generals, top bureaucrats and administrators lived. Surrounded by high walls, each home was in its own exclusive compound attended by servants and with guards at the gate.

His heart was heavy as he walked. Fergus was concerned for his friends. They faced great danger, if they were not successful tonight all of Fabia would soon be like Pasidia. A few people in power enjoying a grand lifestyle, served by the rest of the population which existed as little more than slaves. Poverty. Greed. Hunger. Pain. Anger. Hatred. Crime. Immorality. And the whole society overlaid with the forced worship of Kuman and his stone idols. Sacrifice of infants. Endless laws, rules and regulations on how, when and where to appease the gods.

He had heard the tortured cry of a mother whose infant was torn from her arms and thrown into the fire. The anguish of Tamara joined the scream of the child in a horrid chorus that haunted his soul. Women treated as less than men. Children taken from their homes and forced to work for Kuman. He thought of Petrina, and felt her pain. On and on... Heaviness surrounded his heart. It deepened his resolve to fight for the breastplate. To restore love and goodwill to Fabia. When he was sure that he wasn't being followed he crossed the street and turned back toward the palace. He stayed in the shadows carefully until he reached the pier.

The guards on the pier stood as he approached. "Good evening, Fergus," said a muscular man with a bushy beard.

"Good evening," he replied. "Beautiful evening, isn't it?"

"It's nice now. But by the looks of those clouds moving in," the guard nodded toward the western horizon where a dark bank of clouds was moving toward them. "It'll be raining before morning."

"That's something I haven't been able to get accustomed to," said Fergus. "This rain. How long do you think it'll be before it starts?"

"Should be a few hours, at least. I hope it holds off until our watch is over. I hate being out here in the rain."

"I can understand that. Mind if I go check on my boat?"

"Go ahead. But I wouldn't go out on the river. You could get caught in the storm."

"I'll be careful, thanks." He walked past the guards and down the pier. The boats rocked gently as the cool evening breeze stirred the water. On his right Fergus saw the large bamboo enclosure that housed Kuman's regal fleet. Several large boats with intricately carved images of large animals on the bow and stern. The main boat was covered by a large linen canopy and the carving on the bow had been removed and replaced with a large Kuman statue. The boats were built so that twenty oarsmen could sit on each side and propel the craft through the water at great speed. Beyond the fleet lay a large work area where fast boats were being built for Kuman's army.

Fergus turned left and followed the pier to the spot where he had tied the boat. He stared in disbelief and shock. It was empty. Frantically, he looked around. The boat was gone.

TWENTY THREE

Kuman threw back the delicately embroidered silk blanket and jumped out of his elegant gold bed. A deep restlessness stirred his soul. He couldn't sleep. He paced around in the large bedroom trying to calm the agitation he felt in his innermost being. He jerked the rope beside the bed. A few minutes later a sleepy-eyed female servant entered the room.

"You rang, highness?"

"Yes," he replied curtly. "Bring me wine." The servant bowed, then left the room.

All the palace servants had been ordered to refer to him as 'highness'. But, since he was not yet king, he didn't require this beyond the living quarters. In the government and elsewhere he was the great leader of the alliance. Soon, however, he mused, *everyone would call him highness*. He only needed a few more provinces to join the alliance, then he would be declared King of Fabia. *Those who refused to join with him would be destroyed.* He relished the thought.

A few minutes later the servant returned with a jug of wine and two gem encrusted goblets on a silver tray. She set the tray on the small table beside the bed, poured wine into one of the goblets and then held the tray in front of Kuman.

"You first," he said. He knew that many people hated him. He didn't trust the servants. She set the tray back on the table and put the goblet to her lips. Kuman watched her carefully as she drank.

"Okay," he said. She poured wine into the second goblet and held the tray before him. He picked up the wine.

"Anything else, highness?"

"That'll be all for now." She bowed and left the room.

Kuman paced the room as he warmed his veins with the wine.

The uneasiness had settled upon him earlier in the day, as he left the hall-of-justice. And it had followed him all evening. Since Tamara's death he did not eat the evening meal in the palace living quarters. Instead, he invited a rotating list of administrators, officials, priests, their wives and guests to the palace banquet hall each evening for a lavish meal. Several secretaries were kept busy preparing the guest lists and distributing the invitations.

Each evening the guests consumed great quantities of wine, beer and tekara until their actions became animated and the banquet hall was filled with gales of boisterous, giddy laughter. Following the meal musicians and dancers entertained the audience. The male and female dancers wore skimpy, sheer tunics as they performed their sensuous and provocative routines. They encouraged the drunken audience to participate, and the evening would slowly progress to a massive orgy.

The camaraderie, food, music, dancing and rampant sex helped Kuman relax at the end of a busy day. But this day was different. When the dancing began his restlessness increased, so he left the banquet hall and went to his private quarters. He was agitated, short-tempered and aroused.

He rang the bell of his chief steward, Abidan. A few minutes later a short, fat, swarthy man appeared at the bedroom door. "You rang, highness?"

"Bring me a virgin," Kuman barked.

"Yes, highness." Abidan bowed and hurried from the room. A few minutes later he returned with a beautiful but frightened girl. She had long, straight limbs, a full, round soft body and a sweet, perfectly shaped, oval face. She cringed as Abidan led her into the room. Her bright blue eyes were filled with terror.

"Leave," Kuman ordered. As soon as the chief steward left the room Kuman tore the skimpy tunic from the cowering girl's body. He grabbed her and pushed her toward the bed where he fell upon her like a ferocious animal. She cried out as he ripped into her. Her cry enraged him. He slapped her face repeatedly until blood poured from burst lips. He tore at her breasts savagely. She screamed. He cursed her and beat on her body with his fists as he raped her.

Once relieved, he ordered the stricken girl from the room. She left, shaken and chagrined, trying desperately to cover her naked body with arms and hands. But nothing could cover the pain in her heart.

The release of passion did not calm the restlessness. He gulped more wine. Then he left the bedroom and staggered to the bronze altar in the palace shrine. He lit a clay incense lamp standing on the floor in front of the large stone image of the shadow's double plates. Then he folded his legs and sat on the soft carpets with his face toward the icon. The spirits had been quiet for several weeks. Perhaps they were behind the restlessness, he mused. "Come to me," he said softly. "Come to me. Come to me..." He repeated over and over until a dark shadow floated through the window and filled the room with a cold, thick presence.

***

Time passed slowly in the dark storeroom as Omar and Morven breathed the stale air and massaged their stiff limbs.

"It feels strange in here," Morven whispered. "Like the rest of the world doesn't exist anymore. The danger out there doesn't seem real."

"Step out of here and reality will strike you with a sharp sword," replied Omar softly.

"I know. But I have to keep reminding myself of that. I've never been cooped up like this before. It's making me feel weird."

"Think of home. Think of what'll happen to Fabia if we fail in our mission tonight."

"My heart aches at the thought of Elita and our children living in an environment like Gara."

"And our daughters, like Ester, sacrificed to the gods."

"I sure hope Nadine can get her out of there."

"She will."

"Do you think Fabia will ever be the same again? I mean, once we get the breastplate back."

"Nothing will be the same. We still have Kuman and his great ideas," Omar said wryly.

"How will we deal with his armies?"

"The people will unite behind the breastplate," said Omar with confidence. "There is strength in our traditions."

"But many are forsaking them."

"When we have the breastplate it'll be different. The people will honour that."

"And Kuman's armies?"

"We must pray to Elconan for wisdom and insight. If we have to fight to save Fabia, then we'll fight. Better now than when his army of giants is mature."

"And kill?"

"If that's what we have to do to stop this evil, we'll do it."

"It's only because I have seen the evils of Gara that I can bear that thought. Do you think the people back home will understand?"

"My father's murder got the attention of the nation. I think they'll understand."

"I keep thinking about Elita. I'm glad that she's unaware of the danger we're facing. She'd be worried sick."

"You've never told me how you met. How did you meet Elita? She's from Soleb, isn't she?"

"Yes, I went to Soleb to help them with the harvest. I was picking apples when we met."

"Let me guess," said Omar, as if thinking aloud. "She was in the apple tree?"

Morven laughed quietly. "Not quite. She was serving meals to the harvesters."

"And you were smitten by the most beautiful girl you'd ever seen."

"Something like that."

"You and Elita are very close."

"Yes. And Elconan has blessed us with two beautiful children. I'm missing them a lot…Can hardly wait to get back to them."

"It must be nice to have someone to go home to. All I have is Sigmund."

"Soon you'll have Ester."

Silent pause.

"Nadine was given a very difficult assignment," Omar reflected. "I pray she and Ester are okay."

TWENTY FOUR

Nadine steeled her emotions not to grimace as Sacar fondled and kissed her. She pretended to respond, but remained alert and moved her body toward the Kuman statue standing on the table beside the bed. Sacar was focused on his passion and unaware as Nadine reached for the statue. She grasped it firmly, and with a powerful stroke, smashed it against the keeper's head. Crack! Sacar slumped. Nadine pushed him away and got up quickly. She felt the pulse. It was weak. Sacar was unconscious. Quickly, she tore the bed sheets into strips and bound him securely. She stuffed a rag into his mouth and then secured the gag by tying a strip around Sacar's bloody head.

Nadine picked up her black tunic and slipped it on. Her hands were shaking and her breath came in quick, short gasps. *Calm down*, she told herself. *Calm down. Steady.* She paused, closed her eyes and breathed deeply until the panic subsided and she was able to collect her thoughts.

She searched through the scrolls frantically until she found a list of all the rooms and who was in each. Ester, she found, was on the second floor near the end of the pool. "Good," she whispered. Nadine picked up the key to Sacar's room, grabbed a second black tunic, slipped out the door and locked it behind her. She moved quickly but carefully along the darkened corridor and up the steps, very carefully avoiding Talga and the other cleaning servants. The full moon shone brightly over the courtyard, bathing it in a soft, cold light. A cool, gentle breeze rustled the leaves. Nadine was glad for its fresh breath against her body, which was covered with perspiration.

She found Ester's door, opened it and stepped in. Ester was

asleep. Nadine clasped her hand over Ester's mouth and shook her gently. "Ester, wake up. It's Nadine."

Ester woke with a start and began tearing at the hand at her mouth.

"Shhhh...," Nadine cautioned. "It's Nadine. Be quiet." Ester blinked in the dim light of the moon that came through the small, high window. She nodded recognition. Nadine released her mouth.

"Nadine," Ester gasped in surprise. "What are you doing here?"

"I've come to rescue you," Nadine whispered. Ester jumped out of bed and threw her arms around Nadine. The girls embraced each other warmly. Tears coursed from Ester's cheeks as questions poured from her lips.

"How did you find me? What are you doing in Gara? How did you get in here...?"

Nadine held a forefinger to her lips. "Shhhhh, I'll explain later. We have to move quickly. Be careful. Here, slip on this tunic. If someone sees us they'll think we're cleaning servants."

Ester slipped the black servant's tunic over her head. She shook her long, full, auburn hair and it fell over her shoulders.

"Come," whispered Nadine. "We must hurry." Using the dark shadows of the corridor as a covering they carefully made their way back to Sacar's room. Nadine unlocked the door and they slipped in. She bolted the door behind them.

Ester gasped when she saw Sacar lying on the bed, bound, with blood oozing from his skull. "What happened to him?" she asked.

"I'll explain later, we have to get out of here." She grabbed a bed sheet and thrust it at Ester. "Here, take this sheet and make it into a rope. I'll be right back." Nadine slipped out the door, locked it and hurried to the dressing room where she grabbed her purple tunic with the dagger still wrapped in it. She grabbed a second purple tunic for Ester. Voices sounded in the hallway. A cold fear coursed through her. She crouched in the shadows.

"Sacar asked for the new girl tonight," said the voice of Talga.

"Must be having a good time," said another voice, sarcastically.

"She's been in there for quite a while."

Nadine breathed very softly as she waited. Her heart beat in her head. The voices passed. She waited. The corridor was quiet. After several minutes she peered out of the dressing room carefully. She couldn't see anyone, so, very cautiously, she made her way back to Sacar's room. Once inside, she locked the door behind her.

"How's this?" Ester held up the bed sheet tied with many knots.

"That's great." Nadine paused, then reached for her friend and the girls embraced. "We need to hurry," she said quietly. "Omar and the others will be waiting for us at the pier, with a boat."

"Omar?" Ester asked with surprise. "Is here?"

"Yes. He came for you. Here, slip on this purple tunic." Sacar groaned and rolled on the bed. "See that window?" Nadine pointed above the desk. "That's our escape. The doors are heavily guarded. Here, take this." She picked up a dagger lying on Sacar's desk and handed it to Ester.

"What would I do with that?" Ester asked innocently.

"Just take it. You may need it. Here, like this." She tied her dagger to her thigh.

Ester tore a piece of bed sheet and did the same. Nadine tied one end of the roped bed sheet to a leg on the desk. She got up on the desk and looked out. She couldn't see anyone, only the still darkness of night. She picked up the rope and threw it out the window.

"Hurry," she urged. "Get up here and I'll help you out." Ester climbed onto the desk. "It's not far," said Nadine. "You go down first. I'll follow you." Nadine helped Ester climb through the window. Ester grabbed the rope and, hand over hand, let herself down. When Ester was safely on the ground Nadine crawled through the window and quickly climbed down the rope to join her. As they were catching their breath the shadow of a man moved around the corner of the building in the bright moonlight.

"Get down," Nadine motioned with her hand. They quickly dropped to the ground and lay along the bottom of the wall in the shadows. The guard came around the corner.

TWENTY FIVE

Fergus searched the pier quickly. Cold sweat dropped from his forehead. One of the guards paused from his gambling and eyed him suspiciously. He got up, walked down the pier toward Fergus. "What are you looking for?" he asked.

"My boat is missing," said Fergus.

"Where was it?" Fergus pointed to the empty space.

"Had some stuff in it, didn't it?" asked the guard. Fergus nodded. "Maybe it was stolen."

"Someone would steal a boat?" Fergus asked in surprise.

"Remember, this is Gara," said the guard dryly. "Maybe some slave, trying to escape. He won't get far. The river's well guarded. Lots of slaves trying to escape."

"Do any of them get away?" asked Fergus, trying to keep his voice calm. This was new information. He hadn't counted on the river being guarded.

"A few. Most are caught and returned. But a few make it?"

"Where do they go?"

The guard shrugged. "Who knows? Maybe to your lovely Cormath? Aklavia? Perhaps. Some live in the bush like animals." A sense of desperation crept around Fergus's heart. He had to find a boat. And he had to find a way past the river guards.

"How is the river guarded?" he asked casually.

"Boats with soldiers cruise the river."

"At night?"

The guard shrugged. "Always."

"Mind if I keep looking around?" asked Fergus. "Maybe the boat got moved."

"I think it's gone. But go ahead." The guard returned to his game and the jug of tekara that he shared with his comrades. Fergus continued to search in the moonlight.

***

Omar and Morven slipped out of the closet quietly and stepped into the dark hallway. They each carried several pieces of strong papyrus rope. Ahead of them, underneath a torch hanging from a wall sconce, they saw the guard slouched in a chair. His arms were folded across his stomach, his chin rested on his chest. His eyes were closed, his breathing slow and deep. "He's asleep," mouthed Omar. Morven nodded. They crept up behind the guard quietly. Morven slipped a rope around him and, with a sharp yank, pinned his arms against his body. Omar quickly tied a heavy cloth across the startled guard's mouth as Morven bound him to the chair.

The guard struggled awake and began thrashing around, his feet kicking the air. Omar grabbed one leg, Morven the other. They wrestled with the flailing limbs until they succeeded in tying them together, then they secured them against the chair. Immobile and silent, the guard glared at them in the dim light.

Omar took the brass key hanging on the guards belt and unlocked the door leading to the hall-of-justice. He remembered the last time he was in the room, grovelling on the floor before Kuman. *Never again*, he thought. It was dark inside, except for a warm iridescent glow from the table beside the throne. It filled the room with a soft presence. "There it is," Omar exclaimed, his voice filled with excitement. He grabbed the torch and led Morven through the dark room to the glowing breastplate. "Hold this," he said excitedly as he handed the torch to Morven. He picked up the heavy breastplate. "I've got it," he said. "Let's get out of here."

They moved out of the room quickly. As Morven passed the bound guard he reached for his sword and yanked it from the sheath. "We may need this," he said. Then he blew out the torch and dropped it at the guards feet.

"I better put this on," Omar remarked. "That'll be the easiest way to carry it."

"Good idea."

"Can you help me with it?" Morven reached for the golden icon. As Omar handed it to him he slouched forward and fell to one knee, almost dropping it.

"Wow. This thing's heavy."

"Sorry, should have warned you." Omar laughed. "Strap it to me." Morven straightened up and, with Omar's help, strapped the breastplate to his friend. The brightness of the icon hurt his eyes and he had to keep his face turned from it.

"Good," said Omar, when the breastplate was firmly attached. "Now it's just the guards outside. Then we're off to the pier."

"Sure hope Nadine gets there."

"She will," replied Omar, with forced confidence. They moved down the corridor carefully in the darkness until they came to the large entry lobby. They stopped at the door and listened.

"I don't hear anyone," whispered Morven.

"Remember, they patrol the perimeter of the building by walking around it and meeting in front of this door. We don't know where they are now. So we better wait until we hear them outside. Then, when they walk away we'll know we can slip out without being seen."

"Okay," replied Morven. He ran his hands around on the door. "I've found the lock," he said.

"Good."

TWENTY SIX

The cold, thick darkness floated in through the window and settled around Kuman like a heavy, toxic vapour. Electricity pulsed down his spine as the familiar presence enveloped him. His chest heaved each heart beat. He bowed his head and waited in tense expectancy. The shadow had come to him many times before. He waited eagerly for his mentor. *What great wisdom would be given to him tonight?* He wondered.

Surprise, then fear, shot through his heart as the dark mass thrust his body forward and slammed his face into the plush carpet. His body jerked and twitched as the spirits tore through him. Tonight, instead of wisdom and accolades, the shadow taunted him. It pawed him like a cat playing with a mouse. It ridiculed him. It spat vile curses at him until he became numb and cold. He quivered on the floor. Foul foam seeped from his lips.

"Incompetent fool," hissed the shadow. "The breastplate has been stolen."

The breastplate! Kuman jerked his body upright. Panic surged through him. He jumped up from the floor. As he threw on his robe the darkness let out a piercing, hideous cry and slithered out the window.

***

Nadine prayed silently as she pressed her body into the cold damp earth beside the harem house.

"Elconan, protect us. Don't let him see us." The guard peered into the night casually, then turned and walked back to the front of the building and out of sight.

"That was close," whispered Nadine. "Come on, let's go."

Staying low in the shadows, they crept toward the wall that surrounded the palace complex. Then they crawled on the ground along the wall toward the hall-of-justice.

A piercing cry, like an animal in pain, pulsed through the air. Ice cold shivered through Nadine. "What was that?" she gasped.

"I've heard it before," whispered Ester. "It comes from the palace."

"How awful. This place gives me the creeps."

***

Crouched in the darkness inside the justice building, Omar and Morven also heard the scream. The hideous cry pierced through the stone walls. A cold icicle of fear poked Omar's heart. "Something out there is very angry," he whispered.

"Whatever it is, I hope I don't meet it in the dark. What kind of vile creatures exist around here?" As Morven spoke a dark, cold heaviness seeped into the building. "Sure is spooky in here," he said quietly.

Footsteps outside. Muffled voices.

"I hear the guards," said Morven. Omar nodded.

"A few more minutes and they'll leave to walk around the building. Then we'll run for the pier."

"Fergus better be there with the boat."

***

The haunting cry streamed across the palace grounds in the cold, dark night. It floated toward the river and over the pier. Fergus shuddered. Icy, clammy fear wrapped around his heart and compressed it like a vise. His mind went numb. His heart beat crazily. Panic surged through him like bolts of electric lightening. It shook his body like a reed in a gale. He staggered, caught himself, and stood against the waves of terror sweeping over him. "No," he said firmly into the night. "It will not overpower me." Fergus locked his feet to the pier. "Elconan, give me strength," he prayed. He breathed deeply. Drawing in the fresh night air, again and again. The terror slowly drained out of his system; his erratic heart calmed and resumed its beat. The numbness in his mind cleared as he stood on the pier firmly. "I need a boat," he said to himself. "Any boat...with oars...that can carry five people. I need to hurry." His body sprang to life and he began searching the pier urgently.

***

Kuman burst out of the palace and grabbed the guard lolling at the entrance. He yanked his tunic and shook him.

"Quickly," Kuman yelled. "Sound the alarm. Get others. The breastplate's in danger. Secure the hall-of-justice."

The guard leaped into action. He blew his whistle frantically as he grabbed a torch and ran toward the justice hall. Within a few minutes guards were streaming across the palace compound in a moving mass of torches, shouting and curses.

***

"Something's gone wrong," said Nadine anxiously. "We better run for it. Keep your dagger ready." She pulled the weapon from her thigh, nodded to Ester.

"I don't know how to use this," said Ester as she reluctantly retrieved her weapon.

"Here, I'll show you," Nadine gave Ester a quick lesson on holding the dagger, and how to use it to cut, pierce and slash. "We'll have to watch their swords. If one of them comes after us, you distract him and I'll attack him with this." She held her dagger in front of her triumphantly. "Got it?"

"I'll do what I can. I don't know anything about fighting."

"Just distract him. Keep him focused on yourself. I'll do the rest."

"Okay."

"May Elconan go with us."

"Yes. May Elconan go with us," Ester repeated quietly.

TWENTY SEVEN

Morven jumped back as the door slammed open. Guards poured through the entrance in a wild rush of torches, bodies and fear.

"There," someone shouted. The torches turned toward Morven and Omar.

"Run," yelled Omar as he dashed out the door. Morven slashed at the guards, slipped through them and followed Omar.

"Get them," a frantic voice yelled. The guards stampeded after Omar and Morven as they ran toward the gate that led to the pier.

***

Nadine and Ester ran toward the gate. They saw the pier beyond in the moonlight. Then they saw the torches and the guards chasing their friends. Nadine stopped suddenly. Ester banged into her so hard Nadine stumbled forward.

"Get down," urged Nadine. They dropped to the ground.

***

Fergus heard the commotion in the palace compound. *They've been found out*, he realized. *I need to get a boat now—any boat*. In the dim moonlight he noticed a small boat...oars. It'll have to do. He untied it quickly and moved it to the end of the pier. The guards, distracted by the commotion, did not see him move the boat.

Morven and Omar reached the pier where they met the startled, drunken guards. "Hold it, right there!" one of the guards barked. Morven faced them with his sword. Other guards caught up and surrounded them. Morven ran at the guards with his weapon. They jumped back.

Omar rushed past the distracted guards and ran down the pier. Several guards ran after him. He heard swords clash behind him, then Morven cried out and dropped to the pier, blood gushing from his chest.

"Over here, Omar," yelled Fergus. But it was too late. With the guards panting behind him Omar rushed past him off the end of the pier and hit the water with a mighty splash.

"After him," yelled a coarse harsh voice. Six burly guards dropped their swords and jumped into the water.

"Here's another one," piped a guard, in a thin frantic voice, pointing at Fergus.

"Get him," ordered the harsh voice. Four guards jumped into the boat, their swords pointed at Fergus.

Wrapped in the heavy breastplate, Omar plunged down into the cold inky water. He tried to swim, but the weight pulled him deeper and deeper. His lungs screamed for air as he went down, down, down.

***

Meanwhile, back at the harem, the guards had been electrified by the hideous cry. When they heard the whistle and the commotion around the hall-of-justice their curiosity was piqued.

"We better check the harem," said the leader. "Make sure everything's okay there." He pointed to a short, red-haired guard, "You walk around this side of the building, and you...," he pointed to another, "Go 'round the other way. Check the building carefully. The rest of us will stay here to guard the entrance."

***

Omar tore at the breastplate, found the clasp and released it. Down, down, down it plunged. He surged up, gasped for air at the surface and plunged down again. *Have to get away*, shot through his mind. He swam frantically under water, but the need for air forced him to break the surface. He was surrounded by boats filled with guards. They closed in on him quickly.

***

"Sound the alarm," yelled the red-haired guard as he rushed back to his leader. "There's been an escape."

"Where?" cried the leader.

"Out the window, over there." The excited guard pointed to the rope hanging from Sacar's window.

"That's the keeper's room," thundered the leader. "Go check inside. See what's going on." As the guard hurried into the building the leader blew a bugle. Sleepy harem guards roused quickly and ran toward the entrance. Torches flamed. Other guards, returning from their chase on the pier, joined the harem guards.

"Sacar's been clobbered on the head," gushed the red-haired guard as he raced back out of the building. "He's tied up, and someone escaped out the window."

"They can't have gone far," barked the leader. "Let's comb the entire compound carefully. He pointed to the red-haired one. "Take six men with you, go back in there and find out who's missing."

"Yes, sir," beamed the ruddy recruit.

***

Several hours later, in the deep darkness of night, before the first rays of dawn, Eran, a young, short, muscular guard with closely cropped, black hair and dark, blank eyes, stumbled across Nadine and Ester hiding in the shadows of the compound wall.

"Lie still," he ordered, with his sword pointed directly at Nadine's heart. Then he yelled. "I've found them. Over here." Footsteps pounded the cobblestones as other guards rushed toward Eran. The girls were quickly surrounded by a cadre of angry guards with their swords drawn.

TWENTY EIGHT

Dark clouds hung low in the early morning light. A strong breeze rustled the leaves. Soft ripples danced across the Yaseb River as Kuman met the palace guards in the courtyard in front of the hall-of-justice. The governor's face was fierce, clouded with anger. Cadmus, Shobal and Phelan had been roused for this early morning meeting. Captain Remus and his guards were to give an account of the night's events. Kuman seethed with rage as he paced among the men gathered in several straight lines on the immaculate lawn still covered with early morning dew. He was wearing a fresh white linen robe, his long, golden hair flagged and rippled in the wind.

"Fools," he screamed. "Idiots!" He cursed and yelled at the group. The men stood subdued and afraid of the violent anger that raged before them.

"Where are the intruders now?" he spat at Remus.

"Shackled and locked in the dungeon, Majesty," replied the captain.

Kuman pointed an accusing finger at Remus. His eyes wild and bugged. "Where is the breastplate?" Kuman's spittle struck the captain's face.

"We don't know, Majesty," he replied stoically.

The veins bulged in Kuman's neck. "Don't know?" he glared. "Don't know? You're the captain of the guard, and you don't know?" The men shifted nervously. Remus stood resolute. "What do you know?" Kuman screeched.

"The prisoner was wearing the breastplate when he ran down the pier. When he surfaced the breastplate was missing."

"Have you sent divers down to look for it?" Kuman demanded.

"Yes, Majesty," Remus replied in a hollow voice. "But the water is too deep. They can't reach the bottom."

"So are you saying that you can't retrieve the breastplate?" Kuman fumed.

"That's correct, Majesty. The divers will try again when the light is brighter, but we're not hopeful. The river is very deep at the end of the pier."

Kuman shook his fist. His temples pulsed each heartbeat. He paced and raved. "Fools! Incompetent idiots! Useless women, all of you...Which of these wimps were guarding the hall-of-justice and the harem?" he demanded.

Remus nodded, two rows of guards moved forward and fell on their faces before Kuman. He cursed the frightened men vehemently. He spat on their heads and kicked them viciously with his heavy sandals as he berated and ridiculed them. The terrified men took the abuse with low moans and muffled gasps.

Finally, Kuman yelled, "Get up." The guards struggled to their feet quickly. "Drop your swords," he demanded. The men pulled their swords from their sheaths and dropped them on the ground.

"Who found the girls?" Kuman asked harshly.

"Eran did, Majesty," Remus replied.

"Eran, step forward," ordered Kuman. Eran's short hair bristled and his blank eyes sparked with fear as he stepped forward. His face was a mask of terror. "Pick up your sword and move away from the others." Eran scooped up his sword from the ground and moved back, away from the others.

Kuman pointed his finger at Remus. "You," he said. "Execute these men." He pointed to the guards. Remus hesitated. "Here!" Kuman screamed. "Now!" The guards fell to their knees crying and begging for mercy. Kuman's face was fierce as he waited for Remus to act. With forced motion the captain pulled his sword, walked behind the line of men and one after another, thrust it through each kneeling man's heart. Soon the ground was covered with dying men flailing in their own blood. When he finished Remus turned to Kuman, his face hard, like granite, his sword running with blood.

"Drop your sword," ordered the governor. Terror flashed across the captain's face. He fell to his knees, his face to the ground.

"No, no, no...," he wailed pitifully. "Mercy please, Majesty." A faint grim smile broke Kuman's lips. He turned to Eran.

"Kill him," he ordered.

Eran's face paled in the soft early morning light. He hesitated...pulled his sword...stepped forward awkwardly...Kuman stared at him with a dark, mean scowl. Eran steeled his face and thrust the sword through his captain. Remus gasped, fell prostrate as blood gurgled from his mouth.

"Well done," said Kuman with relish. "Come here." Eran stepped toward the governor and dropped to his knees, shivering, his face ashen. Kuman placed his hand on Eran's head. "I pronounce you captain of the palace guard. You may rise." Eran stood to his feet, bewildered, but relieved. Cadmus and Shobal shook his hand and congratulated him.

"Your first priority," Kuman interrupted. "Is to secure the palace compound. Make sure the prisoners don't escape." He looked at Eran intensely. "Your life depends upon it."

"Yes, Majesty," Eran clipped. His knees were shaking.

"Then," Kuman continued. "Find the breastplate." He turned to Cadmus. "Give him all the resources he needs. I want that breastplate."

"Yes, Majesty," Cadmus replied brightly. "He'll have whatever he needs." Kuman turned to leave.

"Majesty?" said Cadmus. Kuman turned to his deputy. "The body of the dead intruder, Morven. What should we do with it?"

"Burn it with the trash," Kuman replied coldly. He turned and walked toward the palace.

TWENTY NINE

Lorna rose early, as usual. The pale morning light was soft and warm, birds greeted the rising sun with resonant songs, chirping and trilling in the trees outside her window. Her sleep had been troubled. As she tossed on her bed she kept thinking of Omar and his mission in Gara. She yawned and stretched, her muscles were sore and tight from her body's fidgeting throughout the night. An uncommon heaviness lay on her heart. Her usually bright mind felt clouded, confused. She walked to a small table and splashed cold water over her face. Then she ran a metal comb through her long, black hair, now streaked with grey. The viceroy slipped on a light linen robe, picked up a scroll and walked out into her vibrant flower garden. This was her favourite place to meditate and pray, early each day while the rest of the household was still asleep.

She opened the sacred scroll and began to read. She could not shake the uneasiness in her spirit, nor could she absorb the words on the scroll. Finally she laid it aside, closed her eyes and began to pray. For Omar. For Gara. For Fabia.

***

Omar sat on the damp stone floor in the cold, dark cell with his feet shackled and his hands securely locked behind him to a heavy wooden pillar. When he leaned back against the pillar the shackles on his wrists dug into his spine and he was forced to hunch forward. His body grew numb from the cold and lack of movement. Faint torch light flickered through the small window cut into the heavy, wooden door that marked the cell's entrance. He heard the guards talking outside the cells, a heavy sorrow settled over his heart when he learned that Kuman had executed the guards because of his attempt to retrieve the breastplate and free Ester. His sorrow deepened as he thought about Morven, a good friend, lying on the pier in his own blood. His heart ached for Elita and the children. *They will be devastated*, he thought. *And I'm responsible.*

He knew that Fergus was in the next cell. They were brought in together. But the guards, and the thick stone walls prevented communication with his friend. His hopes that the girls would somehow miraculously escape were shattered when he heard the guards bring them into the dungeon several hours after he was incarcerated.

His body shivered in the damp tunic, still wet from the river. The heavy tiredness of exhaustion wrapped itself around him like a blanket of lead. His stomach burned with hunger and his mind was faint from lack of food and sleep.

"Where are you, Elconan?" he whispered in the darkness. "Don't you care?" Rodents scurried about in the shadows. A rat sniffed his feet. He talked to the rat quietly, calmly. Perhaps they could be friends. But the rat only stared at him with fierce, hungry eyes that sent shivers down his spine. "These animals are cursed," he whispered to Elconan. "They are not like the animals we've always known." He wiggled his feet in the shackles, the rat jumped back. But the beastly eyes stayed fixed on Omar.

Voices echoed in the hallway. The bolt on the door released. The door creaked open. Light from many torches flooded the cell blinding Omar momentarily. He squinted, looked up. Kuman was standing there, dressed in a shimmering white silk robe trimmed with gold thread. A multi-gemmed pectoral hung from a heavy, gold chain around his neck. His long, yellow hair was frizzled and bushy. Cosmeticians had carefully rubbed his face with fragrant oils but had not erased the tired, haggard lines of a face deeply stressed. His deep blue eyes flamed at Omar.

"So, friend," he said sarcastically. "This is how you treat me. Pretend friendship. Then sneak into my private areas and steal what's not yours. Where is your integrity? Your honour? That you would steal from a friend? I offered you the finest hospitality in Fabia. Treated you like someone of significance. And you treat me like this? Hypocrite. Nobel Omar, nothing but a hypocrite."

New adrenaline shot through Omar's veins. "What I took wasn't yours," he replied forcefully. "You killed my father and stole the breastplate. And Ester was promised to me."

Kuman's face flashed red. He spoke in sharp, forced accents. "How dare you accuse me of killing the king. It was done by others. They brought the breastplate to me."

"Others, yes," Omar retorted. "Others that you paid. Their hands were soiled with my father's blood, but your heart Kuman, your heart is soiled with the guilt of his death. My father loved you like a son. How could you do that to him?...And to Fabia?"

Kuman signalled to one of the guards holding a torch who quickly stepped out of the cell, then returned immediately with a chair. He placed it behind Kuman. Without taking his eyes off Omar, he sat down. Then, in a soft, flat voice, he said, "Okay, Omar, I'll admit it. I hired the killers."

"But why?"

"It's simple. I want to be king. I knew the council would favour you or someone else, over me. So I just did what was necessary to fulfil my dream."

"But what about our customs and teachings that come from Elconan? The sacred scrolls direct us to live for the highest good of all—for Aoght. Your actions violate the basic underlying principle of Fabian society."

Kuman snorted. Then he looked at Omar intensely and said, "Where is Elconan? Have you seen him?"

"Elconan is transcendent," Omar countered. "And he speaks to us through the sacred scrolls."

"Transcendent. Yes. And invisible. And silent. And those sacred scrolls, as you call them, are old-fashioned and outdated. They might have been valid for another age. But not for today. We're in a new era; the people want a god who is visible, and present. One they can touch and feel, and who will respond to them."

"A self-made god."

"Yes. One who frees us from the restrictions of old customs and traditions."

"What do you find so restrictive in our culture?" asked Omar softly.

"That I must live for the highest good of all," Kuman shrieked. "This is a principle of bondage. It's outdated, Omar. I want freedom. The freedom to choose to do whatever I please."

"Even if it causes others to suffer?"

"I do what I want to do. If that hurts someone else..." Kuman shrugged. "That's their problem."

"But when you enslave others you deny them their freedom."

"Listen, Omar. This business of equality—that's really out of date. True freedom means I can force others to serve me. I can have whatever I want, when I want it. As king, my rule will be absolute, and everyone in Fabia will serve me. I will have all the zorn I want. All the women I want. And all will bow down and worship me. My army will enforce my will ruthlessly, and I will be the centre of the world."

"But the people strain under your yoke of bondage. I've met many who are tired and angry because of what you're doing."

"A few complainers. Every great and noble venture has been opposed by a few detractors...those who can't dream big dreams."

"It may be a big dream for you, Kuman, but it's a painful and heavy reality for your servants and slaves. You have robbed them of their freedom."

"Freedom for what?" Kuman mocked. "To follow outdated customs? I offer them a new freedom. The freedom to be greedy, to hate and to lust. And they love this freedom. Didn't you see them on the high hill? How they bowed down to me and then danced and celebrated the new freedom?"

"I saw a woman die on the high hill, her heart broken because her child was thrown into the fire."

A fierce anger flashed across Kuman's face. He jumped to his feet. He pointed his finger at Omar and shouted, "How dare you speak to me like that? As if I caused her death. She chose to die, to humiliate and embarrass me. Just like you chose to steal from me. You'll die Omar, and your body will be consumed by flames. Except you won't be dead when the fire eats your body. Tomorrow morning you'll be sacrificed live. Just like the child you're so concerned about."

Kuman's outburst shocked Omar. A cold numbness settled around his heart. "What about the others?" he asked with a brave voice. "Can I call upon our years of friendship to ask you to release the others?"

Kuman laughed derisively. "They helped you, didn't they? You stole the breastplate and lost it in the river. My best divers are unable to reach it. Ten men have died trying."

"You threatened them?"

"Yes. With death if they didn't surface with the breastplate. They chose to stay under and drown themselves. And you're to blame, Omar. For that you'll die." He paused...laughed. "But you wasted your time, you know. My best goldsmiths are at work right now designing another breastplate. It'll be bigger and better than the one you dropped into the mud at the bottom of the river."

"You can make another breastplate, but it won't glow with the presence of Elconan."

"So much the better. That glow was just a nuisance anyway. Made me uncomfortable whenever I wore it. Let it glow in the mud. That's actually a good place for it." He laughed. "So you see, you're going to die for nothing. Nothing at all."

He paused, sat on the chair, then turned to Omar and said. "But I am not a man without mercy. I'll let the girls live. Ester I'll take as my concubine." Sharp pain stabbed Omar's heart. Kuman laughed hilariously.

"Every time I take her I'll think of you, and how you humiliated me, and I'll take my anger out upon her, in ways you haven't even imagined," he said with a threatening voice. "Then, when I'm done with her, I'll give her to the temple as a prostitute. Any man in Fabia that pays the price will have your precious Ester. And as they wear away her beauty the price will drop and she'll become the plaything of the base and ugly. Those who grovel in the dirt like animals will have their sport with her."

Omar's heart flooded with intense pain. He became oblivious of his chains and the death he faced. "I beg of you," he pleaded. "Don't our years of friendship mean anything? Do what you want with me, but please don't do this to Ester. She's innocent. Her escape was my idea."

A sadistic glee settled on Kuman's face. He forced laughter, then in a voice filled with sarcasm he said, "Beg all you want, old friend, but what I have spoken shall be done."

"No!" cried Omar, despair filled his voice.

"But you should be thankful," continued Kuman in a hard, emotionless voice. "She'll be treated better than the other one."

"Nadine?"

"Yes. She tried to kill the harem keeper."

Omar was surprised and saddened by the news. "Are you sure?"

"Yes. Bashed in her head with one of my statues. For that she should die. But I'll be kind to her, I'll let her live. I'll give her to the palace guards as their play thing. Their sex toy. Each of them will satisfy his urges upon her as he wishes. She'll be kept busy." Kuman laughed sadistically. "Oh, yes. I can just imagine them lined up, one after the other, waiting to get at her. From her belly many children will come for the fire." Kuman cackled loudly.

Omar's senses were numb. His heart ached. His mind reeled. He bowed his head and whispered quietly to Elconan. The cell became quiet. Kuman sat on the chair, gloating. Omar dug deep within his soul for strength. His eyes were filled with sorrow as he turned to Kuman and spoke softly, "What happened, Kuman? You've changed from the person I knew when we were growing up. We were the best of friends, you were like a brother to me. Remember how we spoke about the future? We talked about how we'd serve the people and contribute to the highest good to keep Fabia great. We watched our parents getting older and we talked about how the mantle of leadership would soon fall upon us. We even talked about how one of us might someday become king. Remember when we agreed that, if one of us became king, the other would be the king's closest advisor? What happened, Kuman? How did you change from living for Aoght to thinking only of yourself?"

Kuman paced around in the cell like a caged animal. Omar waited quietly. After several minutes Kuman spoke in a bitter, distant voice. "You say all are equal, but we're not all equal, Omar. None of us are equal. We're all different." A heavy silence hung between them as Kuman paced. Omar waited in silence until Kuman spoke again. "It started when we were boys, in school with Kara. Remember how I struggled with his assignments and exams? You always learned more quickly than I did. He loved you for it and lauded you with recognition and attention. Which, deep down in my heart, I resented. But we were friends, so I didn't say anything. Then your father was chosen to be king. You moved to Aklavia, while I remained in Gara. Your father was a very talented ruler, and the people loved him. You, Omar, are much like your father. You have many of his talents and abilities. I knew that one day you would be king, and I wouldn't. And I resented that. We would no longer be equal."

"But," Omar interrupted. "You're wrong, Kuman. True, we are given responsibilities according to our talents and abilities, but in Fabia we're all equal in recognition and privilege. The king has no special privileges."

Kuman ignored Omar's outburst. "I wanted to be king, Omar. And I knew I would never get elected ahead of you or several others on the council who were favoured by the people. But I kept my desire a secret deep in my heart until I was elected as governor of Pasidia. I had learned how to put on a good front and pretend that I was following the teaching of Elconan, but inwardly I was angry with him for not gifting me with the same leadership and administrative gifts you had."

Kuman returned to the chair, sat down and faced his old friend. "I sat up late into the night, feeding my resentment and plotting how I might become king. To be honest with you, I was very discouraged, and didn't know how I'd ever do it." He paused. Waited...as if deep in thought. Then continued. "Until late one night I received a visitation."

"A visitation?" Omar asked in surprise. "From whom?"

"Spiritual forces."

"From Elconan?"

"I didn't know where they came from, and I didn't care. They told me that they understood my pain, and were willing to help me become king."

"How did they come to you? In what form?" asked Omar with interest.

"Remember the flying shadow that appeared at the dedication of the monument on the high hill?"

"How could I forget?"

"It came to my window, night after night. Voices spoke to me from the shadow. Often I was drawn up through the window and into its belly, where my mind was filled with all kinds of wisdom and understanding."

"Incredible," said Omar softly.

"They showed me how to win the hearts of the people through mystery and fear. I received instruction in how to build the great monuments you see in Pasidia. The people revere me because I can build as no one has ever done before. They look upon me as a great superman. But reverence does not necessarily lead to obedience. To accomplish my goals I needed a people who obeyed without question. Severe, painful and public punishment for those who questioned me cowered them into compliant people."

"That's why you humiliated Tamara by exposing her naked body and burning it publicly."

"You're catching on, Omar. And when I'm through with you and your friends the people will fear me even more."

Hot pain flashed through Omar's soul. He closed his eyes and waited to control the emotions tearing at his heart. After several minutes he asked quietly, "Was the army their idea?"

"Yes. They taught me about war, and how to build a strong army to carry out our wishes."

"Our wishes?"

"Yes. I made an agreement with the forces. They would help me become king; I would follow their instructions, in everything."

"So the embryo, the army of giants, the weapons of war, and the temple...are all their ideas?"

"Yes."

"And the alliance?"

"Yes."

"And my father's murder, was that their idea?"

Kuman's face clouded. Deep darkness filled his eyes. "No. They wanted me to wait until the army was mature. Then, they said, we would strike quickly and conquer all."

"But you didn't want to wait."

"No. I knew that if I got the breastplate, I could sway Fabia to follow me."

"You really believe that Fabians would give up their freedom?"

"Haven't you seen what's happened in Pasidia? The people are in awe of our great building projects. They've never seen anything like this. And I've given them a god who is present and visible. They're following me." Kuman became animated, rose from the chair and paced in the cell. "And, haven't you seen the people coming here from the other provinces? The alliance is growing and following me," he stated triumphantly.

"What about those who don't?"

Kuman cursed violently. "They'll be forced into slavery. They'll learn to obey. If they don't, I'll kill them!"

A dark cloud of despair settled around Omar's heart. The fate of Ester, Nadine and all the oppressed people weighed heavily upon him. How could someone he had known so well and loved like a brother, become so evil? "Jealousy and pride are harsh taskmasters," he said in a low tone.

"But at least now I'm free from the guilt of not living for your precious Aoght. I can do whatever I want. And I have powerful spiritual forces at my disposal to help me reach my goal."

"Could you please clarify something for me?" asked Omar. Kuman shrugged. "Was slavery your idea, or did you get it from these spiritual forces?"

"It's theirs. They teach that equality is stupid. It's an outdated relic from the past. In my new kingdom the talented and gifted rise to the top and are rewarded accordingly. The rest must serve them."

"Do women rise as well?" Omar asked.

"No," Kuman spat. "Their role is to serve the men. They'll do as they're told. We're done with those old archaic ideas of Elconan's...that men and women are equal...and that a man should love and honour his wife. Why, in my new kingdom a man can have many wives. All to serve him. Serve the master. And if he doesn't like her—well, he can just get rid of her."

Kuman's words caused a deep sadness to settle over Omar. It crushed down on his spirit until he felt pressed into the cold stone floor. A gloomy silence hung between them. Finally, after several minutes Omar spoke. "When I was riding to Aklavia, after my father was killed, two men jumped me and tied me to a tree. Were they acting under your command?"

"Yes. They were supposed to kill you, but they failed. You got away. They must share the blame for the trouble you've caused. They'll burn with you tomorrow morning."

Omar shuddered. *Is there no end to this man's evil*, he wondered. Then he spoke: "Why didn't you kill me when I came to visit you?"

"Believe me, I wanted to, but I couldn't do it publicly or your father's death would be traced to me. Until I had more of the provinces on my side I couldn't risk the wrath of the people. And you were always surrounded by your friends. So I waited..." He paused briefly. "Then you seemed to show an interest in what we're doing in Pasidia. I thought that perhaps I could enlist you as an ally, and then I wouldn't have to kill you. You see, I do have a heart," Kuman snickered.

"An ally? After you killed my father?"

"Don't the followers of Elconan specialize in forgiveness?"

"But forgiveness is not the brother of evil."

"Oh well," sighed Kuman. "These arguments don't matter anymore, anyway. What you have done to me cannot be forgiven. Tomorrow morning you'll burn in the city square. My couriers are travelling throughout Gara inviting people to witness the death of a traitor. They'll cheer as you burn, Omar." Kuman walked toward the door.

"Before you leave, can I ask one more question?" Kuman stopped, faced Omar.

"Go ahead."

"What will you do with my friend, Fergus, will you release him?"

"Fergus will burn with you in the morning." A sharp pain stabbed Omar's heart. Fergus was a good and trusted friend. Omar felt a heavy weight of sorrow for the plight of those who had been loyal to him. His heart ached for Elita. He knew he must ask Kuman for at least one small act of kindness.

"If our many years of friendship mean anything to you, would you please embalm Morven's body and return it to his widow in Cormath?"

"Sure," said Kuman sarcastically. "Treat a traitor like a king." He paused. Then: "Morven wounded one of my guards. His body was burned on the trash heap this morning."

"Ohhhhh...," sighed Omar painfully. His head dropped. Through his mind flashed a picture of Elita, broken and crying.

"Before I leave, Omar," Kuman began in a strong firm voice. "Since you are an old friend, and I am not beyond compassion, I'll make a final offer. I'll release you and your friends...I'll even release Ester to you..." Omar's attention was piqued. But what he had seen of Kuman recently prevented his hope from rising. However, he listened expectantly. "On one simple condition."

"What's that?"

"Bring Cormath into the alliance. Join me."

A heavy darkness rattled through Omar's heart. "But joining the alliance also comes with other conditions," he said, dryly.

"Yes. You'd do the same as what the others have done."

"Which is?"

"Swear allegiance to me. Provide me with choice virgins for the embryo."

"And your shadow god?"

"Yes. Of course he replaces the old-fashioned, outdated, repressive religion of Elconan." Omar thought of his friends in the other cells. *They could all go free. And, after all, where was Elconan anyway?* Doubts flashed through his mind. *Could he sacrifice his friends for belief in a transcendent, invisible and silent deity? Was allegiance to Elconan really worth it?* He turned to his old friend. Kuman's eyes bored into him like flaming arrows. In those eyes Omar saw the pride and the greed that was suffocating everything in Pasidia that contributed to the highest good of all. No, he would not turn from Elconan and lead Cormath into slavery. "I can't trade good for evil," he said firmly. "I won't lead Cormath away from Elconan."

"Fool," Kuman hissed. "Not only are you a fool, but you're also my enemy. It's your choice. You will die tomorrow, and Ester is mine. And soon I'll march against your lovely little Cormath. It'll be mine too, regardless of your choice...." Kuman paused, looked at Omar severely. "You won't see my face again...Farewell." His voice dropped. "Old friend," he said derisively.

Omar looked directly into Kuman's eyes. Behind the cold hardness he saw fear and emptiness. His heart ached for the man who was once his friend. "Farewell," he replied sadly. "I'll pray that you experience the love and peace of Elconan."

"Don't bother." Kuman turned and left the cell. A guard bolted the door. Omar sat alone with his thoughts in the dim light. Son of a king. Governor of Cormath. Tomorrow he would be roasted alive. Ester. Nadine. Tormented by the lust of men. A dark heaviness crushed his spirit. Despair tore his heart. The hours passed slowly in the damp, quiet cell. He prayed for strength, for Kuman, for the others in the cells with him. He prayed for Aklavia. His body grew tired. He nodded.

Sharp pain jerked him awake. He kicked his shackled feet. A rat scurried into the darkness. Blood poured from his foot. He stared at it in disbelief. "He's eaten my toe," Omar muttered. Vicious animals around here. The pain surged up through his tired leg. His toe throbbed. Although he was hungry and tired, he forced himself to stay awake to keep the rat from eating more of his body. The hours passed slowly. Outside the sun set; torches were lit as darkness settled over the city.

THIRTY

"Omar, is that you?" a soft voice called through the small opening in the door.

"Yes," croaked Omar, with a parched throat. The bolt slid back and the door opened slowly. A guard stepped into the cell holding a torch. Through eyes clouded by fatigue and pain, Omar recognized a familiar face.

"Alix," he said weakly. "What are you doing here?"

"Keep your voice down," Alix whispered as he knelt in front of his old friend.

"What are you doing here?" Omar could hardly contain his excitement. "How are you doing?"

"I'm a member of Kuman's palace guard. I heard you were locked up in here last night. I had to be careful, but I was able to arrange things so I could be on this watch." Alix reached for the leather pouch hanging from his waist. He held it to Omar's lips. "Here, have a drink." The cool wet liquid fed new life to Omar's dry cracked throat.

"Thank you," he gasped, when his thirst was slaked. "It's good to see you. What are you doing here?"

Alix placed his hand on Omar's shoulder and looked directly into his eyes. "I've come to ask for forgiveness."

"Forgiveness? For what?"

"For leaving you, and joining Kuman. I thought he was a great man with exciting new ideas. He offered us the freedom to live for ourselves without regard for others. This was the way to true happiness, he promised."

"What changed your mind?"

"I saw that Kuman's freedom enslaves people in their own

greed. It causes people to hate each other, to fight, steal and kill. His freedom is like a rosebush that hides a venomous snake. It smells good on the surface, but when you get close, it bites with a deadly sting."

"Strange words for a palace guard."

"If Kuman knew how I feel he'd kill me. He rules by ruthless intimidation. The people's hearts are filled with fear. Anyone that speaks out against him is killed."

"I'm supposed to be burned alive tomorrow morning."

"I know. The couriers are inviting the whole city to watch your execution."

"How are the others?"

"Fergus is in the next cell."

"Have you seen Ester and Nadine?"

"Yes. They're in a cell down the hall."

"Are they okay?"

"Yes. They're fine. I gave them some water."

"Have you heard what's supposed to happen to them?"

"Yes. The guards are anxious to get at Nadine. But Kuman's forbidden anyone to touch her until your burning. Then they get her as a celebration."

A deep pained sigh escaped Omar's lips. He felt responsible for the plight of both Nadine and Ester. The thought of the abuse they faced sent frozen jolts of anguish through his body.

Alix's voice broke his melancholy. "You haven't answered my question."

Omar's mind was fogged with fatigue, stiffness and hunger. His foot throbbed where blood still oozed from the severed toe. "What's that?" he asked dimly.

"Do you forgive me?"

Omar fixed his eyes squarely upon Alix. He saw a face etched with remorse. "Of course I forgive you, friend. Forgiveness flows from the heart of Elconan, and from my heart as well."

Alix reached forward and hugged the captive. His cheeks were wet. "Thank you, Omar," he whispered. "You're a true friend." A warm sense of forgiveness and love flowed between the two men. Finally, after several minutes, Alix straightened back on his knees. He wiped his face with the back of his hands. "I'm going to get you out of here," he said with determination.

***

The palace banquet hall echoed with the forced laughter of Kuman's guests. Servants in sheer, skimpy, purple tunics moved around the tables with trays of wine, beer and tekara and kept the guests' goblets full as they feasted on a lavish banquet that featured roasted cow heart as the main dish. Kuman sat at a large rectangular table, on a raised dais along one wall, facing the crowd. Cadmus sat on his left, Jahaz on his right. Scattered throughout the room were key administrators, priests, army commanders and guests from other provinces. Each of the men was accompanied by a woman. A few brought their wives, but others, aware of the sexual orgies that concluded these evenings, left their wives at home and brought a mistress instead. Kuman arranged the seating carefully so that couples were separated when they arrived and seated at different tables.

A heavy restlessness settled upon Kuman as the evening began. His stomach constricted so that he couldn't eat. Colour drained from his face. "You don't look well, Governor," said Cadmus when he noticed his leader's ashen face. Kuman glared at him. He asked for more wine, drank goblet after goblet until the room spun around like a universe gone mad. When the music started, each drumbeat pulsed through his head like a thousand hammers.

Kuman turned to Cadmus. "I must leave," he slurred. "You'll have to entertain the guests." He stood up and rocked on his feet like a sapling in a storm. Cadmus noticed Kuman's dissonance and jumped to assist him.

He took his leader by the arm, "Let me help you to your quarters." As Cadmus led the governor out of the dining room Kuman waved a limp hand at the crowd.

"Something's wrong," Kuman stammered as Cadmus led him to the bedroom.

"Yes, there is," Cadmus scoffed "You're drunk. Everything will be better in the morning. I'll order the servants to give you a bath and massage. Then a good sleep, and you'll feel better. It's been a full day."

"No," Kuman groaned. "Something's wrong. I can feel it here." He pounded his heart.

***

Kuman's servants bathed him with hot, scented water and followed this with a massage of fragrant oils. Then they helped him into his massive bed where he lay in a drunken stupor. The restlessness, however, continued. He wrestled with the blankets like a wild boar in a trap; his bedclothes were soaked with perspiration. Over and over he cried out like a terrified animal in great pain. The servants shuddered at the cries that pierced the night air and echoed off the plastered palace walls.

Two hours past midnight a heavy, black shadow settled over the palace and covered it with a deep, malevolent darkness, as deep and as cold as the overlapping shadows of a thousand ghosts. As it seeped through the windows it sucked the air from the room; the servants screamed in terror and scrambled through the palace frantically seeking places to hide. Some ran out into the dark night, while others hid under beds and in closets.

Three kitchen servants were so terrified by the oozing, creepy shadow that they ran into the kitchen and thrust knives into their chests. They collapsed on the cold tiled floor with blood spurting from their torn flesh.

The large shadow, shaped like two plates facing each other, hovered over the palace and sent long tentacles through the window into Kuman's bedroom. It grabbed him by the throat and shook him. He awoke, gasping for air, his eyes wide with terror. The shadow lifted Kuman from the bed. "Fool," it hissed. "They're getting away." Kuman struggled with the shadow. He tore at its powerful grip around his neck. In desperation he grabbed the rope that rang the servants bell and jerked it madly.

***

"We have to hurry," said Alix as he loosened the shackles on Omar's legs and wrists. He took Omar's hand and helped him up off the floor.

"Ohhh, they're so stiff," said Omar, rubbing his limbs.

"Limber up while I get the others."

"What about the guards?"

"I put a mixture of henbane and opium in their drinks. They'll sleep for a while, but we have to get out of here quickly." Alix reached into his waist sash, pulled out a small container and some cotton rags. "Here, put this salve on your wound and wrap your foot in these." He handed Omar the container and rags. "I'll leave this torch." He stuck the torch in a sconce attached to the wall. "I'll go get the others." Then he slipped out of the cell.

Omar worked carefully to put salve on the wound. The blood had crusted and the bleeding had stopped. He wrapped the foot so that he could still slip on his sandals. He had just finished when Alix returned with Fergus, Nadine and Ester. Omar rushed to Ester, they embraced hungrily. "Are you okay?" he whispered.

"Yes, thank Elconan. It's so good to see you." He kissed her full on the lips.

Alix tapped him on the shoulder. "I hate to break up this party, but we need to get out of here." Omar released Ester, then he hugged Fergus and Nadine. Alix handed each of them a sword.

"The dungeon guards are all drugged," he said. "But you'll need these once we get outside."

"What happened to your foot, Omar?" asked Nadine.

Omar grimaced. "A rat bit my toe off."

"A rat? How bad is it," asked Ester with concern.

"I'll be okay."

Fergus interrupted. "Do we have an escape plan?"

"Yes," replied Alix. "Once we're outside we're close to the

compound exit. It's watched by four guards but they're usually drunk this time of night. But even drunk, they can put up strong resistance. We'll have to rush them quickly and overpower them before they know what happened."

"Then the pier?" asked Omar.

"No," replied Alix. "It's too dangerous. It's well guarded. We'll head toward the city until we're out of sight of the pier, then break toward the river where I hid a boat in the bushes. Stick with me."

"What if we lose you?" asked Omar.

Alix dropped to the floor and drew a map in the dust with the point of his dagger. He pointed to a rectangle in the diagram. "That's where the boat is," he said. "Just down from a large warehouse, away from the pier. If we get separated, meet here, in front of the warehouse. Do you understand?" He looked around at the group. Heads nodded. He stood up. "How are your limbs?"

"A little stiff," said Omar. "But anxious to leave."

Fergus pumped up and down on his legs. "I'm ready," he said.

Nadine flexed her muscles, alternately bending each knee. "I can outrun any of Kuman's guards," she said confidently.

Ester was holding Omar's hand. "I'm ready," she said.

"May Elconan be with us," said Omar.

"May Elconan be with us," echoed the others.

Alix turned toward the door. "Follow me."

***

The servants did not respond to Kuman's frantic ringing. Most had run out of the building. The few remaining were paralyzed with fear and wouldn't move. He struggled with the shadow as it held him by the neck. It hissed. It spat. Then with a fierce shriek it lifted him into the air, shook him, then dropped him to the floor. Thud. "Aww...," he moaned as he collapsed in a heap. Dazed. His mind still groggy from the wine, his heart pulsing with fear. He struggled to get up, then stumbled to the door. "Abidan," he groaned. "Abidan...."

THIRTY ONE

The dungeon hallway was lit with only an occasional torch flickering in a sconce on the wall. The prison was constructed of rough stones and mortar with heavy wooden doors marking each solitary cell. Omar and his friends stepped out of his cell; as they cautiously began walking on the damp, cobbled floor, a desperate voice cried out across the hallway. "Help me."

Omar turned to Alix. "Let's release the others," he urged. "Are there many?"

"No," replied Alix. "Kuman keeps the dungeon population down with frequent executions. These men," Alix pointed to the eyes peering at them through the small opening in the door, "are scheduled to die with you tomorrow."

An icy cold flashed through Omar's veins. "My father's killers?" he asked, astonished.

"Yes. Scarface and Duff. I don't imagine you want to free them." A charged silence hung in the air as Alix waited for a reply. Omar stood, silent, deep in thought, fierce emotions tore at his heart.

"Let them die," Fergus said gruffly. "We need to get out of here." Omar bowed his head, his eyes were closed. He searched deep within his soul for strength, for wisdom. His friends were restless, anxious to get going.

"Please...release me," said the voice. "I regret doing it. It was Kuman's order. I believed in him. But now I know he's a crazy madman. I want to help make things right."

"Cry of a condemned man," said Fergus gruffly. "False penitence to receive mercy. Let's go."

"Omar?" Alix looked at his friend with raised eyebrows.

Omar hobbled to the cell door and peered through the small opening. "Are you Scarface?"

"Yes."

"You killed my father?"

"I did," replied Scarface sadly. "In ignorance. I was following Kuman's orders."

"You were supposed to kill me. Why didn't you?"

"Your father was a good man. Killing him left a deep hole in my heart. I couldn't bring myself to kill the son."

"What were you going to do with me?"

"We hadn't decided yet. We didn't know what to do. We were caught between Kuman's orders and the holes in our hearts."

"What about Duff? Does he feel the same as you do?"

"Yes," came from deep within the cell. Omar turned to his friends.

"Let's go," Fergus chaffed. "We need to get out of here."

Omar's soul struggled within him. Anger, pain. His father's face flashed through his mind. Smiling, happy. Then the sudden surge of pain, and the tortured face turned cold in death. The king's son shivered in agony. He wanted these men to die. *But what is Elconan's way?* he asked himself. *And what had Ulis taught him about forgiveness?* His soul groped through cobwebs of sorrow as he sought in his heart for an answer. Finally, he turned to Alix and said, "Let's release them. I forgive them."

Alix moved quickly to unlock the door. Scarface and Duff fell at Omar's feet with their faces to the damp cobbled floor.

"Thank you. Thank you... ," they murmured.

"Get up," said Omar. "We have to get out of here." Scarface and Duff rose, still bowing to Omar and muttering, "Thank you...thank you...."

"Let's go," said Alix.

They walked down the narrow hallway in pairs. Omar held Ester's hand and tried to ignore the pain raging in his foot as they followed Alix. Behind them walked Fergus and Nadine, followed by Scarface and Duff, their faces beaming with the joy of release.

JOURNEY TO LIGHT

At the end of the hallway they walked up a set of stone stairs. Omar reached for the crude iron railing and hoisted his damaged foot up each step carefully. Dim light shafted through a doorway at the top of the stairs where two guards slumped on the floor in a drug induced sleep. Alix pulled their swords free and handed one to Scarface, the other to Duff. "Take these," he said. "You know how to use them, come lead the way with me."

They were in a large entrance lobby behind the hall-of-justice. Two guards were seated behind a table near the exit. Their bodies arched over the table, their faces pressed into the highly polished oak surface. A line of drool led to each gaping mouth.

As Alix pushed the door open they heard faint cries of, "Abidan, Abidan," from the direction of the palace.

Alix's face startled. Fear flashed behind his eyes. "We better hurry," he said. They stayed in the shadows and moved toward the compound exit as quickly as Omar's wounded foot allowed. The cries from the palace shot courage through Omar's veins and the pain in his foot subsided. When they sighted the gate Alix motioned the group to stop.

"There are four guards at the exit," he whispered. "Fergus, you and I will take the two on the left. You two," he pointed to Scarface and Duff. "Take the two on the right. The rest of you," he turned to Omar and the girls. "Stay behind us. We may need you for back up. We'll all rush the gate together." He surveyed the group. Ester's face was white, but a firm determination shone from her eyes. Nadine sparred an imaginary enemy with her sword. Fergus's eyes were restless, his body flexed. Omar's face was resolute, but his eyes shone with peace. Scarface and Duff were well-trained in close contact combat. They licked their lips, their eyes signalled readiness. Omar closed his eyes and said quietly, "May Elconan be with us." Torches flashed from the palace. "Let's go," he urged.

They ran toward the gate as fast as Omar could hobble. The guards saw them coming, jumped to their feet and drew their swords. Metal struck metal. Grunts. Strained curses. Scarface cried out and collapsed on the ground, blood pumped from his chest.

"Good work, Jalam," cheered one of the guards. Jalam? Petrina's pained face flashed through Omar's mind. He turned to the right. A hideous grin and a bloody sword surged toward him. Omar raised his sword. Clang. Clang. Metal against metal. The bloody sword plunged at him. Omar jumped aside and buried his sword in Jalam's stomach. A hideous curse screeched from the guard's lips as he fell to the cobblestones. Blood and intestines poured from his stomach. His last breath a series of painful gasps.

The palace compound flared to life with shouts, guards and torches. "The dungeon's empty," a frantic voice yelled. "The prisoners are gone." Curses and orders were shouted. Men ran to the gate.

"Run!" Alix commanded. Omar turned to Ester. Her face was gripped by fear and terror shone in her eyes. He grabbed her hand. Pain shot up from his foot. He shuddered, steeled his emotions and, holding Ester's hand, ran after Alix away from the pier in the darkness. Behind them, guards stepped over the dead bodies at the exit and rushed toward the pier. It swarmed with torches, shouts and violent curses.

***

A soft, faint light was breaking the eastern horizon as Eran walked toward the palace. His stomach was tense and his head throbbed with fear as his mind projected to the meeting ahead. He dreaded facing the governor with the report of the night's events. His delight at being promoted to captain had dissipated quickly when he faced Kuman's angry tirades. He had seen Kuman's anger, and he feared it.

His mind was still tormented by the sound of his sword tearing into Remus's flesh. The contorted face of the captain taunted and tormented him. Earlier in the night he had tried to sleep, but he sat up in his bed screaming hysterically, his bed clothes soaked with sweat. His wife, terrified by his horror, ran from their home through the dark streets of Gara to the house of her parents. Now this. How could he tell Kuman that there would be no sacrifice, the prisoners under his care had escaped. At the steps to the palace he removed his sword and dagger, and stashed them in some bushes. He knew Kuman carried no weapon. Better to face Kuman without a weapon that might be used against him. Kuman's anger would be severe, but if he survived the tirade, he surmised, then he would find some way of dealing with tomorrow.

Kuman was waiting for his captain in the large palace library. The walls were lined with shelves that contained scrolls of literature, science and history. "The captain of the guard," Abidan announced, his face strained, ashen. Kuman had viciously berated him for running from the palace and hiding under a tree when the flying shadow visited Kuman's bedroom. The cries of his master calling him by name had loosened his paralysis and forced him into action.

"Send him in," Kuman chipped. Eran entered the room and dropped to his knees before Kuman, his face to the floor.

"While you're down there," Kuman sneered. "Tell me you have the prisoners in your care."

"One of the guards betrayed us. The prisoners escaped," Eran mumbled into the plush carpet. "But we'll keep looking for them. I'm sure we'll have them by morning." With his face buried in the rug, he never saw it coming. Kuman picked up a large stone statue from his desk and smashed it into the back of the captain's head. Blood and brains squirted out over the elegant floor.

"Abidan," Kuman called. The chief steward stepped into the room. "Clean up this mess," Kuman barked. "Send his body to be burned on Omar's pyre." Kuman left the library, went to his bedroom, poured a large goblet of wine and paced the room as he tried to calm his anger with the alcohol.

A cold, heavy silence settled over the room. Kuman felt it first as calmness in his soul, but that lasted only for a few moments. Then his skin crawled with little bumps, he felt cold and clammy, he shivered as he reached for a robe. A deep, cold dread grew in his stomach and seeped through his body like cold tentacles of spreading ice. Kuman gulped more wine. He threw the goblet against the wall, it smashed in a splatter of red on the clean, white plaster. He reached for a bottle of tekara, tore off the top and raised the bottle to his lips. His throat burned as he guzzled the fiery spirits fiercely, but his stomach grew warm. As the power of the intoxicant spread through his veins he began to relax. His head reeled. He dropped the bottle. It shattered at his feet, the precious liquid soaked the rug. Kuman fell backwards on the bed and faded into unconsciousness as his body slackened and the world swirled around him.

THIRTY TWO

"Here's the boat," said Alix as he led the group down a grassy slope to the water's edge. He stopped at the boat and turned around. "Are we all here?"

"Scarface died at the gate," Omar said sadly. "Duff's not here, but I'm sure he escaped."

"Has anybody seen him?"

Nadine spoke: "I saw him running toward the city. Did he know about the boat?"

"I told him," replied Alix. "After we broke from the compound I told him to follow me to the boat."

"He must of had other plans," Omar suggested.

Alix shrugged. "Guess so."

The shouts at the pier grew louder. Torches began moving away from it and spreading out along the river.

Concern flashed across Omar's face "We have to go. Get into the boat. Hurry." As they scrambled into the boat an ominous, dark cloud ghosted across the sky and slithered over the moon, casting the night into an eerie, ebony darkness.

"Looks like another Pasidian storm coming," said Omar as they quietly paddled away from the shore.

"Good," said Alix. "The boat patrols won't stay on the river during the storm. They'll be heading for shore."

"Can this boat make it through a storm?" asked Omar.

"I'd rather face the storm than Kuman's patrols."

"And I'd rather drown than be burned alive."

"Neither one is much consolation," Fergus remarked.

"Oh, Fergus," scolded Nadine. "Don't be so negative. We'll make it."

A gust of wind rocked the boat, a wave broke against it and drenched the paddlers.

"Turn into the wind," yelled Omar. The sky rumbled, light flashed from the clouds. Then, like a dam suddenly broken, the rain deluged down upon them.

"One of us will have to bail," Alix shouted above the storm. "Nadine, use my boots, get the water out of the boat." The others paddled frantically as Nadine tore off Alix's heavy guard's boots and began scooping furiously.

***

Kuman jolted out of his drunken stupor as the dark shadow shrieked through the window and poured into the room. It hovered over the bed and bellowed, "You've let them escape, imbecile. First you lost the breastplate, now the girl, and the king's son. Incompetent moron!" it screamed. "I gave you all kinds of wisdom and knowledge. I helped you become rich, famous and powerful. Because of me, Pasidia was at your feet, worshipping you like a god. I taught you how to replace the archaic law of living for the highest good of all with self-indulgence, having your own way, and getting everything you want. I chose you as my human emissary, to deceive the world and bring it under my control. But you failed, idiot! You allowed selfishness and pride to consume you until it became your god, instead of me. The power I gave you to enslave the world, you used to promote yourself, and like a stallion smelling a mare in heat, you ran your own way. Fool, now you've lost it all!"

Kuman's anger flared. In drunken boldness he faced his tormentor. "Shut up, stupid shadow! How dare you speak to me like this. I laid the plans, I did the work. I built Pasidia. I built the great structures. I built the alliance. All you did was float around in the air and give me orders. Well, I'm tired of your orders. And I'm tired of you!" he screamed.

The shadow hissed, spat, then grabbed Kuman by the throat and threw him across the room. Bones snapped as the governor hit the wall. Blood spurting from his nostrils left a bloody track as he slid down the white plaster and collapsed on the floor.

"I'll show you what I can do, insolent one," the shadow jeered, as it slithered out the window and shot away in the double plate.

***

"What's that?" cried Ester. They all heard it. A deep rumble vibrated low in the belly of the earth and began shaking Pasidia violently. Animals ran through the fields in crazed frenzy. Dogs howled hysterically. Mothers screamed in the night and ran to their children. Frightened men ran into the streets, their eyes wild with terror as buildings crumbled around them. The ground shook violently, like a stormy sea. On the high hill the Kuman statue rocked precariously. Jahaz and the priests ran from it, their eyes wide with terror. The statue teetered back and forth as the earth shook. Then, with a mighty bang, it crashed to the ground. Kuman's rock face smashed as it struck the stone pavement.

Light flashed in the sky. The clouds rumbled violently. The wind drove fierce rain hard against the small group clustered in the boat as it tossed and bobbed on the rough water. They paddled like men possessed, but the wind pushed them back, again and again with mighty gusts, as they struggled with failing strength.

Then, suddenly, as quickly as it started, the raging storm grew quiet. As the clouds lifted the wind died and the air became still. The daggers of rain eased, then became a soft drizzle. The river stopped its fearsome tossing and became smooth, lapping softly against the sides of the boat.

"Paddle!" cried Omar. They leaned into the oars with renewed strength and hope. As they reached the far side of the wide river the sun broke in the east and splashed the breaking clouds with red ochre across the horizon. As the boat hit the river's edge Alix jumped out and held the boat steady while the others scrambled ashore. Fergus helped Omar climb up the steep bank until they reached the top, a flat, rocky area at the edge of a meadow that stretched toward the nearby forest. Exhausted from paddling and the steep climb, the group collapsed on the slippery rocks. They lay there, panting; absorbing the early sun and allowing their tired bodies to rest.

After several minutes Nadine turned to Omar and asked, "What if Kuman sends soldiers after us?"

"We'll disappear into the forest. They won't find us there. Then we'll make our way back to Aklavia."

"But what if he attacks Aklavia? What if he brings the alliance against us?" Nadine's voice was filled with concern.

"Kuman doesn't have the breastplate anymore. Without the breastplate, I'm confident the other provinces will not join him in an attack on the capital."

"But he could attack with just Pasidian soldiers," Fergus interjected.

"I guess he could. But some of the provinces would come to our defence. Sorna will have to stir the provinces to join us in standing against him."

"Against his army?"

"His army is immature. Better now than later, when he has an army of giants."

Nadine shuddered. "That would be scary."

"Look." Omar pointed across the river. A fierce dark cloud formation, as dark as a sour bog, was collecting above Gara. The cloud had a strange shape, all bent, twisted and angry. It blocked the rising sun and bore down upon the city as if to smother it in its hideous grip.

They sat up and gazed at the spectacle developing on the other side of the river. A strange excitement and fear coursed through Omar's veins. He put his arm around Ester and pulled her close. As she leaned into him he noticed that she was shaking. He squeezed her tightly and kissed her forehead softly.

"It's going to be okay," he encouraged her. "We're together now, and nothing can tear us apart."

"That cloud's scary," she whispered. "What if it comes across the river?" Scenes of Cedric and white stones flashed through Omar's memory. He braced himself against a cold shiver that ran down his spine.

"I'm sure it won't," he said, with assumed confidence. "We've never seen one like it outside of Pasidia." He turned his attention back to Gara. Suddenly, plate shaped shadows burst from the cloud. Light flashed across the sky as they careened over the city.

"There must be hundreds of them," cried Fergus. "They're going to smash into each other."

"What are they?" asked Ester.

"Kuman's mentors," Omar replied sadly. "One of them appeared on the high hill when he dedicated the statue, and a mighty voice boomed from it telling the people to follow him. They're enemies of Elconan. Enemies of everything that's good. They've taught Kuman how to build his own empire by enslaving the people."

"Why?"

"They're motivated by pride, greed and hatred," said Alix. "They offer us the freedom to grasp for everything we see, to plunge our bodies into fulfilment of every kind of pleasure, even if that destroys us, and they teach us that some people are superior to others."

"Where do they come from?" asked Nadine.

"They represent spiritual forces of the deepest darkness," Alix replied soberly. "The most violent evil. Their leader disguises himself as an angel of light, of knowledge and wisdom. At first, what he offers sounds good, but when you follow his ways you soon find that they lead to suffering, misery and death."

"Why would anybody follow him?" asked Ester.

"Eyes blinded by bitterness, greed or envy find his message attractive," said Omar.

A horrendous growl rose from deep within the earth and interrupted their conversation. Omar struggled to his feet, then helped Ester rise. They clung to each other and looked toward the city. The growl grew louder and louder until it filled the air with the anger of a thousand volcanoes. The buildings in Gara began rocking like grass in the wind. The ground shook violently. Then, with a mighty, thunderous roar, the earth beneath Gara exploded. Buildings shattered as they were thrown into the dark sky. Bodies of people and animals flew through the air in clouds of dust and debris. Giant trees were torn from the ground and flung into the exploding melee like sharp arrows.

As Omar and his friends watched in horror and disbelief, the earth parted and the once proud city of Gara slid into the giant abyss of the ruptured earth.

Hideous screeches and gleeful howls pulsed through the air from the flying shadows. They danced with joy as giant mountains of earth slid into the chasm and covered the city in a swirling cloud of dust. As the earth shook the whole province began to sink. Screams of pain and hysteria pierced the air as Pasidia sank below river level. As the earth fell away before it the Great Sea heaved and roared up the mighty Yaseb until the land of Kuman was completely covered with water.

Omar stared into the emptiness of the sea where Gara once stood. Fierce emotions tore at his heart: unbelief, wonder, amazement, deep sorrow. As the full realization of what he had just witnessed swept through his brain Omar's heart pulsed with intense, crushing sadness. Paralyzed by incredulity, the group stood silently, like stone statues, and stared into the barren void across the river. Ester clung to Omar and began sobbing.

Fergus was the first to speak. "This must be a nightmare. I can't believe what I've just seen. A whole province has just disappeared. All I see is water."

"This changes everything," Nadine said excitedly. "We're free. He won't come after us now." She paused. Her face clouded. "But all those people. Gone. Why?" She wiped tears from her eyes. "They were deceived by Kuman. Why did they have to die?"

"Kuman's gods are very ruthless," Omar replied.

Fergus shook his head. "I still can't believe it."

"Look out," yelled Omar, as he pulled Ester down. Three flying plates swooped across the river and dove at Omar and his friends. Frantically they dropped on their bellies as the shadows careened toward them, cackling and hissing as they swept over the frightened group cowering on the rocks. They spun through the air in broad arcs and plunged toward the earth, again and again, screaming curses, hatred and bile. The ground trembled each time a shadow descended with a thunderous roar and screeched over the backs of the huddled group.

As the rage above him continued a steely resolve began creeping through Omar's veins and pushed toward his heart. *Who are these shadows anyway?* he asked himself. *That the followers of Elconan should cower before them.* He dug deep into his soul for every speck of courage he could muster and stood to his feet. "In the name of Elconan, be gone!" he shouted as he shook his fist defiantly at the shadows' onslaught.

The attackers bellowed like angry bulls. "Be gone," Omar shouted, over and over. "In the name of Elconan, be gone." They swooped and dove at Omar as he stood bravely and continued to shout. The confrontation grew more intense. Again and again he felt the evil wind of the plates as they grazed the top of his head. But he stood against them, strong and resolute, commanding them to leave, in Elconan's name. Finally, with horrific screeches that shattered the air and shook the trees, they disappeared into the clouds.

The air became quiet.

Omar's friends raised their bodies from the rocks cautiously.

"Will they come back?" asked Fergus with a shaky voice.

Omar looked out across the expansive ocean and watched the waves rolling over the site where Gara once stood in its pride and arrogance. He sighed deeply. His tunic was soaked with sweat and his body trembled. He turned to Fergus. "Only if we let them."

THIRTY THREE

Soft, warm light filtered through the city as the sun slowly broke the horizon. A gentle breeze rustled the leaves as Sorna rose from a fitful sleep. She slipped on a bright silk robe and walked out into her fragrant garden, vibrant with the early morning clamour of lusty songbirds.

Omar and his friends had arrived in the capital late the previous evening. They arrived hungry, tired and dirty, their clothes ragged from the long journey through the highland forest from Gara. Omar met with her late into the night and shared an amazing but very troubling story about the events that transpired in Pasidia. She thanked Elconan for their safe return, but her spirit was deeply disturbed by the story of evil and the tragedy that swallowed Pasidia and all of its people in an angry display of indescribable violence.

She wandered around in her outdoor sanctuary restlessly as she meditated and prayed. She asked Elconan for strength in her soul, and for wisdom to know how to lead the nation. Without the golden breastplate, she realized, life would never be the same again in Fabia. The manifest presence of Elconan, his visible, tangible expression, was gone. What would now capture and hold the peoples' hearts and imaginations? Would they remain faithful? Or would they seek another god that is visible, and present?

Deeply concerned, Sorna wrestled in her spirit for several hours as she roamed in the garden. When her family started to rise, the viceroy returned to the house and prepared herself for the day. After a quick breakfast of fresh fruit, cheese and bread, she walked to her office to meet Omar and his friends.

***

"What I don't understand is, where did this evil come from?" Omar's voice had a hard edge. "How did it enter Fabia?"

"Elconan gave us both the privilege and the responsibility to take care of the earth," Sorna replied thoughtfully. "If we love each other and live for the highest good of all, evil has no power. But one man chose his selfish interest above that of the community. This decision provided a doorway through which evil entered and destroyed a people."

"I guess Fabia will never be the same."

Sorna's face darkened. Sorrow etched her soft features. "No," she said quietly. "We've lost a province. But we've lost more than that. Fabia lost its innocence. Remember that some of the governors were committed to Kuman. They were enticed by their own greed. It's still here with us."

A deep sadness crossed Omar's face. He felt responsible for the loss of the icon. "What about the breastplate, can it be replaced?"

"Unfortunately, no. It shone with the light of Elconan that was given to us at the beginning of time, to help us govern with love and justice. Without the visible symbol of his presence it will be more difficult to lead. We'll struggle with unbelief, lust and selfishness."

"Where was Elconan in all of this?" Omar's voice was full of frustration. "Why didn't he protect my father? And why did he allow all those innocent people in Pasidia to perish?"

"As children of Elconan, we have the power to love, and the freedom to choose. Unfortunately, if we choose our own selfish interest and violate the principle of Aoght, innocent people suffer. We have seen how the selfish choices of one person can have a disastrous effect on an entire province."

"But why isn't that freedom limited, so we can't choose evil?"

"Would that be true freedom?"

Omar's reply was slow and thoughtful. "I think I see what you mean. If our freedom is limited to choose only that which is good, then it's not really freedom at all."

Nadine interjected: "So, even though it breaks Elconan's heart when someone chooses evil, he won't prevent it?"

"For our choices to be truly free we must have the power to choose good or evil," Sorna replied.

"So, if Scarface and Duff weren't free to kill my father they would've been little more than puppets."

Sorna nodded.

"I'll have to confess," Omar continued. "I've been angry at Elconan for not protecting my father. But I think I'm beginning to understand. His love for the killers would not allow him to take away their freedom to choose."

"Nor did he force them to choose what's right in the dungeon."

A deep heaviness rolled from Omar's soul. His face brightened as the light of new understanding shone from his eyes.

Sorna looked around at the group soberly and thoughtfully. As she looked into their eager, young eyes hope sprang up in her soul. These young friends had faced the breath of evil. They had been tempted and threatened, but they remained faithful to Elconan and the highest good. If they could, she concluded, so could others. "Love what's good," she said with new confidence. "And love one another. That is the journey to light. That is Elconan's way."

They were interrupted by a knock on the door.

"Enter," said Sorna as she arose.

The door opened and a courier stepped in. "A message for Governor Omar," he said with a bright smile.

Omar rose from the cushion and walked to the door. The courier held the scroll in front of him and bowed as the governor approached. Omar took the scroll from the outstretched hand and said, "Thank you. May Elconan be with you." He unrolled the scroll; as he read the message a smile broke his face.

Ester jumped up. "What is it, Omar?"

"It's a wedding invitation." His eyes danced as he faced the group.

"Who is it?"

"Petrina and Zared are getting married."

"Wonderful," exclaimed Nadine. "I'm so happy for them."

Omar looked around at Sorna and his friends, then, in a voice gentle, but strong, he said, "The light is still with us."

***

The End

***

for more steps on the journey see: www.journeytolight.ca

PEACE PORTAL ALLIANCE
CHURCH LIBRARY